DRAGON IN YOU

A MEMOIR

MARIAH DAWN

© Copyright 2024 Best Life Infinity, LLC

ALL RIGHTS RESERVED

No part of this publication may be reproduced, stored or transmitted in any form or by any means, electronic, mechanical, photocopying, recording, scanning, or otherwise without written permission from the author. It is illegal to copy this book, post it to a website, or distribute it by any other means without permission.

For information, address Best Life Infinity, LLC, 1755 Telstar Drive Ste, 300, Colorado Springs, CO 80920: info@militarysurvivor.com

ISBN: 978-0-9815958-9-4

Table of Contents

Introduction x
    Dragons and Thieves Analogy xiv
1992-2004 1
    Aspiring Eternal Love 1
    Unbearable Academics 2
2004-2006 8
2006-2010 13
    Vulnerability to Speak 15
    Shallow Encounters Felt Safe 16
    Impermanence of Life 19
2011 27
2012 37
2013 45
    Suffocating Proposal 46
2014 52
    Unconditional Love 52
    Coffee, Lemon Cakes, and Flowers 53
    This Job Serves No One 56

    Nostalgia Wins 58

    Success in Recentering 61

    Double Shake Up 62

2015 .... **64**

    Picked First To Play 71

    Life Is Beautiful 72

    Extended and Expanding Family 77

2016 .... **82**

    My Turn to Ride 82

    For Time and All Eternity 84

    Ronan 85

    God Be With You 90

2017 .... **92**

2018 .... **94**

    Speechless Pregnancy 94

    April 96

    Birthday Surprise 100

    May 102

    June 107

    Moving Day 110

    Hypervigilance and a Handgun 111

    Live Your Truth 116

Raela 117

McFly 122

Christmas Day 125

2019 127

123... Breathe 127

Raela RSV 129

Traveling Home 131

Tired To My Bones 134

Letter I Never Sent 135

Don't Be So Dramatic 139

The Ideal Situation 144

This Is "My House" 146

Gauging Reactions 148

Zoloft 150

Cleaning Company 153

Driving Companion 154

2020 And then. Covid 159

Crooked Glasses 160

March Easter 161

Drops of Hope 162

Last Birthday with Michael 164

May 165

v

The Month We Separated 170
June 12th 172
June 13th 173
June 15th 175
June 16th 177
June 17th 178
Torrential Rain 181
Fresh Baked Cookies 183
Home 187
Misfired 187
The Dragon's Reign 190
They Needed Snacks 191
I Exhaled 193
No Small Talk 197
Kite String 199
Looking for Fairy Tales 201

2021 .... **206**

Zoloft No More 206
Concussion 208
Hiking 209
First Date 211
Battalion Agreement 214

Our Last Hug 215

"Wellness Check" 230

Nightmares 233

First Breakup 239

Martial Arts 245

Shove 246

Can I be 30 yet? 249

Mandated Rehab 253

Mouths To Feed 253

Question of The Day 255

Not Going To Be Undone 258

Let The Truth Be Told 262

September 2021 265

Run and Hug Him 266

I Don't Want It 267

October 270

October 4th 271

October 5th 272

Airport Tarmac 287

Our Final Goodbye 289

Graveside 291

Opening a Time Capsule 297

vii

    My Body Said No More 300

    Back at It 301

2022 .... **304**

    Heart Grow Fonder 304

    Michael's Birthday 305

    Army Presents Their Investigation 307

    The Killers Concert 317

    Communication Breakdowns 320

    Dichotomies of My Grief 326

    Taps Family Camp 330

    Positive for Everyone 332

    Work Events of 2022/23 333

2023 .... **334**

    It Was Zero Percent 335

    Do You Believe in God? 337

    At Their Mercy 339

    A Crushed Soul 341

    Promise To God 348

    Date with Doug 351

    Gingerbread Houses 355

    Christmas Eve 369

INTRODUCTION

You can call this a prologue or a warning label, you decide! My hope for this book is that it will convey the suffering I have experienced and the ensuing peace I finally achieved from the trials and tribulations I overcame and the positive mental shifts that occurred – all of which consumed every last ounce of my being to definitively stand on my own two feet and feel that I am a person worth loving.

I have lain broken down on the backs of many people until I could once again stand. I attribute most of my 'drive to thrive' to my children, Ronan and Raela. Some might say it wasn't fair to my children, for a parent to place that kind of pressure on them. But they lived through my tragedy alongside me, unfortunately. My will to give them a fruitful life, despite what they both witnessed and experienced, brought me to a place where I could do the same for myself. I am not ashamed of this, and actually, I am so very grateful for it. They give me deep love every day, and I hope I have done well in giving that back to them.

I have had multiple therapists shovel me out of bottomless pits. Friends have sat with me or invited me to play dates for the kids, while I was still a shell of a person. I have walked into grief support groups and received the great blessing of feeling normal in the midst of my horror. Sitting in those circles with others, I would say things like, "I was going through a divorce when he died, so I'm not really a widow. I'm just here for the kids." I was trying to defend my right to be there because I feared I wouldn't be accepted. But I was humbled when my defense was met with, "Yes, you are allowed to be here. We were going through a divorce as well. We are here for ourselves and also for our kids."

I hadn't realized that other people had a spouse deep into addictions, or had lived through life-threatening domestic violence, or had begun the divorce process only to end up with the title of widow. Just. Like. ME. I sat at another table in another group and said, "I feel like I'm actually addicted to chocolate. I self-soothe with it so hard. And it works." I felt so awkward admitting it, but it was the hard truth. And it was met with a quiet whisper of "Me too."

My hope for you is this; to offer you a place where self-soothing with chocolate is acknowledged as reasonable. And where the deep pain of admitting that you almost died multiple times at the hands of the person you said, "I do" to is acknowledged and understood, rather than met with "Why didn't you leave sooner?" I did not leave sooner, but I hope to show the next generation they can. In fact. Leave.

I have had many, if not daily, divine interventions. Finding myself and my footing has been a team effort between me and God, who has placed many people and opportunities in my path. To have the life I dreamt of, I had to actively put in the work and take myself there. I have applied this to every aspect of my life. I wanted a happy, peace-filled, and loving life, so I've taken myself there. I have had to be brutally honest and vulnerable with myself, as much as my healed mind and body have allowed me to be. With this vulnerability, I want to warn you that I will be sharing some highly uncomfortable truths in this book – my truth, from my experience, only my experience, as I've lived through it. I am in essence putting myself on trial. I offer, for those who wish, to reach out to me. If reading this becomes challenging and it feels like I might be out of my mind, understand that I might have been. Just know that this is okay. It is part of the journey of healing.

To truly be the change I wish to see and to acknowledge the narrative that destroyed my self-worth, I need to explain my thoughts and experiences in the moments they were happening. I then interject my current, more grounded, more compassionate, and humbled perspective of this pulled-apart-at-the-seams life we are all experiencing.

My final request is that you be aware that in reading this book, you might find yourself thinking, "Wow. How dare they do that to her!" or "Would she just suck it up for once in her life?" The truth, though, is somewhere in the middle. How dare they for sure. But also, how dare I. I also use the analogy of thieves in this book, for which I believe we all are.

Please read knowing that I deeply love everyone mentioned in this book. I strongly stand behind the notion that if you say you hate anyone, then you are actually incapable of love because love knows no bounds. Love understands that we just might not understand. Love is embedded throughout this story. It may not seem that way, but I promise you it is. This story is about how I 'got there' and how I learned to love. For to truly love one person, you must love all.

Dragons and Thieves Analogy

My sense of autonomy and identity, stolen. When others assumed things about me negatively, or only praised me when my actions aligned with their values, this encouraged me to perpetuate attributes I knew would win me those praises. This was done by those who loved me dearly and I do not believe maliciously. But it was done over and over again. And all without me knowing it was happening, even at thirty-one years old.

This pattern of people pleasing subconsciously controlled me until I healed enough to recognize my authentic self-held value. Not just in the fragmented parts that seemed to win me affection from others.

I have come up with the analogy of thieves. Being a "thief" means to tell yourself a story about someone's intentions to make it make sense in your reality. By writing someone else's story I was robbed them of the chance to explain themself, from their perspective. I allowed them to steal a part of my mental wellbeing with the narrative I wrote for them instead of asking. This is what thieves do to you. I have created many thieves in my life.

That's why we must always try to have compassion, ask for clarification, and do our best to understand or at the very least acknowledge their experience and feelings. When I felt it was not a healthy option to ask them I wrote their story with grace instead. To give my mind rest.

I am love. It is who I am. It is who you are as well.

Love for me is a table full of fresh food for all to eat (security). It is a house full of walls that have come down (vulnerability). It is crafts with my kids for days and days (creativity). When my therapist asked me what my dream is, I said that it is looking through my sliding glass door into the backyard, watching my children play (peace).

And I was right. That has brought me so much peace. But at that time, I answered the question anxiously. I now know, my dream is to play in the yard with my children (being present), not just watching them. That is my peace.

My hope for this book is to show you who I am and how my reaction to my surroundings unknowingly led to adorning myself with armor. And you thieves didn't know either. For that is the great dichotomy: that the victim is the perpetrator and the perpetrator the victim. Welcome, thieves, for I am one too.

As a little girl sitting in Sunday school each week, I was aware that my dad worked fourteen-hour days, seven days a week; that my mom was 'checked out', and that my grandparents never invited me over. But I had no idea that they were all carrying burdens of which I knew nothing about. I intuitively felt that something was off despite being told everything was fine. This was the beginning of a pattern that took me into my thirties before I consciously recognized it and am now trying to actively break. Before, the pattern ran subconsciously. It was learning and then accepting that gaslighting equated to love, that by shielding me from the truth and reality of life, I was somehow being shown love. Instead, it confused me and threw my navigational compass off.

Gaslighting, although perhaps done with good intentions, confused and taught me to accept even white lies as truth. This pattern became my destructive dragon. When I recognize the pattern and run it mindfully, I can understand myself and my desires and why I crave what I crave and then release the damaging behaviors in exchange for strength and authenticity.

The "Dragon in You" is a metaphorical dichotomy. Unleash your dragon's power intentionally and with purpose so that whatever you do is done with love. It is a lot easier to have compassion for others when you know their intentions are pure. Even if their actions still hurt you. If you are reactionary (fight, flight, freeze, fawn response) you risk falling captive to your dragon aka coping mechanisms (the opposite of your desired outcome), thus bringing forth destruction. I lived much of my life in reactionary response to things. I wasn't always aware that I was operating this way, but I felt if I let my guard down my safety would be at risk.

If you don't take the time or have a chance to understand other people's dragons, that can lead to feeling hurt by them. Maybe their intention was to hurt you. They have fallen captive to their coping mechanism. Coping mechanisms almost always achieve the opposite of what our heart actually desires.

An example of one of my dragons:

I love quality time. I love hosting parties and going places with others. Meaningful connection and intentional conversations bring me so much joy. This is an honest and loving quality of mine. My self-sabotaging dragon would tell me I was bothering people and that I needed to entertain and make it worth peoples while to grace me with their presence. I viewed others' time as more important than mine. I would take whatever people gave me and whatever worked for them at the expense of my wellbeing and availability. I operated in a scarcity mindset that told me to say yes to what others initially offered instead of bringing up what could make the time/place work better for me.

A mutual compromise on both parties allows for a mutually great time. Instead, I fell victim to my dragon and made a thief out of others. When I was in a state of alchemy I knew that planning fun outings, hosting others, and having conversation are what people admire about me, and how I want to live my life. I learned to trust that others could handle themselves, entertain themselves, and enjoy their time without me having to facilitate the entire event. I find beauty in life when others were excited to spend time and get to know me because the feeling is mutual.

I begged to be dropped off at church in hope to find some sense of community there, maybe someone to call on me in class, ask what I thought, to listen to the words that came out of my mouth. I desperately sought the church to validate my words that seemed to fall on deaf ears elsewhere. But at the same time, I was terrified of being called on to read scripture and to have all eyes and ears on me.

I lived in the shadows most of my life. Now, I am trying to be seen; to air out my side of "the story"; to find people who have felt this pain, and to let them know they are not alone. I realize that I may upset people who misunderstand the intentions of my story. I may be abandoned by these misconceptions. I was "the girl who got everything she ever wanted" according to my mother at one point in time. In reality, everything I wanted was based on everything I got; it was assumed that whatever I had, whatever was given to me, was what I wanted. I made it fit my wants because I thought that any chance at love and survival meant doing just that. Fitting into their box; sitting at their table. For twenty-nine and a half years it worked, for them at least. And a little for me too.

So let's get to it. After years of feeling like people didn't know me, I have accepted that they just didn't know how to show up in my life in the way I needed to be shown love and in a way that would have helped me understand that what I was receiving from them was in fact love. My mother described me as feral, a label that I believe was easier for her to slap on rather than acknowledging that she didn't know how to connect with one of her five children. As a result, I made a thief out of her and rebranded myself to her compliance standards.

My father's work life seemed to be more important to him than being with his family, or at least that's the thief I had come to know. Perhaps work was his coping mechanism for having had a family in the first place. I have yet to be offered a different explanation from my parents, so I will stick with my own conclusions as they make the most sense to me.

I have written my life experience to try and find meaning in my ambivalent childhood. I know my parents did their best, but I was nevertheless deeply hurt and wounded by their actions. Now, I am desperate for relief, for self-discovery. For Light. For Peace. And to re-brand thieves.

1992-2004

ASPIRING ETERNAL LOVE

`To sum up my childhood, it seemed fairly typical. I had food, four walls, and a roof over my head. My parents were trying to figure themselves out, and I coped by finding my own world inside my head to receive acceptance and security through daydreaming. This search led me to my faith in The Church of Jesus Christ of Latter-Day Saints (LDS or The Mormon Church).

The LDS church claimed that my eternal salvation depended on my ability to have a husband and children "for time and all eternity," and that I would find happiness and love in this. Even as a little girl, this doctrine appealed to me because I craved someone who was devoted to me. This devotion would prove that I was lovable.

I wanted someone to sacrifice for me, to find this life promised by the LDS church, and when I failed to find a man who would choose me, I became fiercely independent while my self-worth dwindled.

I realized that I manifested my biggest fears instead of focusing on how to make my dreams a reality. I ended up learning that my fiercely independent dragon was my greatest strength. I knew I had everything I needed within myself. So when others did sacrifice and make time for me it was a sacred gift, not a need.

In my late twenties, while sleep-deprived with my newborn son, I asked my mom why this part, the hard part, the desperation, wasn't mentioned in church. If I could have seen how this question would foreshadow the tragedy that was yet to come on my young and growing family, I would have found myself crumbling to my knees a lot earlier.

Unbearable Academics

In elementary school, I thrived socially. Academically, it was unbearable. My 3rd grade teacher would hand out goldfish crackers to those who finished a book, while I often sat there empty-handed. I watched as all the kids around me stood up time and time again to trade in their books for gold fishies, but I was frozen. My body tensed as I tried to form any thought or read the words on the pages, but my mind was completely blank. I could read a sentence 10 times and still have no idea what I was reading. I would later learn that I needed more than one kind of sensory input to understand something. Listening to someone read aloud while moving my body was how I took in information. At the time, the school could not accommodate me in this way.

Instead, I sat in the classroom holding back tears, calling myself a loser and stupid. I worried I would never make it in the real world. It was a lot of pressure to put on myself, but I didn't know what was happening or what was wrong with me. I was hyper-focused on the reward, the goldfish, and what it would mean to my self-worth if I got them. I wasn't upset with my classmates, but rather, with my glaringly obvious dunce hat; that everyone knew I wasn't leveling up with them. Shortly after this, I was placed in the Special Education program.

I wish I had realized what a blessing Special Education was at the time. Instead, I felt like the dunce hat now came with a siren that would go off, and all of us "Special Ed kids" would stand up and walk out of the class to the smaller classroom. I was given less homework to keep up, which was a liberating respite after drowning underwater for so long. I had one-on-one attention, with the occasional kid-biting-teacher incident kept to a minimum.

When I turned eight years old, I was baptized. This was the happiest day of my life, at that point in my short life. Everyone was there: my family, my friends, my grandparents. I felt that I was doing the right thing! One of the adults was trying to make me nervous. But I felt brave. I could do this! I wanted it so bad. Finally, it was my turn. All the songs about "I can't wait until I'm eight!" ran through my eager mind. This was a chance to prove myself! So into the water I went. And it was warm! I got baptized and we all went home and celebrated. With the next sunrise, though, everything was back to normal. I lay in bed wondering if I had already sinned. I knew I could repent on Sunday, but I worried about the short time in between, waiting for Sunday to arrive.

I went downstairs and everyone acted like this big thing hadn't even happened. Didn't we just throw a party for how good I am? Was I still good? I guess I could wait until people saw me taking the sacrament on Sunday, knowing that I was still good or trying to be. At least I still had that much. I was continually searching for approval but not sure where to find it.

I believe it was around this time that I started sleepwalking. I still don't know the underlying cause of it, but I assume it was from severe stress. I recall waking up in the middle of the street multiple times, and I'm not certain I even told my parents about it. Maybe I just went back to my room. I have a specific memory of being held from falling down the stairs by a blanket. Dustin was holding the ends of it and kept me from rolling down. I think we both just went back to bed after that.

I made friends. I always did. I loved people. In fourth grade, I would go to after-school care which was fun for me. But I was aware that I was always also the one who arrived first and stood in the cafeteria line for breakfast. I was grateful for cereal that wasn't infested with ants like it was at home. I was grateful for food that I didn't have to fight for with my siblings. I was grateful for standing in that line with my band-aid-colored tray, being able to sit down and eat in silence. The problem, though, was at night when the sun went down. Everyone would get picked up from after-school care except my little sister and I. I would wait.

I just wanted to go home. It felt like I was never able to just be home. Home was where I could retreat, and it was also where I had four siblings who loved me and loved to torture me. There was Vanessa, the oldest; then David; Dustin; myself; and my little sister Savannah. At home, there was always someone to play with. And I played with whoever was in the mood to play. I don't think this was a bad thing. I believe it taught me to be well-rounded and flexible. Throughout my life, I have made friends with many people with varied interests. I am grateful for them and to be in their world, understand them, experience their life, and to see how special each person is because of their differences. With that being said, combined with years of therapy, I discovered how waiting and accepting whoever would play with me deeply affected my self-worth.

I saw myself as transactional, believing that when someone wanted what I had to offer they would come to me. It was as if I could only fulfill a need for people instead of standing alone as my own person. My self-sabotaging dragon told me that this served me well. It felt good to be around people, but it kept me from being authentic. I was filling a role instead of being in my own body. I only allowed the parts of myself that suited a specific moment to come forth. These were the fragmented pieces of my soul. I was being true to myself but lost myself along the way.

2004-2006

In middle school, I attended a charter school about thirty minutes from home, so I again began riding the bus. I felt like I was at school all the time. If I wasn't at school, I was on the bus for an hour each way. And if I wasn't on the bus, I was doing homework or going to bed.

The bus rides were long and pre-MP3 player/iPod/iPhone days, but I had my CD player. I also had two brothers who were familiar with LimeWire. I'll let you look it up if you don't know what that is. They burned albums for me, and I would gaze out the bus window with the view of the city of San Diego while listening to David Bowie, Queen, the Shins, and many, MANY indie bands. My imagination ran wild. You could say that I was meditating. When my CD batteries ran out of power or when I was talking to my friends instead of listening to my music, those were Wild West times.

It still freaks me out how many hours I spent on a bus without a seatbelt. On the first day of school, the bus driver said, "The seat you sit in is your seat until we get to the next bus stop." My seatmates and I would play Frogger: tracking the driver's attention in his long rearview mirror and switching seats whenever he wasn't looking.

Frogger turned into sitting in the front seat and evading the bus driver on the days when I had to get off at a different stop for my martial arts class. My mom had forgotten to sign off on this change. We weren't allowed to get dropped off at an unauthorized location, but I got off anyway! I think the bus driver knew he couldn't chase after me or grab me, and I don't recall getting written up for this. But now as an adult, I can only imagine him telling his friends, "Yeah, another girl ran off the bus at the wrong bus stop. Nothing I can do about it." I mean, that had to be stressful for the bus driver, but what could he do? Tackle me? I also wonder if the bus driver let me get away with this or if my mom signed the paper and I didn't know. I even wondered if the bus driver had been messing with me!

I am naturally an introvert, so it gave me some time to myself. It also gave me an unrealistic gauge of how long it takes to get places. One day when we attended "back to school night" I was amazed at how quickly we drove to school. I think it also helped me to never feel rushed when I drive.

Riding the bus also gave me new friends, none of whom I still talk to. Lori at my bus stop made me walk her home some days (in the opposite direction of my house), but I didn't mind. I'd walk Emily home sometimes too. And the days Randy took the bus, he was on my walk home we walked together. One day he gave me a necklace he had taken from his mom. I wore it home and immediately lost it. The next day he said his mom found out and she wanted it back. I searched everywhere but it was gone. Oops!

During this time that I also met my childhood best friend, Emma. We had a great childhood together. I recall that we had just gotten a camcorder, and we decided to make a movie of a candy shop with all of our Halloween candy. When we watched it again, Emma's dog Gracie had eaten all the candy in the background! We taught each other to play guitar and wrote the most innocent songs about train rides and love, things we knew nothing about. There was a big rock in her backyard that we would paint, and when it rained, we would paint again.

We learned to rollerblade, unicycle, juggle – anything we thought to try, we did it. We watched movies in her mom's bed. We rode bikes all through the neighborhood. We would find spare change in the couch cushions and the dryer and then walk to the gas station to spend it.

Summers with Emma were one long day of tortilla chips and shredded cheese in the microwave for nachos. Eating way too many vitamin C gummies. An endless supply of otter pops and popcorn. But most of all, summers were laughter.

Emma taught me that rules could be dumb, like no rollerblading in the house. That wasn't allowed at my house, but it was at Emma's. We rollerbladed all over, inside and out, but nothing bad ever happened. In my twenties, I had indoor rollerblades I would use in the house to make cleaning fun. My kids now have rollerblades for cleaning. Emma and I also learned that some rules were non-negotiable, like no cranberry juice on the carpet or placing a tarp down when you paint.

During summers, there was a permanent futon in her bedroom just for me. I only went home when my mom absolutely insisted, which wasn't very often.

When I think back to that time, I wonder if that's when I started believing that people don't miss me. Unfortunately, I didn't have the vocabulary, understanding, or foresight to express this to myself or anyone. Recently, I was hypnotized by a psychologist and directed to walk through my childhood home. My mom in was in the living room, but my dad wasn't home. I ran to the top of the hill in the backyard and then back to the house, under the closet stairs. I waited and waited for someone to notice that I was missing. The hardest part about this psychological attempt for attention as a six-year-old was the moment I realized that no one was looking for me, and I had to come out of hiding. My attempt to be missed failed. I asked people to play a game they didn't know they were playing and with rules, they unaware of. Who knows if I was in there for ten minutes or an hour. But I perceived it as life went on without me. And with that feeling, I made myself smaller and smaller.

2006-2010

In high school, I attended a different charter school. I also started going to morning seminary with the LDS church, meaning I was up by 5:50 a.m. to sit in a classroom for an hour and learn scripture every day before school. It was torture. My dad drove me daily, talk radio blasting against my still-asleep brain. To say that I'm not a morning person is a gross understatement. Only recently have I been able to tolerate conversations before 9:00 a.m. Having to wake so early for seminary and then be back home by 7:00 a.m. for carpooling produced a lot of resentment toward my parents.

High school continued to be a good place for me. I'm not sure I would have graduated if it hadn't been for my friends and my teachers. High Tech High Media Arts is a project-based, hands-on learning school. The classroom size was small, and the teachers knew and listened to us. I loved all my classmates. I tried to sit with someone new at lunch every day. I loved getting to know people. I classified myself as the "unofficial and undercover popular kid." Anyone could sit with me, and if I saw someone sitting alone, I would say hi.

I recall once, as a Junior when a friend's mother unexpectedly gave me a pair of rollerblades. I loved those rollerblades! I put them on as soon as I got to school, hoping to take my "free will and fancy-free spirit" to the next level. No one stopped me. In fact, my friends and teachers alike would take turns pushing me across the classrooms. I remember the exhilaration of being able to fly past other students in the halls, laughter bubbling in my chest. This freedom only lasted a week or so when my teacher regretfully told me that rollerblading was actually prohibited on campus. I'm still grateful for the kind-hearted teachers who allowed and encouraged me to be myself for as long as they could.

Another way this school encouraged innovation was that instead of Physical Education, there was a free elective period where you could choose between various classes that fit your interests. If you had at least 20 students signed up and a teacher supervisor, you could do whatever activity you wanted. I invented a game that I named "Spies." It was a lot like hide-and-seek with a few extra roles.

When it came time to sign up for block periods, over 100 people signed up for mine! I was amazed. For a whole semester, "Spies" became a legendary name, like we had taken over the entire school. It made me feel loved and accepted that I could contribute to my classmates' happiness. Until then, I had never felt the validation of affecting so many people at once. It is still a precious memory that I treasure.

Vulnerability to Speak

I can recall one classmate in my sophomore year who never spoke.

When it came time to read in class, he straight-up refused. No one had ever heard his voice. Instead of getting in trouble or marked down, my teacher pulled him and me aside.

She said that we were to go to a private area of the school and that he needed to read out loud in front of me from just one page of the book we were reading in class. So we did. We moved to the corner of the common area and sat cross-legged on the floor. It was just us, sitting in silence. I started to read and then indicated that it was his turn. Nothing. So I read again. It was his turn, but again, nothing. I continued reading further down the page that he should have been reading. I told him to read just one paragraph but was met with silence. Giving up, I said, "Okay, just a sentence." To my surprise, he then read a whole paragraph. I smiled, and we walked back to class together.

The teachers never asked me to do that again, nor did they ever ask him to read in class. But I was happy for my friend. He continued to not talk through the rest of high school. But at least I knew he could communicate if necessary. And especially, we each knew for sure that he could talk to me.

Shallow Encounters Felt Safe

I looked for attention from strangers who thought I was fun because I *could be* fun. And when it was time to go home, I didn't have to feel hurt by a stranger "abandoning" me because it was part of the social contract. Simply two strangers going their separate ways after a short interaction. That felt safe. No obligations to call back or make plans. Shallow encounters that made me feel like I was in a community, without any commitment to another. I thought Emma and her family were the exception to this, that I could allow myself to be vulnerable and dive into deeper waters without being afraid of being left to drown. When she left, my brain had to rewire itself as I pulled myself out of the depths of trauma and hurt.

With Emma, I made her and her family my new home. When we stopped talking it felt like it happened overnight because it all happened so quickly. This family I invested in didn't materialize. It hurt me so deeply and rewired my brain traumatically. That's not to say that Emma wasn't hurting as well. But she is the one who got to choose not to have me around. I had to be told to go away. This was the thief I knew. In my mind, she stole the only sense of family I had known up until that time. The only comfort and security I had were suddenly, deliberately, taken away. She never reached out to give me a different version. Her version.

Looking back, the fracture in our friendship likely began when her mom got into a severe bicycling accident. She was riding and a car hit her while she was riding on the side of the street. I wasn't given any other details, and at the time, I didn't ask. I had just gotten home from our carpool when Emma called, in tears, asking if I could come back over.

I hurriedly explained the situation to my brother, David, who drove me to Emma's house. I'll never forget her standing out on the porch as I ran out of the car, which hadn't yet stopped, to launch myself at her. She cried on my shoulder. She shook in fear as I held her as tight as possible. I remember thinking if I squeezed her tight enough to stop her shaking, then her fear would cease as well. After a few minutes, my body gave out and we went inside shaking, heartbroken, and confused. Her mom was still in the hospital. We lay in her mom's bed, rewatching Big Fish to pass the time. No words passed between us.

When her mom finally came home the next day, it was the first time I had seen severe road rash. She had a broken hip and pelvis and could barely walk. She spent most of her time in bed. I can still feel myself hugging her.

A few days later, Emma and I were watching a movie with her brother Brad. From my seat on the couch, I thought I had caught a glimpse of a figure going outside through the kitchen, but I didn't dwell on it for too long. I turned my attention back to the TV screen. Emma's dad came in about 30 minutes later asking if we had seen their mother. The three of us immediately ran outside, splitting up to look around the block. She was nowhere to be found.

Brad got in his car, Emma in the passenger seat while I got in the back. They had no idea where she could have gone, especially driving while injured. Immediately, I suggested that she may have gone to where her biking accident had happened. Brad thought it was unlikely because of how traumatic that must be to revisit the sight of your injury, but we had nowhere else to start. We raced off to the accident scene.

She wasn't there. I then suggested the park that was closest to their home. Maybe she wanted some space to be alone and think. With no better leads, we rushed off again. Brad pulled up to a stop sign before crying out so loudly my head snapped over to the left side of the car. "Mom!" He yelled. Her car sat alone on the side of the road. We all jumped out of the car, hastily throwing the car into park on the road, and tried to get their mom's attention. Brad screamed at her while Emma and I shook the car trying to open the locked doors. There was no response, her eyes empty. Eventually, Brad's screaming got her attention. She said she went to the accident site and then to a park to be alone. My relationship with their family seemed fractured after that. I can only assume we were all trying to find this new normal and trying to process it.

Impermanence of Life

Two months later, I received another life-changing phone call.

There was a quiet student named Will in my class. He was tall and always wore baggy clothes. He did his best to try and to not stand out. But when it was his turn to read in front of the class, those efforts were for naught. One day, he read aloud a poem he had written about dirt. Although slightly monotoned and the topic mundane, the description of grains of dirt and the worms poking through and around the dynasty of the anthill thrilled me. Our class was silent as he masterfully transformed the image of something dirty into something melancholy and beautiful. Maybe I was projecting my pain onto him, but his words held a bittersweet anguish hidden in a routine English assignment. Writing was also my safe place where the world inside of me could come alive. When I heard Will's words, I connected to him in our suffering and how we managed it. Maybe I felt like one of the worms he talked about in the anthill. I deeply wanted to help him somehow; I wanted him to keep writing and have an outlet for whatever tormented his heart.

    That night, I went to a local bookstore and found a leatherback journal with a compass on it to give to him. The cashier rang me up—$30. My stomach dropped because I only made money by babysitting, and those gigs didn't come often. Despite the price, I knew I wouldn't regret my purchase.

    The next day, I wrote a note on the first page explaining that his poem was so moving that it inspired me to pursue writing as enthralling as his. I didn't say who it was from. During lunch, I entered our classroom and placed the journal in a brown paper bag on Will's desk. I watched, but he didn't touch the bag even though I had written his name on it. Finally, when the bell rang, Will quietly slipped the bag into his backpack and walked out.

A few days later, I saw Will walking down the stairs as school ended. I waved to him, and he looked right at me and waved back. I did not know it at the time, but he walked straight from those stairs to a hotel nearby and ended his life.

Before school the next day, my friend Yoselin called me and told me the news. My heart dropped into my stomach. It didn't seem real. I was in complete disbelief, unable to comprehend her words. I showed up at Emma's door crying. We all piled into her dad's car to pick up Chris, another classmate, down the street. The car was silent. He opened the door, confused about why it was so quiet. Ironically, he asked, "Who died?" He had no idea that he was spot on.

The family announced the celebration of life service at the park down the street a few weeks later. My friends and I all went. When it ended, I approached Will's mom. I told her about the journal and shared that I tried to show him that he was loved. I wish I had given it to Will instead of just leaving it on his desk. I wish he knew that I cared. She grabbed my hands and tearfully thanked me for the journal. She had found it on Will's desk and read the note. Despite her earnest gratitude, it didn't feel like I did enough. To this day, I still think about how I waved goodbye to Will right before he died.

A poem I wrote in the months after:

>Yesterday's challenge meets me again
>Last day of his life, screaming I'm alive
>For him the burden grew inside
>His thoughts were his
>
>And he who holds ownership
>Paper and pen, his friends
>Words unspoken had to look shining in his work
>Locked up, a swallowed key, he wrote with deep   meaning
>
>Shaken up and down the story still inside
>Not a map but the treasure was in him
>In with a drift, out with the school days end
>And that's All I saw of him
>
>You stop, I go
>Thoughts to actions, Ideas to pain
>A different type of world, one I cannot explain
>Always on the outside, I can't fill those shoes
>The people around are the ones who really lose
>
>What were you thinking you didn't tell me

Every time a different story
Every time a different mourning
Arrived at the scene, held your cup of tea

Irregular
To set you "free"

A few days later, Emma's parents informed her that they were getting a divorce, and she stopped talking to me.

Family is family by blood; you have no choice but to be bound together. Friends that become family feel extra special and for me validated my desire to feel like I belonged. Knowing they chose and invested in my well-being and wanted me around brought me a sense of community that filled a deep void in my chest. That is until I realized I was, in fact, not family. And unlike family, they could relinquish their hold on me anytime, whether I was aware of it or not. Although I have done a lot of work to realize that I did my best for Will, with the maturity and tools I had at the time, I still struggle with feeling abandoned by him. That I wasn't "enough" of whatever he needed for him to confide in me. I ache that the narrative had changed when he waved back that day. That he would have walked up to me instead of that hotel, grabbed my hand, and told me he needed support. I would have run towards him head-on. At the very least, I wish I had looked into his eyes that last time and felt his suffering, recognized it, and sat with him through it.

I felt like a causality. When Emma stopped opening her door for me, those feelings compounded. Like I was a painful reminder of the past that, if ignored, would go away. So I did go away. I retreated to my time vault of a house. It seemed like no time had passed. I had long since stopped interacting or engaging with my parents and siblings at this time as if we'd all been roommates since I was ten years old. No one asked where I had been, and I didn't ask where they were, either. I manifested my childhood fears of feeling not worthy of people's time or attention again as a teenager. I'd do it a few more times in life before I'd learn my lesson.

Stephanie became my best friend shortly after. It sounds like she was a rebound best friend, but that was not the case at all. She and I were classmates for three years before we became close. However, my friendship with Emma consumed me until I could get my head out of the sand and truly appreciate Stephanie. She became my sister and her family, mine. I would spend all my time at their house. Her mom's name on my phone was Weekend Mom.

The name of this book could have been "I'm forever grateful for (insert name here)" because that's the truth. I have had so many people come into my life and heal me, support me, witness my pain, acknowledge my experience, and even laugh with me! Stephanie became one of these people.

Around this time, I joined the San Diego Fire-Rescue Department Cadet Program. I had no prior firefighting experience, but gained critical knowledge that would later significantly impact my life. I learned what to do when people were in crisis. I learned that while normal people run *out* of burning buildings, firefighters run toward them. This was exactly what I had been searching for since I was a kid hiding under the stairs—the rescuers. I learned that I could become one.

During my first month as a fire cadet, I attended a cadet academy. This was a week-long academy that mimicked a real fire academy. I was the only girl in the program, surrounded by 15 other boys. These fire drills were the exact opposite of what I did in elementary school, walking out of class to stand in line on the blacktop. These were fire hoses and axes, breaking down the doors to go inside and rescue. I thrived. I kept my head low but my spirits strong as I absorbed everything. At the end of the academy, there was an award ceremony where I was awarded "Cadet of the Academy"; the one who showed the most promise. All of my cadet friends started calling me Chief T. I felt seen.

Over the next year, I would become ride-along certified which meant I was certified to use the equipment on the fire engine and truck for emergency responses. I rode along all over the city, throwing ladders onto burning buildings, assisting in medical aids, and grocery shopping with firefighters.

I received my EMT certificate in my senior year of high school. I would go to school during the day and then college EMT course at night. My teachers would tell me I needed to try harder than getting C's. I would bring my A's from my college class and boast "I am!" I loved EMT classes. I loved cadets.

2011

Through the Fire Cadet program, I witnessed people from all walks of life. People who lived remarkably differently than I did and were not considered terrible or damned for doing so. I ran 911 calls to different churches and local bars, even strip clubs. I served citizens of San Diego who, for the most part, were kind and respectful to me. I could not imagine that all of these kind people were damned to Hell just because they weren't baptized in the LDS religion. I felt a sense of "us vs them" that I had never experienced before, and it rattled me to my core. Although I feel I owe God my life for saving mine mentally and physically, I understand others don't view God this way. I however wouldn't trade the peace I have for a life void of an all-knowing creator. Never before had I challenged what had been preached to me since I was a little girl. For months, these contradicting thoughts spiraled through me. For the first time in my life, I questioned my religion.

In the LDS church, home teachers are two men assigned to a family. The program aims to personally support a person's journey to become more Christlike. I questioned my home teachers in a room below the chapel—a room below all the sermons that I listened to. This church was where I had found familiarity and comfort in the religion and family I chose. I trusted them to take me as I am. I had to.

I looked at the two "suits" in wonder, comfort, and safety but also in resounding desperation. I knew this place, this feeling. This was home. The church was where I kept all my stock, all my eggs in this basket growing up. My hope was here, and it was starting to fade.

My gaze bore into them, like lasers connecting my eyes with theirs. There was fire in my bones, and I strained to keep from jumping out of my skin. With a metaphorical microphone in hand, I started my trial by fire.

"How do we know what's wrong or right if I only do and know what the church tells me," I questioned. The first teacher fanned pages of scripture and started spouting off memorized verses. He then advised me that I should talk with the bishop, the head of the congregation. The second teacher met me outside and gave me his phone number. He told me he worried about me having a safe place to "explore religion" and offered to have me come over to his house. This teacher would later become my husband. Michael.

He presented himself as a safe person to drink with. I was intrigued because it was a possible answer to my questions concerning what was right and wrong. I went to his apartment only a week or so after meeting him. It was a two-bedroom apartment that he shared with one of his friends. The house was clean with candles that smelled of vanilla lit in every room, a scent that reminded him of his mom. I vividly remember a handle of Vodka and a 2-liter bottle of Sprite on the counter. The image is ingrained in my memory; it would be a surrounding factor for Michael for the next ten years. I was nervous, but he told me he was going to guide me through drinking. I was ready to make this choice for myself. After the first shot, I quickly felt the effects of the cocktail burning down my throat, already slightly dizzy.

The walls I built up around my heart came crashing down. It was as simple as a sip of Vodka and

Sprite—cheap thrills. As easy as it was, it was disingenuous and against my better judgment to become so close to a person this soon. I was taken aback by the goofiness I displayed and how it seemed as if my inner child was coming out to play after years of hiding. All in front of a stranger, Michael. In contrast, Michael had a few drinks and seemed unphased. I didn't think too much of it at the time or for the next decade. I thought he had a high tolerance and coupled with the fact he never slurred his words or passed out, I didn't register it as a possible addiction or a coping mechanism at this point. Between drinks, we talked about the Mormon church and its beliefs. We agreed that the Mormon church was mostly true and had solid values. After only a drink or two, I fell asleep on the couch and left the next morning. For months, we continued to meet over drinks, getting to know one another.

At first, he wasn't interested in dating me, and I wasn't interested either. Despite that, from April to November of that year, I devoted all my time to Michael; we spent all day together and then went on casual double dates with different people at night. We were best friends. It wasn't until one double date in

November that we finally felt a pull towards each other that we hadn't felt before; I wanted to be with him, and him only. Not the standard start of a relationship. But then again, maybe our start only foreshadowed what we were to become.

A few months of this went by. When my mom found out that I was hanging out with a 26-year-old Navy guy who had already traveled the world, she had a spontaneous explosion of words concerning her 19-year-old daughter who was very naive to life in general.

Shortly after we began dating, I was thrown into Michael's complicated family. His dad, Jerry, had just been booked as a now two-time felon for grand larceny. Despite not being close to his dad, Michael went to the court ruling in Las Vegas. After the ruling, Jerry contacted him and said all of his childhood things were going to be lost if he didn't pay the storage unit fee. So a few weeks after the court hearing, Michael, his 3 siblings, and I met in Vegas. I offered to pay half of the cost of the storage unit and his half-brother Robert paid the other half. I don't know why Michael didn't pay for it himself, but I felt bad that he was going to lose all of his family photos and childhood mementos.

While we were in town, we stayed with Michael's grandparents. One day, we all planned to spend the afternoon at his grandparents' pool. Before we went outside, Michael cornered me alone in the bedroom. He warned me not to embarrass him in front of his family. I was to act like we were a perfect couple and that I was okay with how he acted all the time.

Most importantly, he told me he could be with any girl but he was choosing me, and I should be grateful for it. So long as I didn't embarrass him. I felt an overwhelming sense of power dynamic between us. He seemed so grown up to me. He was strong, had a career, and lived on his own. I was just a kid trying to make it in the world. I also saw the life he had, his friends, and his grandparents, and wanted a life like that. One where when a family member was in crisis everyone drove into town to get the belongings out of the storage unit. I wanted unity and it seemed like they had it. I didn't feel like I had that relationship with my family, so I was going to do what Michael said because he had what I wanted. In my naivete, I thought that this behavior of aggression was just what came with the package.

By the time we got home from Vegas, he had apologized and blamed it on the stress of being around his family and dealing with his dad. Despite how callous he acted towards me during the trip, he showered me with attention now that we were home. And that's what I craved. If the man who got bored and annoyed of everyone in his life whether in general or romantically, still chose me again and again regardless of how many times he got annoyed and frustrated with me then how special did that make me! I was the one he always came back to. My self-worth was dependent on Michael keeping me, no matter what.

I didn't morph myself into someone unrecognizable. I just dampened the parts he disapproved of. I emphasize this because our connection was real. We really did love each other to the deepest degree we knew how to. We were two people who liked to have fun, so we did that together. We spent our days in boisterous arcades and watching low-rated movies. Drinking became our evening life. We'd get lost in deep conversations about life, religion, and the universe. He liked being loved by me and I liked loving him. We had a good foundation. But we did not have the tools to co-create a healthy relationship. We didn't talk about feelings, fears, or the sustainability of our relationship. Instead of hard talks and boundaries to create a space that encouraged mutual growth, we just saw what we wanted in each other and focused on how we satisfied each other's desire for companionship.

Despite our bliss, Michael's caustic words continued to cut at my self-worth. By allowing him and not telling him how I felt, I perpetuated his behavior. He would later go on to tell me that he really thought there was nothing he could say or do that would make me leave him. He was right. I was loyal and believed every apology and profession of love. I believed deeply that he loved me and wanted a life with me. That we were going to grow together and show up daily to support one another. Every furious outburst was just another chance to be better for him. Although hurt by his delivery, I thought he was trying to tell me how he was hurting in the only way he knew how. That is how I viewed the relationship. That was how I showed up daily. I was too good at masking my feelings and still too terrified of being thrown away that I suppressed any thoughts of advocating for myself. Every time he hurt me, belittled, and slandered me, it imprinted on my soul. It reprogrammed me to eventually believe his version of events and only his. My peace depended on this. It would all be over if I didn't see things his way or act how he wanted me to. I was so terrified of being left behind and forgotten that I could do nothing else but cling to him. At this point in our relationship, we were not at a point where it was dangerous, physically or mentally, for me to say something. I should have.

We were on a walk one day when he had called me a bitch for the first time. Incredulous, I stopped immediately hoping I had heard wrong. I hadn't. At that moment, I made a pivotal decision to stay silent. It was a decision I wasn't fully aware I was making, but it would cost me dearly. By not actively saying I was not okay with being called that, I was passively saying it was okay. I was naive in thinking the hurtful words wouldn't worsen over time.

Later that night, I found the courage to bring the conversation back up again, asking why he had called me such a hurtful word. He brushed it off and said he was just trying to get a reaction out of me. He wanted to see what I would do, see if I would stand up for myself. He rectified that I wasn't a bitch. I should have asserted that I was not okay with him getting a reaction out of me that way. But I thought the innocent thing to do was remain silent. I did not realize that he would always search for that reaction. So when I became numb to "bitch," he would toe the line a little farther.

In November of 2011, I started working in an ambulance as an EMT. It was my first chance for full-time hours, so the Fire Department got put on the back burner. I wanted to move out of my parents' house and needed money to do that. My life path went in a different direction purely because of my short-term desire to move. I worked diligently, fervently. One night, Stephanie confessed that it felt like I'd forgotten about her. I hadn't forgotten her, but this was a very selfish time in my life. I was trying to launch myself into self-sufficiency. I worked full-time on the night shift, and Michael lived down the street from my work. It was a mixture of convenience and money. My blinders were on tight and I would come to regret it.

2012

At this point in our relationship, Michael and I still attempted to attend the LDS church regularly and follow other church rules. Three months into dating, we violated one of the most sacred doctrines by sleeping together. Despite it being looked down upon to have sex before marriage in the LDS faith, I assumed that it would be okay if we ended up getting married.

In April, he broke up with me for the first time right after my birthday. He admitted wanting to break up with me months ago, but I had given him a "cool present" for his birthday, so he thought it was only fair to wait until after my birthday to end things. Doubt churned in my gut. *Who was this man?* I felt so dumb. I sat on the couch in his apartment searching for the signs that led to this moment. My body sunk deep into the soft cushions. I looked at my hands that once held him and felt terribly alone. My face grew red in embarrassment. My mind raced to find a response. Do I march out and leave him or beg him to stay? The way that I elevated his opinions and thoughts above mine left me eventually walking out of his apartment feeling worthless and scared. Had he spent this time not actually loving me? Was I unable to read the social cues of actual love?

That moment wrecked me and would affect all of my future relationships. Years of feeling unworthy of people's love and time, controlled by one flippant comment. I was gaslit into thinking that because Michael had kept me around all these months, he wanted to invest in a relationship with me. This was clearly not the case if he had, at the same time, been planning to break up with me. His actions did not match what I thought he wanted for us.

I wish I had asked him, "What do you mean by that?" I have learned to ask this when someone does something that I perceive as hurtful. Asking that would have allowed him to explain his thoughts and motives. Instead, I became a thief. I robbed him of presenting his own thoughts and instead wrote my own narrative of internal dialogue. The navigational compass to the root cause. He wanted to break up with me. I told myself it was because I wasn't good enough for him, that I wasn't worth his love or time. I wish I had asked so I could understand his actions. Looking back, I now know that Michael's actions were merely the first clue of his true desires. The breakup was just the byproduct.

To illustrate this further, a friend of mine rents a room to a teenage girl named Hindi. As I walked in with my children one day, Hindi saw us, grumbled out loud, and walked away. At first, I felt rejected, like she didn't want us around. But Hindi had always hugged us upon arrival, so this new behavior wasn't normal for her. So, I just asked her to explain the thought behind her actions. She responded, "I was watching a movie, and I know you only let your kids watch TV at certain times, so I knew I would have to turn it off." What initially could have been perceived as hurtful, was actually a huge sign of compassion and respect for me and my children. To further the blessing of the conversation, we were then able to problem-solve where Hindi wasn't the only one sacrificing. I told my kids to play outside for 20 minutes while she continued her movie and then let the kids watch the rest with her. I do have a rule of no TV at certain times, but paramount to that, we have a rule of community and spending quality time together. TV that afternoon turned into a bonding experience that was memorable for everyone.

If I had probed deeper, perhaps I would have realized earlier that our views and dating goals did not align. I longed for a deep-rooted, eternal relationship, and Michael's comment clearly reflected the opposite. Hearing that he wanted something short-term would have hurt, but at least I wouldn't have assumed that I was to blame or that something was wrong with me that caused him to end things. Our goals were just not aligned.

When we broke up, he justified that the temptation to "sin" was too great. This reasoning contradicted when I would find him at church giving rides to other girls or going out with them. Wasn't there still a temptation to sin with them? Or were they all just better than me? My self-esteem continued to plummet. But then again, he would always come back to me. It would always start with a small text for him or running into each other at church. Small conversation of him admitting that he was lonely or had a headache and wanted a head massage. I would come over because he said he needed something and that would turn into staying for dinner or going to the gym together. Sometimes he would tell me that he felt a little suffocated because I loved him so zealously that he just needed time to process that. Every time we reconciled, I hoped I could be a better girlfriend for him. I hoped we were both trying to be better for each other. I wanted so badly to be loved by Michael.

A few months later completely out of the blue, Michael would say that had I not slept with him, he would have married me. We were on our way out to dinner when he said this; I stood in his apartment in a fancy new dress he had just bought me, my bag in hand, and shoes on. I was so stunned that my appetite instantly disappeared. I was denied a husband and marriage all because I had slept with him?! How was it any different in his mind? If we were married, he wouldn't just divorce me after he slept with me. That would be absurd! I started looking at sex as not so much a covenant that two people make, but as a bargaining chip to get married. Is that where I messed up? LDS members believe that getting married and having kids is the ultimate goal. So is that why I was supposed to wait? I was lost.

In the same breath, Michael offered a solution that was the beginning of the end for us. It was the start of something so incredibly shameful and deeply traumatic. He told me if I was willing to be in an open relationship he would still consider having me around. The concept of an open relationship baffled me. I always believed that a relationship should be between two people only. I don't mean to be ignorant or hurtful to those who choose this lifestyle; I can only speak from my experiences and feelings. It is something that I still don't understand, even after many heated and heartbreaking fights over the years.

Michael pulled up a website for couples to hook up with other couples. He had already created an account and had uploaded photos of us on it without my knowledge. He had also already invited a couple over to his apartment for the next day, all before I accepted his offer. I was in or I was out. My head spun. A double date where we were all dating each other? I was powerless to have a say or even have a moment to process—the date was happening in less than 24 hours. There were two paths before me: agree to be in an open relationship or leave for good. I knew Michael was not the type to miss me if I refused. He would have gladly shown me the door. Maybe he would have taken me back if he felt sorry for me. He had done that before. But I never gave him that option.

The next day, as evening approached, I started to drink. The alcohol barely tamed my fears and disapproval of the situation about to unfold. Michael was so excited and gave me so much undivided attention. He told me how cool this was of me and showered me with compliments. He helped me choose an outfit and never left my side all day. He assured me that nothing weird would happen, we would just meet them and hang out. I was already drunk by the time the couple arrived.

That evening, a very nice couple waltzed in holding a bottle of wine. I am a social person and love meeting new people. so the first part of the night was surprisingly enjoyable as we made small talk and drank their fancy wine. Then the couple pulled out a card game. I don't remember much of the rules, but when one of the cards required Michael to kiss the other woman, I must have looked so horrified that the other couple decided to end the night right then and there.

Michael was nice about it when they left, although he said he was disappointed. He didn't make me feel too bad, but he said he was going to see if they could come by another time. I hated it. I told him this and we dropped the conversation. Instead, he just asked me to tell him stories about things happening like if the night had gone differently. I asked him why it couldn't just be about us. He said that it was "too vanilla." For the time being, it seemed that we had found a compromise by meeting them. But all it meant was that he could bring it up again, just like when he called me a bitch. I was being eased into something that I wasn't comfortable with over a long period of time and before I knew what was happening, my life was unrecognizable. When I brought this up to him, he told me this was just part of life and that I shouldn't ruin our connection because I was being "a prude." We fought so much over the years about this. It was the thing he brought up all the time when he wanted me to do anything I didn't feel comfortable doing. "Stop being a prude" was his go-to line.

2013

In 2013, Michael and I moved to Las Vegas, Nevada, after he graduated from his program. He wanted to move because an Army chemical unit was looking for officers. When he was commissioned to work in Nevada, I also transferred within my work. I was two weeks shy of turning 21 and uprooted everything I knew to move with my boyfriend to another state. I continued to center my self-worth around whether Michael loved me or not. I was afraid that I would never find anyone who wanted to be with me ever again. He was my first boyfriend and the first person I ever slept with. I had essentially left my religion for the lifestyle he offered me. It would have also forced me to look at my relationship with God at that time and realize I did not have any faith in my religion. I attended the LDS church with little accountability for actually practicing or believing in what they believed.

I was able to receive the benefit of the community while gaslighting myself into believing in their version of God.

Suffocating Proposal

When we first moved to Vegas, we lived with his grandparents. At some point, I accidentally discovered the ring in his gym bag. I nearly screamed with joy! My heart overflowed at the thought that he had chosen me. All my hard work to be good to Michael had finally paid off! We were finally going to be married. Or so I thought.

A few days later, Michael and I were at his aunt's house, where his cousin, Jack, lived. While hanging out, Michael insisted to Jack that he and I would never be married. My face burned like fire as my heart shattered into sharp pieces. *What was the point of the wedding ring then?* My thoughts raced. *Was it all just the brunt of an elaborate joke? To humiliate me?*

I stormed out of the house without a word, wanting to leave as quickly as possible, but Michael followed me to the car.

Before he could say anything, I told him it was over; I was moving back to San Diego. For once, Michael was the one shocked into silence. He had never seen me respond this way before. I started the engine, put my favorite M. Ward CD in, and drove. He sat in the passenger seat. He never really liked M. Ward, but with particular liberation, I was taking my life back. *It doesn't matter what he likes anymore*, I told myself. I was done pleasing him, so I turned up the radio and drove. The notion lasted until shortly after the end of the drive. Neither of us uttered a word the whole drive home.

The car came to a heavy stop as I parked in front of his grandparents' house. My footsteps were heavy as I exited the car. Tears streamed down my face as Michael rushed to the driver's side. His hands placed tightly on my arms. He was looking straight into my soul. If you have ever had someone look straight into you, into your very essence, you know then that time stops. The world stops spinning. He looked right at me. At my pain. It was undeniable. With my keys gripped tight, I turned the lock to the front door. Twenty steps and I was in our bedroom. I turned to sit on the bed, and there he was, down on one knee. Of course, I said yes. Of course, this meant I wasn't the brunt of the joke anymore. Of course, Michael used the moment I was done with him to propose, which meant I couldn't be done with him anymore. Of course, getting engaged in fear of losing me wasn't an issue. We did not talk about our issues. He just put a huge band aid on my ring finger. In the end, I would get what I wanted, right? A husband who chose me.

At lunch the next day, I asked him when we should get married. He said he felt suffocated and did not bring it up again. So I didn't.

When we finally got our own place in Nevada, Michael didn't have a job yet because he was waiting to go to basic training for the Army. When rent was due for the townhome, he went to a title-holding bank and traded the title to his car for a few months of rent. He came home with the money and a bottle of vodka. I was heartbroken because every penny counted.

Every night he drank vodka, and my heart sank. Despite my first drink being with Michael right out of high school, I rarely drank now. It was something I did socially and was not something I craved. Alcohol did not mean the same thing to him that it did to me. As embarrassing as it is, I did not understand that he was drinking more than was advised as safe. I did not know what alcohol abuse looked like. I was easily pacified with downplayed comments like "It just doesn't affect me like others." I felt that was true because I saw him slur his words and pass out only once in 10 years. In my naïveté, I watched him drink so much alcohol and thought little of it. I just knew it was ruining us financially. This became the silent dragon in our house.

While visiting San Diego for Christmas, we were at his friend's house. Michael made inappropriate advances on one of my friends right in front of me. Even worse, she was underage, but he gave her a beer. Then they started cuddling on the couch, unashamed that I was in the same room. I was so upset, I got up and walked out the door. He called after me saying I embarrassed him and that sometimes friends do cuddle like that. I kept on walking. He followed me in his car and demanded that I get in. When I got in, he grabbed my hand and tore the engagement ring off my finger saying that I didn't deserve it. At this point, I should have realized the relationship needed to be over; I would never approve of underage drinking.

When we returned to my parents' house, where we were staying while in town, I cried the whole night thinking about the cuddling, the ring, and how I uprooted my life to move to Vegas with him. I felt the projection of my life was too far gone to make myself successful. I had abandoned my Fire Department career and felt that no one at church would ever want to be with someone who broke the law of chastity. My identity as a fiancée confirmed my belief that I was lovable. Now that I was no longer engaged, I was no longer worthy of love. I lay there all night while he slept next to me.

Because we were just visiting, the next day we drove back together. He told me to drive. He broke my heart and still made me drive. At the stoplight down the street from my parents' house, despair tore at my heart. I realized that I was unable to respect myself enough to end this cycle of feeling hurt and disrespected by still getting back together with him. Now I was in the car with him for five hours. I knew we were going to forgive each other, and I hated that I knew that. By the time we got home, we had swept our feelings under the rug. We walked in and unpacked. I made dinner, and we ate and watched a movie without discussing what happened or how either of us felt. He just kept the ring. I kept the shackles around my body, not knowing where I should even begin looking for the key to unlock and release me from this mental torture I perceived as love.

2014

Unconditional Love

When I was 21, a friend offered me a kitten for free. She was the runt of the litter, and I loved her. Pepper Ann provided me with unconditional love during a time when Michael was gone half the time for training and was soon leaving for boot camp and officer school. Unfortunately, it was only a few short weeks later that Pepper Ann displayed signs of increased frailty and sickness, and despite my best efforts, I knew I needed to take her to the vet.

When everything was said and done, I sat down and reflected on my grief process of Pepper Ann. I could vividly remember each stage of loss and grief. Denial that she was going to recover fully, anger at myself and the doctors for letting her die when there was probably more to be done to save her. Depression when everything reminded me of her, and I shut people out. Eventually leading to acceptance, where I could move on and love another kitten in honor of Pepper Ann. My love for animals couldn't end with her death; I needed to share it by loving and giving another kitten a good home.

In the end, I was grateful for struggling through those stages of grief. It helped me recover and become whole again in a healthy way.

Coffee, Lemon Cakes, and Flowers

It was time for Michael to leave for Basic Training with the Army. He was leaving for five and a half months for Basic Training and then Officer Candidate School. He got up early the morning he was leaving for boot camp, got coffee, lemon cakes, and flowers, and put the engagement ring on them. He then placed all of these things on the kitchen counter. This was his way of saying we could get married again. It had been seven months since he had taken the ring away during Christmas. And yet, I couldn't deny how loved I felt. It felt like he was trying. He chose to give the ring back on his own volition. And he chose me. I once again had validation that I was worth loving. He was a hurt person, and I was a hurt person, and we tried to love each other. I hoped.

When he left for Basic Training, I stayed in Vegas as his fiancée. Basic Training was good for him. He finally felt like who he wanted to be, or so he said. When I got my first letter from him, it was exhilarating. Reading back on those letters now, it's evident that my responses seeped out pure stress. My letters to him were too short. They weren't sexy enough. He told me he would write to Kelsey instead.

Kelsey was one of the girls Michael would give rides to church back in San Diego when we were broken up. She had been sending him provocative photos, and when he got home from training, he showed me the photos and letters. Seeing them deeply scarred me. Kelsey knew me, knew both of us. We were friends on social media. She knew we were engaged. Over the years, Michael and I had broken up many times. It felt like every time I started to get over him, he would come around and ask me out again. Up until this point, I had never fully processed any of our breakups; I was always welcomed back into his arms before then. All I had known was the pain of the breakup, but never the healing and self-discovery of autonomy that comes after. All this to say I was scared of losing him to Kelsey because my only association with us not being together was deep heartache. This would soon change. He threatened in his letter that if I didn't step it up, he would use his phone time to call Kelsey instead of me.

What's heartbreaking and confusing is that in those same months, he wrote to me about a dream he had that confirmed his decision to marry me. He told me he had to go to Basic Training to figure that out, while still saying he intended to find attention elsewhere. He said that if I wanted him to pursue me, I better step it up. Prior to him knowing he wanted to marry me, he had already given me the ring — twice.

He made up stories of hooking up (he admitted in his final letters) with women there. He was supposed to go to Basic Training to know he was supposed to get married. But that didn't necessarily mean he needed to marry me, he clarified during one of his phone calls. The dream was just to show him that was capable of marriage and that he could marry anyone. Marriage was on the table for him and he now saw that as an opportunity — maybe to marry one of these girls from Basic Training, or maybe me, if I stepped up.

After Basic Training and before Officer Candidate School, I flew out to meet him in Georgia. We spent the weekend in Georgia and on a lake in Alabama with Chris, a friend he made at Basic Training. Michael said when he saw me at the airport, he knew I was the one. We took pictures for our wedding. It's hard to look back at that time and wonder what he was thinking because a month later, he once again called off the wedding. He left for Officer Candidate School (OCS), and I flew home. OCS was where he would get massages from other girls late at night and make out with another girl out in the forest. He would confess this all to me just to say that he felt bad about it later. While at OCS, I broke up with him for the first time ever. Distance from him made it easier.

This Job Serves No One

Although I enjoyed my time working in the ambulance, politics were not for me. And that is me trying to say it in the most political way possible. I loved the ambulance in San Diego. Las Vegas, however, ran things differently. One day, during the Emergency Vehicle Operator Course (EVOC), my coworkers were discussing the pay scale and asked if I made more money in Las Vegas than in San Diego. I was uncomfortable answering, but I didn't think any harm would come from contributing to the conversation and didn't think anything of it. A few weeks later without any notice, I was pulled into the Human Resources office and told I was bragging about my pay at work and was in trouble for it. They would have pulled me in here sooner, but the instructor who reported me died of a heart attack.

At the time I was very upset. I didn't have a way to defend myself because the person who said it couldn't defend himself. I saw posts on the internet of what a great person he was. Maybe he was. I didn't know him. I just knew I was mad at someone I wasn't allowed to be mad at.

I wrote the general manager about this and delivered the handwritten letter to him. In it, I expressed how I felt uncomfortable being brought into a room with three men and having the door shut behind me. I had no union rep. I was told what was what and then ushered out to do a lift test. I walked to the ambulance bay to do this and failed.

I was so upset that I went straight to the bathroom. I thought for sure I had just lost my job. I also felt pain in my back. The gurney that I tried to load into the back of the ambulance was a lot heavier than I remembered it being. As it turned out, it was over-weighted. The person who took the test after me noticed a large weight under the mannequin and removed it. He told the supervisor, who then got me out of the bathroom and told me I could take the test again. I don't remember what happened after that. What I do remember is shortly after I was in a room with Human Resources and two other people who said my letter to the general manager was retaliation. A sick and twisted corporate move to say you are not allowed to disclose your own experiences. This was the separation of the white-collar "thieves" who had their titles as managers, heads of departments, and the ones who signed my paychecks. I felt the power they held and that I wasn't valued as an employee there. I labeled myself "gray collar me" and felt backed into a corner.

After all of this, I stood up and quit. I could no longer work in a place I didn't belong. Fortunately for me, word travels fast in Emergency Medical Services, and by the next day, I was already offered two jobs. They had heard what happened and sought me out. Most of my friends from the ambulance stopped talking to me. I'm sure they were worried about their careers. I don't hold negative feelings about them trying to protect themselves. But it did hurt.

Nostalgia Wins

After quitting AMR, I began my employment at the Las Vegas Motor Speedway. I worked there and for a special events company. I started going on dates. I dated a few race car drivers. A driver named Matt would always come over and talk to me. It was fun, and he was funny. So when he asked me on a date, I agreed. Michael was still at OCS, and we were attempting to be apart.

Another person I dated took me to the stratosphere, and he kissed me at the top. I wasn't ready for a kiss, but it was nice. He came over a few more times, and I went over to his house with his roommates. It was a fun time, and I was grateful for it.

Then, I met Zane at a country bar. Later, we would make the connection that we were in the same room at work a few weeks prior. I still remember walking off the dance floor, where he pulled me close and kissed me. Magic. He asked me out the following week. Zane would continue coming over after work, bringing me smoothies and other treats. I told Zane that Michael reached out to me and told me it was okay that I was dating, but that when he came home, he wanted to be with me again. Zane looked at me, holding me tight in the kitchen, and said, "If you were my girl, I'd never let another guy touch you."

Looking back, I feel like I let Zane go, and regret it greatly. But I think a very important distinction to understand is that time has gone by. We are two very different people now, and we no longer share the space we did back then. I wish him well. I thank him for treating me right even though I was too lost in myself to accept it. I apologize for that. I also know he is probably doing just fine and doesn't need my apology.

In the fall, I enrolled in a certified nursing assistant (CNA) class in Mesquite. When I started the class, Michael and I were together. Two months later, he would call off the engagement again. One of my classmates, Camrin, invited me to her church event for Halloween. I drove up and met her. Getting out and being with her and her family was lovely. Her husband and three children were so kind. We had dinner, went to the event, and then afterwards, Camrin said one of the single guys from her church asked if I wanted to go on a date. I agreed, and then he picked me up at my Camrin's house on his horse! We went for a horse ride, and he showed me how to use his guns in the desert. I had shot guns before, but the unexpectedness of the night was thrilling! He gave me an amazing Halloween night under the full moon, shooting guns at soda cans.

I was determined not to get back with Michael — or so I thought. My mind wrestled with the fact that he wanted me back. We both spent years wanting and then not wanting each other. We also had this townhome together. We had a lease that I had no way of breaking. Michael came home, into the townhome. And like water down a stream, there was little resistance. It was my turn to cave back in.

Success in Recentering

While at the Special Event Company and The Las Vegas Motor Speedway, I heard about a training company called Joint Tactics and Medicine, or JTM. They trained military members for pre-deployment certifications such as Tactical Combat Casualty Care or TCCC. I became a part-time role player. This meant Heather, the moulage artist, would paint wounds on me and 5-10 others. Then we would dress in military clothes and be dropped in the desert to be rescued while the rescuers (Navy Seals and Pararescuemen/PJs) were shot at with paintballs. We would sometimes get to use abandoned hotels on the strip for our training, and occasionally, some events led to the actual hospital, where they would give turnover reports to the emergency room doctors. It was wild! I'd also go with my boss to the desert with raw pig meat, shooting holes into it so they could practice suturing. One of the perks was I got free training and my concealed carry license.

I had three part-time jobs that I absolutely loved. I wish I had learned sooner that I didn't have to stay with the ambulance service while I was unhappy there. Management wasn't a good fit for me, and I wasn't a good fit for them either. They didn't benefit from having me there and I didn't benefit from being there. I thought the ambulance was the only way to go. I was powering through when I could have been thriving somewhere else. I was so unhappy there that I wish I had thought of applying to a grocery store instead. I did not need to be in emergency services. I could have focused on college. I could have done anything else while I recentered. As it turned out, those good-for-me jobs quickly found me when I gave up how I thought things should be.

Double Shake Up

One night in December, Michael and I went out on the Strip. We met some people we had recently become friends with at the Excalibur Hotel. They invited us to their party in the suite. It was huge! There were three bedrooms and an upstairs. People were constantly coming in. At one time, I think there were about 40 people in the suite.

At some point, I started to not feel well. It felt like a stomach ulcer flare-up or something. I was ready to call it a night because I had a history of stomach pain. Looking back, my chronic stomach pain was usually due to stress and ignoring my intuition. The guy who invited us, came storming down the stairs and out of the room. I went upstairs to find his girlfriend holding a clump of her hair in her hand and a shattered drinking glass. Her head was bleeding. She said that they had left to go to another club and she forgot her ID so they had to go back. He was angry at her because they had to leave the club and come back for it.

Michael came upstairs shortly after. I got into the bed with her and held her as she cried. Shortly after, the boyfriend came back. He was still angry. Michael told him he wasn't allowed back in. Back into his suite. He got angry again but left. Later when the girl seemed to be ok, Michael and I headed home. We stayed up until the sun rose because I was so shaken up.

About a week later, I found out the reason I wasn't feeling well was because I was pregnant.

2015

With the positive pregnancy test, Michael decided to finally get married. He suggested that we should go out that very night and tie the knot. After all, we did live in Vegas and had been semi-engaged for a year. I put on a dress while he got the keys. All I needed to do was walk out of the bedroom, down the stairs, and into the car. My knees gave out instead. Inside the four walls of our bedroom, I sobbed. This was not what I wanted my life to be. I never wanted to elope. I wanted to be swept off my feet and adored. I felt the dream I had for my future crumble. I knew Michael thought he was doing the right thing by marrying me, but tears splashed hopelessly on our bedroom floor at the thought that I was forcing this marriage by getting pregnant. I felt like he was going to resent me and in the same breath, I was ecstatic to be a mom. It was what I'd wanted for so many years. Michael grabbed my hands and set the keys down. He held me until I fell asleep instead.

We announced to our family and friends that the wedding would be three weekends from then and that whoever could make it was welcome. I would be eight weeks pregnant by then, but my dress would still fit. I remember driving down Rainbow Drive, and I spaced out so hard that I missed my turn. It scared me. But that was part of pregnancy, right? When I got home, I had spotting, but it wasn't a lot. Maybe an ounce of blood at a time. When I asked my mom, she assured me it was spotting, even after being seven weeks along.

The big day was fast approaching. Both my family and Michael's family were present. We went to the chapel and paid the deposit. $200. I had my white dress which I paid $90 for months earlier. It was the perfect dress. The day before the wedding, we went out to eat with my family, and afterward, I went back up to my parents' hotel for a few minutes. My side had been hurting the whole night, a stabbing pain that would come and go every few minutes until it was constant pain. It was getting harder and harder to move. My mom said it was my ligaments stretching due to pregnancy. I lay down on the bed.

Because I was spacing out sometimes, I tried to drive as little as possible. Michael came to pick me up, and we went home. When we got back, I sat on the couch and asked for a heat pack and Tylenol. As he handed them to me, I felt a sinking despair that something was not right—I needed to get to the emergency room. He got me in the car, and we rushed to Summerlin Hospital.

As soon as I entered the lobby, black spots flooded my vision before all went black. When I awoke maybe a few minutes later, I was in a wheelchair in the waiting room. The nurse brought me to the back to get an ultrasound. I lay there terrified for my baby and felt at the mercy of the doctors to tell me what I needed to do and when to do it. Afterwards, the doctor came in and informed me that I had an ectopic pregnancy. They were going to start preparing me for emergency surgery.

As I lay in the hospital bed, I looked over at Michael's wide eyes. He tried to assure me that an ectopic baby was only a lump of cells; it wouldn't have been a viable pregnancy no matter what we did. It was not helpful. But he was scared and trying to comfort me. They wheeled me back to the operating room in the early hours of the morning. Before they started anesthesiology, I looked at the surgeon and confidently told him to be quick because I was getting married that day! The doctor looked out at the delusional words drifting across the room and holding lightly in the air. He politely informed me I wasn't going to make it to the chapel today. I politely held my ground. The doctor looked at the anesthesiologist placatingly and said, "Pump her full of whatever you have to; she's getting married today!" They suctioned out a pint of blood that was sitting in my abdominal cavity from the rupture and removed my fallopian tube and pregnancy. Then stitched me up.

When I woke up, they said I could leave as soon as I could walk, so I immediately stood up, walked to the bathroom, and then asked to be discharged. Michael came back to the post-surgery room and drove me home. It was pouring rain. I actively told myself not to think about losing the baby because I needed to focus on the next few hours. I told myself I would process this later. It slipped my mind that my friend, Liz was waiting at the house to do my hair for the wedding. We were obviously not home when she got there, but she had still waited. After a brief breakdown of everything, she nodded, understood that we needed to get moving on getting me to the chapel, and we walked into the house.

Liz washed my hair and styled it. Every time I would pass out from the heat of the blow dryer, she would hold me up until I came to and started again. She put my makeup on, painted my nails, shaved my legs, zipped up my wedding dress, and sent me off. It was the perfect dress because it did not touch the stitches at all.

Our car pulled into the parking lot 20 minutes late. As I stood before the chapel doors, frustrated employees glared at us, ready to cancel our time slot. You have a specific time in Vegas and they stick strictly to it because they have so many weddings every day, especially on Sundays like ours. They admonished us for being so late. I responded by lifting my dress to show my stitches and iodine-covered stomach. Michael gave them a summary of our night and morning. They quieted up and reverently ushered us into the chapel. The minister marrying us said, "We will get you married, and if we need to cut it short you just nod at me and I will wrap it up." I thanked him and walked to the bridal room. Unbeknownst to me, Michael stood in front of the congregation and explained that we had just lost the baby, and I was three hours post laying on the operating table.

The doors opened, and I walked down the aisle unaware everyone knew I was no longer pregnant. We got married, took photos, and were supposed to go out to lunch after, but I needed to go home and rest. We had to pay the minister, so I took the cash to the receptionist and handed it over. The receptionist looked at me kindly and said that the minister had already left and was told not to take my money. I paused and thought how gracious that was. It briefly crossed my mind that someone wouldn't do that unless what I just went through was tragic. But I wanted this to be a happy day so I stuffed my feelings down again and reminded myself that I could feel the heartbreak of this later. It was a miracle in and of itself that she didn't take the money because it was all the money we had. We would use that money for gas the following week to make it to Missouri.

We went home, and I guided my ever-so-aching body into bed. My family came over and hung out in our bedroom. All the medication had worn off at that point, and it was painful to move. My stomach felt ripped apart at every turn I made. I could feel the stitches, and every time I looked down at them, I burst into tears. I was confined to the bed and aching to get the iodine off of me and take a shower. My sister took my phone and pretended to look through it, knowing it would upset me. I told her to stop, and she threw my phone onto my stomach. I yelled at her to leave in front of everyone, anxious and hurt because the phone landed on my just sewn-up stomach. Had I not just been cut open, our relationship would have quickly recovered. Instead, we did what we usually did: ignore each other until enough time had passed, or we were forced into a room together because of a family function. We didn't talk until it blew over. It was all we knew how to do. It was how we learned to handle issues all growing up. We didn't know any better, but I wish we did, and I wish it didn't take so many years to learn a new way of expressing disappointment.

Michael was totally lost on how to help me. I was totally lost on how to ask. I can't imagine how he felt while I recovered. The only time he helped me through recovery was one night when I told him I really needed a shower. He helped me into the tub, then turned on the shower water for me. His hands gently scrubbed shampoo and conditioner on and then off of my hair for me. I sat there unable to do this for myself. He cleaned me up. Then helped me up, sat me down again, and then brushed and dried my hair.

That night I was torn between excitement and grief. On the one hand, I was finally married! Michael still chose me, and since I was no longer pregnant, it wasn't just for the baby's sake. But, in the back of my mind, I wondered if we were so pressed against time, we just went on with the wedding without pausing to think about it. My thoughts flipped between feeling like he didn't actually choose me and trying to convince myself that he had. My thoughts would be verified in later years when he admitted that he married me because I was pregnant, and then when he saw how I persevered through the surgery, he felt he couldn't call it off.

On the other hand, I found myself pulled into the grief of losing our baby And not knowing if I would be able to get pregnant again since they removed one of my fallopian tubes. I was now a wife and was almost a mom. For closure, we decided to name the baby we lost Mason James.

Picked First To Play

The following week, we packed up and moved to Fort Leonard Wood, Missouri for Michael's Officer school. We were there from January to June. I made friends and helped him with his homework. We lived in a one-room hotel with one burner and no oven. I made a lot of soup. We ate a lot of pizza. On the weekends we would go explore different surrounding cities.

One weekend we went to St Louis for a Cardinals game. We walked into the stadium and Michael said he didn't feel right not wearing a jersey. I will always remember that because he knew how to make things fun. So we got shirts and sat in our seats supporting the Cardinals.

When I look at the past and the future of this moment, this was the time when we felt the most connected. In a rural town. I was the one to go out with him. I felt like his first choice. We were unplugged from the city. He was busy with his class and we went out and had fun when he wasn't.

The last thing I will say about our time in Missouri is that I spent it healing from my surgery. Mentally and physically. My journey with a miscarriage is difficult to talk about, not only because it is a sensitive subject, but also because I had children afterward. I was able to become a mother eventually, which had become a deep desire of mine since seeing the positive pregnancy test prior. What I do think is important to address is that I was absolutely devastated when I found out I was not going to be pregnant anymore. The pain never went away until I was holding Ronan. But the pain did go away. My heart is with every single person who is still struggling with fertility. For a brief moment, I knew that heartache; it was all-encompassing heartache.

LIFE IS BEAUTIFUL

Three months after returning from Missouri, the Special Event Company I worked for assigned me to a three-day festival in Vegas. The festival name "Life is Beautiful" became a poetic and meaningful phrase I have said to myself many times over the years. It is a reminder through all of life I've experienced that life is indeed, beautiful. On the last day, while the last band played, I went into the bathroom and stared at myself in the mirror, silent tears streaming down my face. I knew in my heart that I was pregnant. A rainbow baby.

Beside me, a police officer started to wash her hands. I felt a reverent comfort as she asked, "Are you okay?" There was a kindness in her words that I needed in that moment. I was scared, elated, and nauseous. It provided me with space to say for the first time, "I think I'm pregnant." She nodded and asked what she could do to help me. I replied that I was okay and thanked her. The space she held for me in that bathroom and noticing my experience is something I still cherish. I walked out of the bathroom and told my boss. With minutes left of the concert, he handed me a pregnancy test and told me that right before the concert he went to the store for some last-minute things. He found himself staring at the pregnancy tests and thought "Why not?" and bought one just in case. I nervously took it and left. For days, I stared at that test; I couldn't bring myself to take it.

That following weekend, Michael was out, but I heard his cousin Jack, who stayed with us periodically, cleaning around our house profusely. Michael had decided to bring home a girl he had been seeing, unbeknownst to me. Earlier, He had texted saying that I had been acting absolutely insane lately. When he found out I was pregnant, he said that must have been why I was acting so emotional. It all made sense to him; in his mind, I pushed him into the arms of another woman because of my hormones. He was going to bring a girl home; he could either break up with me or I could let him have a night of peace, and maybe then we could stay together. I immediately started to pack a bag to leave him.

When they arrived, they strolled past me into the spare bedroom and shut the door. I sat there with my bag, stunned, listening to her giggles. I couldn't believe what was happening. I snuck out of the house and sat in my car, frozen. I could not drive. I didn't want to be alone, so I called Shawn and asked him to pick me up. We sat in the parking lot. He said, "I hate to be the one to tell you this but your marriage is over." He knew. I didn't. I told him I had a key to my work and asked him to take me there and I'd spend the night on the couch.

He drove and I sat in the passenger seat. I wasn't embarrassed; I'm not sure I even processed what happened. I looked out the window like it was a bad movie. It was a bad movie because in a good movie I would have listened to Shawn. I would have divorced Michael and been on with my life. I was scared to take the pregnancy test that Shawn gave me. Knowing it would be positive. Knowing my husband was in our home with another woman. Knowing he didn't care. He demanded I be in the other room, silent.

We got out of his truck and Shawn hugged me. I grabbed my bag, walked to my office, and fell asleep on the couch. At 6 a.m., I woke up to my other boss opening the door and saying "Well, that's not good." I can't remember if I told her what happened. The work day rolled by, but by 2 p.m. with no other way to get home, I was forced to text Michael asking for a ride. I didn't tell him how I got there and he didn't ask.

When we got home, I pulled out the test and set it on the counter. Michael started and said, "ok so what?" I grabbed it and with the door open peed on it. It went positive instantly. Unperturbed, Michael looked at it and said "I'm not going to get too excited. Let's wait and see if this one sticks." Then he walked away. I stood in the bathroom holding the test and Ronan in my belly. Alone.

I held my rainbow baby tummy so close. When we lost our first pregnancy it left a huge void. I felt whole again and extremely blessed that it had been less than a year and I was already pregnant again.

Michael brought up the open marriage situation again. We had tried attending parties throughout the years, but I was never on board. On occasion, I would agree to go to a party but always leave early because I was against everything happening there. I did have some friends who were fun to talk to, but that was it. I found out later that he would meet up alone with women he met there and sleep with them. It honestly was a smart plan. Those there would have assumed that I agreed to it since they had seen me before at a party. But in reality, it was a deep-seated wound. He accused me of robbing him of the experience that those parties ended in. He felt that the pregnancy now ruined his hopes and dreams of having an open marriage.

It was an ongoing argument that I hated because it always ended with me having to do something for him that I disagreed with. So, he chose to pursue other women without my knowledge instead. He had secretly made more accounts on couples' websites and continued to meet up with them all while I grew our baby. When it finally did come to my attention, or when he would just straight up tell me where he was going, I was already too exhausted from it to care. So annoyed and covered in child vomit and laundry that I just couldn't care. It took energy I didn't have.

Extended and Expanding Family

One night, while watching a movie in the townhome, Michael's phone rang. It was the police. They called to inform Michael that his grandpa "Papa" had died. Michael hung up the phone and told me what happened before rushing over to his grandparents' house. He told me to stay home. I sat in the house brokenhearted and confused. I wish he had asked me to go with him; I wish I was there to hug our family. Instead, I waited for Michael to return. I don't remember when it was decided, but we were to move back in with his grandmother, Anyu, to help her now that she was a widow. Living with Anyu was a time I will always treasure for the love, the laughs, and the living. Cheesiness all the way.

Anyu was the first person to give me wine when I first met her. I told her that I thought it was going to be too strong so she said "Not a problem." She then stood up and poured me a glass with some Sprite. I am not sure if I loved the wine or if I just loved her easy-going attitude. We said "cheers" with big smiles on our faces. Anyu always asked if I wanted coffee. It is one of the reasons coffee is so comforting to me. A hot cup of coffee was always available alongside her company. We were out of milk once, but she handed me a cup with white clumps floating on top. My face probably displayed my terrified hesitance, but her big bright eyes persuaded me to take a sip of the most delicious coffee I have ever had. It turns out that she had taken Cool Whip and used that. It was a perfect balance of cream and sugar! I was forever changed by her creative process. Coffee and Cool Whip is now a staple that my friends know me for. I still cherish all of the care, laughter, and love that Anyu gave to us.

On a Sunday afternoon, Michael's mom, Julie, was over. I heard her ask Michael to make a pot of coffee since he always made it the best. My eyes jolted over to him in endearment. He was the family's golden boy, and they were always impressed with him, praising him even when doing little things. I teased him, making the motions of the simple steps of making the coffee.

Later in the evening, Anyu was still wired from the coffee. I told my observation to Michael and provided a solution. Since Anyu would drink 5-6 cups of coffee a day, I suggested that we reuse the old coffee container and fill it with decaf instead. That way, Anyu wouldn't have to decrease her intake, but her energy and heartrate levels would decrease. I was right, she became a lot more calm. It was these moments with Michael and Anyu that I cherish. Problem-solving and acts of service toward each other filled us with love. We moved in to take care of Anyu, but she also cared for us.

Michael would come home from his job at one of the hotels in Vegas, and I would come home from JTM. We would both come home to Anyu. One day, he came home with a bunch of paperwork that he was far behind on. I told him that if he watched The Voice with me and baby Ronan in my tummy, I would help him get caught up. Months went by of me doing his work as he sat back, claiming he was exhausted from working all day. The paperwork stack seemed to get higher and higher but I still plugged away. I was happy to have this time with him but I wondered why he couldn't have an assistant at work to help him. It was a lot to do and I couldn't imagine how he was doing this all day while still having this much at home. I'll never know the answer to that, but I do know that the stacks continued to grow, and I was staying up later and later to thin the stack.

Then one day, I got a phone call from him while at work. I was walking down the hallway admiring my baby bump when I heard my phone go off. It was strange that Michael was calling me during work hours. He explained that he just couldn't keep up with his work and needed to know if I would support his decision to quit. We would be back to a single income again, but hearing the desperation in his voice, I knew I couldn't say no. I didn't ask follow-up questions. I have no idea what happened before or after our conversation, but he was so relieved and I knew we could make it on one income.

Slowly, our savings decreased as my belly grew. Michael got put on deployment which was great because it was what he wanted to do anyway. I didn't know until he returned from deployment that he had voluntarily signed up to go to Kuwait and Iraq. It would surprise me that he would do that knowing he would be leaving behind his 3-month-old for a whole year. But maybe that's why he did it. Perhaps he didn't know how else to provide for us. I'll never know, but I can thank him for that sacrifice. With deployment on the horizon, we planned our move back to San Diego and into my parents' house to prepare for Ronan and the deployment.

2016

MY TURN TO RIDE

Knowing I was pregnant with Ronan, my hand constantly rested on my stomach. Michael wanted to wait to tell people or to feel excited, which I understood. We couldn't guarantee that this pregnancy would be viable. Still, I was definitely disappointed by his lack of enthusiasm and could not hold back. I had spent the last year thinking about our baby that we lost. Here I was pregnant again, and relieved. There was an all-encompassing light in me that was growing in my belly. Every week, I anticipated the milestones. My baby, the size of a mustard seed, a grapefruit, and then a tiny watermelon! Every second felt closer to his arrival in my arms, my heart bursting with excitement! My small but growing family. It is natural for me to fall into the deep end with loving people. Here I was, with full permission to love this baby coming into the world. I embraced it head-on and in full. I was deeply in love with Ronan instantly.

During my pregnancy, I suffered from frequent migraines as well as intense pregnancy cravings. I wasn't sure why migraines plagued me so often, but I indulged in all of my cravings for protein, especially salty steak. One night after dinner, I went to lie down, thinking I was just aching from pregnancy. I awoke to sharp incremental pulsations of pain in my abdomen. It was difficult to determine what part of my belly was in excruciating pain. With the previous emergency surgery for my last pregnancy still fresh in our minds, both Michael and I were understandably panicked.

My vision became covered in black spots, and I screamed in agony. Fear for my baby encompassed me fully. Anyu ran to my side and in the distance, I heard the 911 operator on the phone. Anyu, inches away from my face assured me I was going to be okay as the paramedics helped my shaking body onto the gurney. The ambulance drive to the hospital felt long and overwhelming. I had driven and rode in the back of an ambulance for years but was never a patient on the gurney. I stared out of the two windows on the back doors, feeling overly exposed as I lay helplessly and prayed for my son. When I got to the hospital, they transferred me to a bed. Once again, I was at the mercy of doctors as they began their tests. When the doctor finally came through the little curtain and sat down, I was relieved to hear that the cause for all the pain was only kidney stones. All the high sodium and dense protein diet had caught up with me. Thank God for kidney stones, I thought as I was discharged. Baby Ronan was ok. I thanked God.

For Time and All Eternity

Soon after, we made our preparations to move back to San Diego. Michael was to leave for weeks at a time for training, and I got the blessing of starting my stay-at-home journey. We went through our checklist. Michael had moved me back to my hometown. We had both gone through to get our endowments with the Mormon temple, a series of vows acknowledging God's purpose and teachings, but we had not been sealed to each other. To be sealed is like a wedding ceremony, but the focus is to "seal you" to each other for time and all eternity. This was something I pushed for.

I grew up believing that if we weren't sealed, we wouldn't be a family in the next life. So, one month before Ronan was born, we went to the San Diego Temple on May 4th and got sealed. What stood out most to me was the hot flashes I had and wanting them to hurry up because my feet were sausages. It did not feel spiritual, just a thing to get done to ensure our stance in the afterlife. As an unromantic forever family, we headed home. I truly felt that I was worthy to be in the temple. Michael explained to me that he disclosed to his bishop that he drank but wanted to be sober. He believed deploying would force him into sobriety. I believed in God, at least I thought I did.

Ronan

The day Ronan was born, I went into labor at 5 p.m. — the peak of San Diego traffic. Michael drove me to the birthing center where the staff checked us in. I loved the idea of birthing naturally here. It was a home converted into a center and there was a warmth and welcoming feel to the entire place. As they walked me into one of the bedrooms, I spied the bathtub I hoped to birth Ronan in. Excitement filled the air as I asked them to open the windows because the room felt too warm. The contractions grew stronger and longer as I labored naturally for 6.5 hours. Toward the end, I begged for any relief they could give me, but they did not offer epidurals at the Birth Center. At one point, it felt like I was watching a movie of the birth. I was the vessel, my mind removed. It was like my hands and feet were duct taped to a bike and I was going downhill. I was captive to my body as it took control and my mind had no say in what was happening.

After hours of laboring and pushing, I stood in a lunge position pushing in the bathtub when the nurse directed me to look down and grab my baby. As he came up to my chest, I came out of my body for a moment and then flew back into it fully once again, with the baby boy I grew in my tummy. Ronan is me, he is his dad, and yet he is his whole identity all on his own. He is Ronan. I got out of the tub and laid on the bed with my baby on my chest. There is no better drug than that.

We left the center around 4 a.m. and I went straight to bed. I must have woken up around 8 a.m.

My first instinct was to walk down the hall to the bathroom. I was in such a daze that when I saw my mom and my newborn baby on the couch my first thought was "Oh right. I had a baby last night." The thought suddenly jolted me back to reality. It was still not enough to keep me from sleeping off the exhaustion of childbirth. When I woke up the second time, I devoured the stack of pancakes that someone had left for me on my nightstand.

On our first visit to the pediatrician's office, they noticed that Ronan had a cleft palate. Meaning the back of the roof of his mouth wasn't fully formed. It would be a quick surgery when he was nine months old, but that wasn't what frightened me. When they weighed him, they noted that he had lost weight. That he had actually not been able to breastfeed since birth. Essentially, I had been starving him for 2 days. I felt like 40 tons had been dropped on my chest. I had already monumentally failed. The doctor promptly brought in a special bottle specifically for clefts, full of formula, something I was sure I didn't want to give Ronan while pregnant. But by then, I was so utterly frantic, that I popped that bottle in his mouth and exhaled, now so grateful for an alternate solution. I continued to exclusively pump and substitute with formula for six months, which had been my goal. I had put a lot of pressure on myself to go for that long, but I had persevered. Interestingly enough, Michael said watching my dedication to giving Ronan breast milk and being Ronan's mom was the first time he actually started to genuinely love me.

Less than a month later, I made this Journal Entry:

July 2nd Journal Entry:

I always knew Michael didn't trust me as a mom. He thinks that I am mentally unstable. He told me that he would take my son away from me and he knows he could win in court to make sure I would never see my child again. After all this time I don't understand him. He is so soft and sweet, yet so cut throat. He hit me so hard and then was choking me. How can I not fear that he will do this to Ronan? He has free reign to call me worthless and the worst mom ever, tells me that he fears me holding his son... Yet I can't even tell him how I'm feeling. I stood by this guy while we were homeless.

All because I saw something special in him. But maybe his past did more damage to him than I let myself believe. I can't undo his mean side. He goes into blind rage mode. He thinks it's good for the military...and maybe it is. But I am not military. I am not stronger than him. I am not smarter than him. He will always win when it comes to hurting. He doesn't think that I deserve an opinion.

This Journal Entry perfectly sums up why I couldn't leave: fear paralyzed me. And Michael was leaving for a year anyway, so what did it matter? If I could just get through the next few months, he would have 10-12 months without me—a year to heal for both of us. He couldn't physically hurt me for a year. I hoped that was the reset we needed. The deployment I was so sad about also seemed like a necessary respite. Thief rebranded. It gave me an excuse to not have to look at what was dysfunctional and I could bank on time healing and saving our marriage instead.

Almost 3 years after he died I had the thought that when he saw me walk into the house with his newborn baby, subconsciously he saw me as his mom. He

> *saw himself as a certain parental figure, and he saw Ronan as himself. Just like a child plays house to process their environment (play therapy), Michael was trying to process his childhood by reliving it. I was an active but not willing participant.*

I acknowledge that when he hurt me and we then reconciled, I was trying to affirm my beliefs about my desire to be loved, at my emotional expense. If Michael still professed to love me, then that meant collateral hurt was okay. I believe Michael was doing the same. He treated me like, from what I've been told, one of his paternal figures treated his mom and what he witnessed and the way he was treated as well. I think in Michael's mind, if he could treat me the way that this paternal figure treated his mom and still love me and Ronan after, then that meant this person loved his mom and him as well.

God Be With You

When Michael left for deployment, I took a photo with him and said, "God be with you." The Michael I knew before deployment was my best friend and sometimes my worst nightmare. But when I look back at the years we spent getting to know each other, everything we did together, and the family that we grew, I really did love him. Not just in the "I love his potential" sort of way, but in a way that was real for me. I showed up every day for him. Michael hurt me consistently and deeply physically, emotionally, psychologically, and spiritually. But our bond was there. At the end of every blowout, we chose each other. So many people over the years have told me that Michael didn't show it through his behavior, and I get that. Countless times, I wished he would have done things differently or that he just would have been kind and gracious. I lost sleep over it plenty of times before I chose to embrace the man I married. And yes, that is enabling, devaluing, and not healthy. But it's what we both did.

During the year Michael was deployed, I remember thinking that it was easier this way. He was fulfilling his dreams, and we weren't fighting about Ronan. He wasn't even in the country.

2017

Ten months later, I picked up Michael late one night from the airport. We have had many airport greetings over the years, but this one was different. I had not been in the same room with him in almost a year. We had lived two completely different lives during his deployment. And now he was right in front of me.

When we returned to my parents' house, where I stayed through the deployment, we went straight to bed. I woke up in the night and panicked for a second thinking there was a stranger in my bed. The adjustment was slow but fun for the next few weeks. We were able to be our small little family. After two months, Michael was assigned to Salt Lake City, Utah. What felt like overnight, we got an apartment out there and moved. I was very excited to relocate and explore a new city. But neither of us knew who the other person was at this point. After getting settled and the honeymoon part of the move ended, I stared at another positive pregnancy test. I didn't know it yet, but Michael, who was a jerk sometimes before the move, would become someone I actively feared in Utah.

2018

Speechless Pregnancy

I took one of Ronan's shirts that said "bro" on it and added the word "big" above it. I had my camera ready to capture the moment when I heard the door open and Michael walked in. He looked at Ronan, read the shirt, and slapped the phone out of my hand telling me to stop recording. About an hour later, he told me to get in the car to get a pregnancy test because he did not believe me. I grabbed two: one to immediately take and one to take in the morning just in case. I went to the bathroom and it immediately went positive. Michael went to bed without saying a word.

    I couldn't help but be excited. I had a baby growing in my stomach. Michael absolutely refused to acknowledge I was pregnant, but I knew deep down that he loved his little girl. He told me one night that he already had so much responsibility, and to add another baby felt overwhelming. As my bump grew, he got more creative in his way to leave bruises on my body. It got to the point where I stopped feeling comfortable if I didn't have a jacket on. I could no longer blame the move to justify the new and old bruises that covered my body.

Michael was no longer nice to be around. I felt like my very presence upset him. At one point, I asked him if he could get a box down for me, and he refused. When I tried to get it myself, it fell on my head, and instead of helping me, he laughed and walked out of the room. I'd wake up to a pillow smothering my face, or he would shove me off the bed so hard, I'd land on the floor after being in a deep sleep. Sometimes, he'd shove me off the bed even when I was awake. I'd spend hours every night massaging him for two or three hours. It was no longer acceptable for me to massage him for an hour. He now needed me to massage him to sleep, and if I woke him up by stopping, I'd have to start again. I began to be so sleep-deprived that I learned to fall asleep while being completely awake. This was a very helpful, but very painful tool.

April

Journal Entry April 19th:

I feel like I'm in this pregnancy alone. Like the guy I used to love now lives in his phone. I sit here and wait for a compliment to break this long run of heartbreak. This guy thinks I'm a horrible mom, just a nanny for him. Yet when he gets off work, my shift doesn't end. Constantly misjudging him, endlessly annoying him. All I want is a friend. I'm not strong enough for him, for my battle within. He doesn't see it. He doesn't look, I say I'm hurt and he physically reacts thinking I'm a piece of shit. His day could be bad, it could be great...until he comes home to me and wonders where he went wrong. I can't take the ups and downs, being pushed around. I see the man that took all of my hope, adventure, faith. I'm on edge around him because I must please him. Constantly judged and put down. I don't want to be around him. He scares me. I have no idea what goes through his head.

He threatens to take my kids away and blames me for every tantrum the two year old throws. He asks me to massage him at night but he "can tell" I don't love him through the rubs. I'm sick, I'm scared. We both think the other doesn't care. He threatens to take my kids away. Tells me I'm a shit mom. He's going to murder me if I try to leave him. He will try to take everything and blame everything on me. He will try to break me and feel like I need him to be successful. He's all I've ever known. Been in my life since I was 19. Now I'm going to have two kids with him and I want nothing to do with him. I will never be what he wants. He's made that very clear. But what do I do now? I don't want to hurt him. But I don't want to stay. We hate each other. I'm judged for everything. I feel like I have completely lost who I am. I don't want to live in Utah with him. I feel like I always have to look out for myself because when he comes home it's all about him. I can't hear him threaten to take my babies away from me. I don't know what to do. I drive my husband insane. He can't stand me or the way I interact with my son. He thinks I am a lazy and terrible mom.

Then he tells me this followed by "And I feel bad for saying that." I drive him insane. I feel like I have to suppress all of myself and then when my personality slips out he goes insane. I am annoying and I am me. I don't know how to coexist. I make him want less and less to do with me. It's best if I don't say anything, but I'm so lonely.

I'm scared of my husband. But if I tell him that he will get mad because he will say that he gives me everything and I'm selfish for making him out as the bad guy. That I always cast myself as the victim. He gives me everything on paper. A house, food, safety. But what he doesn't give me is a sense of myself. I feel like I have to constantly be on guard. Because if I say or do the wrong thing it will turn ugly quick. He asks me why I don't listen to him. I understand it drives him insane. I don't know for sure why I don't listen. I literally feel like I'm insane. Like everything I do I am being judged for. I don't know what to say. I feel so threatened by him. Like he is my support system financially but in the love department I feel like he's choking the *life out of me. Like I have to fight to be loved. He feels the same way I'm sure. Like he isn't getting what he needs either. I just wish I didn't feel like I have to halfway check out to numb the way he feels about me. He would say he feels like I'm a bitch because of the way I act. I feel like that is only partly fair. I'm scared to be around him.*

He makes Ronan call me bad Mama. He tells me that my mom is Ronan's real Mom and I didn't raise him while he was deployed. He says I alienate myself from my family I feel like I am constantly trying to bury my heartache. He constantly threatens that he will take Ronan away from me and that I will have nothing. That my family thinks I'm a piece of shit too. He says I pretend to be stubborn only to get my way so I can actually be lazy. He wants a divorce I know it. He hasn't said it but he has said he feels nothing but hatred for me. The only thing keeping us together is Ronan. How can I relax around him when I feel like I'm going to have to fight for my child?

All I do is try to paint a picture of how happy our family is. All the pictures I take of

Ronan and Michael. It's so I can convince myself that it's worth it. But I'm scared to death. I'm scared that I will look back at all the pictures and think "My husband didn't love me enough to do the same." He never takes pictures of Ronan and myself. This pregnancy is killing me. I feel like I am going to die. I have lost so much muscle tone. I'm stressed about being stressed. That if our child has any issues I'll be blamed for them. Because I couldn't compose myself. I'm afraid that even if we take a separation, things will always end up the same. He will always view me as the shitty person who pretended to be good. The mother who couldn't take care of her child so she has to hire a nanny. I don't want to cause Michael any pain but I do daily.

Birthday Surprise

It was my birthday. It was a day that, no matter how much I didn't want to be disappointed, I was. Then suddenly, a text! The text said my order was almost ready to be picked up. It was for a brand-new Apple Watch! I called Michael and he said Happy Birthday! I was shocked that he had gotten me a gift because we could not afford this. Michael went on to explain that he was out to dinner with Major G, who told Michael that he had to get me a present. I didn't know what to say. I was also hurt that it wasn't Michael's idea, and as the day went on and no other present came, I was right to assume I wasn't ever going to. Especially if Michael was out getting dinner, which we also could not afford.

I drove down to pick it up, and was genuinely excited. It was a pretty cool gadget! I usually buy things when they're on sale or when I have a coupon, so it felt especially strange to walk in and get something so expensive and brand new. When I got home, I put it on and slowly realized it was actually a tracking device. It soon became inexcusable when I didn't immediately texts or phone calls. With two small children, it was hard for me to keep track of my phone. Michael did not like it when I didn't answer him right away. He said it gave him anxiety when I didn't respond because I was alone with the kids. So I had no excuse; if I didn't wear the watch, then I was ungrateful. If I forgot to charge it, how was a jury supposed to approve me as an equipped parent if I couldn't even remember to charge a watch?

Everything I did was to make Michael happy and give him less ammo against me if he ever tried to take the kids away from me like he constantly threatened.

MAY

Journal Entry May 30th:

> My marriage just ended. He has torn me down to nothing. Told me he is taking Ronan from me. That I have no one to help me. Everyone hates me and the reason he has stayed this long is for Ronan. He has felt pity for me and tells me that I am a manipulator. That I am not there for him when he needs me to be. He told me I am basically just a foster mom to Ronan. We were getting ready for bed and he wanted me to tell him a story so he could "take care of himself" and sleep. I started telling him a story and then I said "I was used and abused" I really thought he would find that sexy since he always talks about how he wants me to be a slut and get taken advantage of. He said that saying that was selfish and he was 10 seconds from coming.

He refused to listen to me when I said that's not what I meant.

He then told me to go to bed and it wasn't worth it. He was going to beat off to Isla's videos. He said that to make me mad. So then I go to sleep. I wake up 3 hours later to pee. When I come back I ask him why he can't sleep. He says because I'm a selfish bitch and I've been laying here thinking of how much I fucking hate you, you selfish fucking cunt. All you had to give me was a paragraph of work. But you couldn't even do that" this is after I rubbed his feet and back for 2 hours. I do this every night, usually for an hour and a half to 2 hours. I said I was sorry and he said my sorry meant nothing to him and to go to bed. So I fall asleep. A few minutes later he takes my pillow from under me and whacks me with it. He yells at me to say something. I can't. I don't say anything. Then he takes the pillow and starts hitting me with it. He whacks my inner thigh really hard and tells me not to cry. Tells me that every whimper makes him more and more done with me. Tells me he is putting Ronan in daycare and I better be in

San Diego tomorrow alone. And I'm not taking Ronan.

Then he starts hitting my arm. Over and over again. He grabs my hair and pulls me down off of the bed. Tells me to stop crying, that I don't deserve to cry. He holds me down by my hair and tells me that I'm worthless. That our relationship is over because of me. That I am selfish and retarded. Then he asks me what it's like to be retarded. I don't say anything. He repeats and says "answer me you bitch." So I say "I don't know." I have no idea what to say or what to do. He says that if he has to be awake so do I. And I can't leave the room. He tells me I have to stay next to him. I go to the bathroom. When I come back he tells me we are over. He's done. No one has ever made him hurt the way I hurt him. The way I don't care about anyone but myself. That Ronan has to throw fits to get my attention. That I do the bare minimum to get by and that's it.

He tells me he feels bad for me that's why he stayed this long. The horrible thing is I feel like that's why I've stayed this long too. I don't want to take Ronan away from him. I don't want him to not have his family. But to what end? For the last few months, I have been scared of him. He drinks hard liquor every night. At least a quarter of a bottle. He plays these violent video games in front of our son and then screams at me for not giving Ronan the attention he deserves. He ignores his child and yells at me to do something when Ronan needs anything. He never steps up and helps out. But he financially supports us and I've been telling myself that that's enough. He never shows me any affection and pulls away when I try to hug or kiss him. He tells me that getting pregnant is my fault, that I knew exactly what I was doing. That Ronan turned out ok luckily and hopefully she will too but that's all I get. I don't even deserve them. That's what he says. I always take pictures of Ronan and Michael. I always print them and post them. Michael even if he takes a photo of us he refuses to show me. Tells me I look ugly or stupid in the photo and then won't let me see it. I have hardly any photos of me and my son.

I want Michael to be a better man. I want him to not drink and chew tobacco. I want him to see everything I do for this family. That I'm here and I do care. But tonight he told me we are done and I believe him. I have not tried to sleep with him in a few weeks because every time we start I start thinking of the horrible things he has said to me or how he's threatened me. I want to be loved so bad. How can I live like this? Always afraid to say the wrong thing? I'm so afraid he will hurt me. I bring out the worst in him. He says all I need to do to fix a situation is be sweet. As he's screaming the most hurtful things to me. He's disgusted with me. I just want his love. I just want him to see me for who I am. Not for all the past people who have hurt him in his life and place that on me. Thinking I'm like that. I hate how he calls me a manipulator. I hate it the most.

I'm totally at a loss and he can't see that. He thinks I'm playing one big game. I'm so tired of being there for a broken person. He calls me broken but I really feel just fine. I don't feel like I have any dark ghosts in my closet.

But I know that he does. Are we really supposed to throw away relationships and people when they are hurting? I feel like we are already doomed, and like he will try to make nice just to sweep the rug out from under me. But he's so much. He gets so angry and out of control. He builds things up into a rampage and says whatever it takes to break me down then tells me "don't you dare cry." I can't do this with him.

June

Journal Entry June 25th:

Michael has made it clear that I will never make him happy. So what do I do? Do I rip the bandaid off or watch him suffer. He told me my lack of sexual drive has driven him into a depression. I hate touching him cause I feel how distant he is. He's distant cause I don't want to touch him. It's a vicious cycle. He says he shows me patience all the time but I don't think that's true. I'm always scared of the next thing that's going to send him spiraling. He's spiraling and depressed and I can't help him.

I know he sacrifices so much for this family. He's driving himself insane. He hates me for all of this. For not being on his page or willing to understand him. He says he told me years ago when I came begging to live with him. He thinks I manipulate just to get my way. He thinks nothing good about me. He tells me he gives me everything and flat out tells me he can't give me exactly what he knows I need. He thinks my cuddles and affection are creepy. He's in the other room and I have no idea what to do. Do I go out there and he's still mad or just needs rubs.

He's got a PT test tomorrow and he's so stressed about it. I'm just so tired of being told by him what a shit person I am. When he gets mad he tells Ronan I'm a bad mom and not to get used to holding my hand. Michael tells me all the time he hates me. He threatens to take Ronan away all the time. He doesn't feel bad for me because he says I asked for all of this. I hold on every day to the human contact I will get when he comes home. If I leave him I lose that too. I feel like that is the most pathetic part of all of this. I have nowhere to go. I wanted a life with him, but what if he's right? What if all of this was a lie?

We were both afraid of losing each other that we held on and now it's so much worse. I think of Michael with another person that would make him happy. I think of how he just wants me to be stronger than I am. How I could be that person but I'm drowning in the resentment he shows me every day. How it's my problem to fix because he feels he's already given everything. What do I do when I see the one I love spiraling? And I'm the cause? He thinks taking Ronan away from me is going to threaten me into "shaping up" but all it's doing is paralyzing me. I can't breathe. I drowning too but it's all my fault. What pisses me off is that I got over him. I moved on. I wasn't happy, but the hardest part was over. I hate him too, but for the sake of Ronan and baby girl, this isn't how I want things to keep going. Or to end.

I have absolutely no idea what to do. I'd like to try therapy and leave all the bullshit from our past behind us. I just want a clean slate so bad. All I want is for when he gets stressed he doesn't resort to thinking of all the ways I've disappointed him. I feel like I have to play it smart and figure out how to keep my kids. Like the ship has sailed with us and it's a matter of time. So I need to start to figure out how to not let him ruin my life like he feels I've ruined his.

MOVING DAY

With the help of my aunt as our realtor, we bought a house in Utah. I was seven months pregnant when we moved. A military spouse in Michael's unit who had become my friend helped me unpack. Michael made fun of me for setting up the magnets on the fridge for Ronan to play with, saying I always make everyone do everything for me. It was the reason he didn't help me with the kids. I needed to learn how to do things for myself and the kids. He told me this was also why he did not add me to the title of the house we just bought and moved into. Thankfully, years later, he did end up adding me as an apology.

Hypervigilance and a Handgun

One night, eight months pregnant with Raela, I was jarred awake around 2 a.m. by Michael yelling. He stood at the foot of the bed shouting that I was making him crazy on purpose. He towered over the edge of my bed, while I was half asleep. Meaning I wasn't quite awake enough to see the gun in his hand. He screamed that I needed to stop organizing everything and why couldn't the socks just stay where they always were? The truth is I had become hypervigilant. I was constantly cleaning, trying to make sure Michael would have nothing to complain about and that I knew exactly where everything was in case he needed anything. I stood up slowly and carefully to try and calm him down, but he slapped me so hard that my glasses flew off. He picked them up and broke them in half. Because breaking my glasses didn't release enough anger from him, he picked up the gun again and sat where I was lying asleep just minutes ago. I started to dial 911 as he kept repeating "You are driving me crazy, I can't take it anymore. You are going to make me shoot myself if you don't stop." The call connected, but Michael snatched the phone from me before I could say anything and hung up.

He crowded up against me as he continued his tirade. I was going to ruin his career. What was I thinking? In his moment of need, all I can think of is myself. He said all he needed was a hug and I couldn't even comfort him. At that point, 911 called me back, but I couldn't answer. They call again. Michael told me to pick up and say that Ronan was choking, but he's fine now. I answered and told them that. When I hung up, he told me to leave the room. I started to walk to the spare bedroom, and he followed me. As I sat on the edge of the bed, he screamed in my face about how we were going to lose everything if I kept this up.

Just then the doorbell rang. "What have you done?" his face glowered in betrayal, "If you don't get your shit together and go down there, we are fu*ked." I grabbed a robe and walked downstairs. When I opened the door, four police officers walked into the house. I stood there trying to act normal and told them what I told the dispatchers. They took my word for it and left. They didn't separate us. I was relieved and also disappointed. They bought the lie that everything was fine, so they left. Michael's career was safe another day. But was I? I silently prayed that this was enough to snap Michael out of whatever was going through his head, and we could get through the night in peace. Michael went to the basement for the rest of the night, and I went back to bed.

Journal Entry September 20th:

You want to be needed, you need to be liked. So you cast stones about anyone that's not within sight.

A stressing desire to fill what is bleak. So you reach right around for the gallon of bleach. To erase what's been done, but just when you feel better you curse it back down. See, the bleach may "clean" but it burns and destroys, instead of addressing and remorsing for those you have scorned.

This hole you've dug, the well you fell down...brings no water when pumped, leaves you stranded and useless in the ground. I've cut the ties and the rope to bring you back up. Because all this dwelling reminds me you don't fill my cup. It's half empty to you, it's lazy it's flawed. It's up to me to fix what you see wrong. But I'm so happy, so loved, I give all of my heart...which is why I'm done with caring what you think, at least that's a good place to start.

Journal Entry September 4th:

I can't keep doing this. I don't understand Michael. We get along so good and then he goes to 100. I'm so scared tonight is going to be another shit show. He came home from work and was so happy. Then when he was getting in his bed he hit his head. I didn't ask him if he was ok. I didn't know he hurt himself. It was so dark and I was laying down. I just didn't put two and two together. He starts telling me what a shitty person I am. How it's unbelievable to him that I have no concept of others. How I just want everyone to hate me. All I can think about is how he never cares when I don't feel good. He just expects me to keep doing everything. Like when I hurt my knee the other day or when I said my back hurts. Why is it that I'm always under the microscope and yet he never has to ask me how I'm doing.

I feel like I'm always walking on eggshells around him. Like he was just laying there thinking "is it time yet for me to divorce her" the way he tells me how shitty I am and tells me I don't know him. It's true. I don't know who he is. I know this pregnancy has been hard on both of us...but I feel like I don't know him. I'm so scared all the time I'm going to set him over the edge. I love him when he's nice and I'm scared of him when I do the wrong things. I'm not on his same page ever. I can't relax enough to get there. He's always drinking and the most I can do is have a glass of wine. I have to try so hard not to be anxious and he just gets to drink as much as he wants till he feels better. He's never going to forgive me for not being slutty. Every time he gets mad it's always going to turn into how I'm selfish and never do anything for him. How I'm the reason he's going to cheat on me. I'm not even scared of that anymore. I don't even care. I don't think it's hot. He's done it before.

I'm sad that he feels like he had to escape this life. Mostly me. I'm sad he doesn't feel understood. I just wish he would be nicer and more understanding to me. I wouldn't clam up as much. I would just like him to get mad and be mad at what actually happened instead of digging deep into my core being. I feel drawn back from him because I don't want to keep getting hurt. But that's also why he feels hurt. It's a vicious cycle and I'm so tired of always feeling like I have to walk on eggshells.

Live Your Truth

Despite all this, I continued to find ways to find joy in my life. My friend, Patricia, whom I met in Vegas, visited me in Utah. I was due with Raela any day at that point, so it was nice to have my friend there. Patricia and I both enjoyed Jordan Peterson, a renowned psychologist, author, and lecturer who happened to be speaking in Utah. He was speaking about his book, *12 Rules for Life*. As we stood outside the venue, an usher asked me when I was due. I loved saying "Any day." It gave me such delight to see people's reactions. The lecture was thought-provoking and insightful as rule number eight, *find and live your personal truth,* sat in my mind. How could I do this while focusing my energy on making sure Michael and the kids were okay? Patricia went home and I continued waiting.

Raela

She was my last pregnancy, my last newborn. There couldn't be any more, and I was heartbroken. I absolutely love being my children's mom. I mourned the loss of feeling cherished as a pregnant woman. I desperately wanted to be held and treated like a princess while I carried and grew my husband's legacy. I was exhausted from chasing validation and forcing myself to feel important. I thought with pregnancy and a newborn, Michael would be nicer, care more, and be more involved. Instead, he distanced himself further. I grew so independent from him that we were already two separate people instead of a co-creation of a family unit. I felt like I had already been training to be a single mom. Life became easier when we separated because I did not know how to be a wife to Michael. When I only had to focus on the kids, and he was no longer someone I had to manage, it was actually simpler. Although it was never my intention, I felt like I adapted to caring for the children alone. I expected it as a military spouse, so when I transitioned to a single mom officially, it did not feel as jarring as it could have.

Michael did not once touch my stomach. The only time he talked to her while she was in my belly was to say that he was sorry he was giving Mama a hard time and that he hoped she wasn't scared to come out because he was acting like he didn't want her. She was born the next day.

The day Raela was born, I went to a thrift store and got the last thing I needed—a baby swing. The store shared the same parking lot as McDonald's, so I let Ronan play in the play place for a bit. As he played, I went into labor. I stood at the bottom of the slide, looking up at my son through the clear plastic bubble window, puzzling out how I was to get him out of the play area. I was not going to have a baby in McDonald's, but Raela was coming, and Ronan was at the top of the playground. With no way of getting him out, I contemplated telling a stranger to please remove him before my water broke. Between contractions, I scanned the room in part panic and part comedy at my predicament. With no other choice, I used my best and calmest voice while being assertive "It's time to go now" to Ronan. As a rambunctious adventure-loving two-year-old, I wasn't sure he would listen to the instruction that his playtime was being cut short. But, he must have understood it was not time to test me. Thankfully, he came down and got in the car with no problems. There might have been a McDonald's ice cream on the way as a bribery.

When I got home, I called Dana, the designated person to call when I was in labor for a ride. But when she picked up, I quickly backed out. Suddenly, I feared I wasn't actually in labor. I didn't want to get in trouble for sounding all the alarms if it was a false labor. It felt much safer for me to drive myself twenty minutes to the hospital instead of uprooting everyone's day just to be told there was no baby coming. That way, if I got there and labor stopped, I wouldn't get in what I thought would be trouble.

As I walked down the stairs with the diaper bag and about to load up Ronan in the car, my doorbell rang. I vividly remember opening the door to find my neighbor standing there. Initially, I tried to tell her it was fine and that I would drive myself. She watched me as I paused, breathing through my contractions.

Then, she took my diaper bag and Ronan's car seat and told me to get into her car.

While on the freeway, my contractions became closer together. I called Michael. I had already set everything in motion. Instead of being excited for my coming baby, I panicked internally, still afraid of inconveniencing everyone. When we got to the hospital, Ronan stayed with my neighbor. I exited the car and walked into the lobby by myself to check in. After they brought me to a back room, I was told I was already 6 cm dilated. But the only thing I needed to hear verbally to calm down was the answer to the question: "Is there a baby coming today?" The nurse immediately assured me that I would have a baby that day. I relaxed, so much so that when Michael walked in, I threw up. It was not a false alarm.

As selfish as it may seem, I looked forward to Michael's undivided attention. It was my moment. I was delivering his baby, our baby. I was supposed to be pampered, cherished, and given his undivided attention. Instead, he sat on his phone and joked with the nurses. He may have done other things, but at the moment, I was hurt deeply and I felt so alone. When the doctor placed Raela on my chest, I felt incredibly united with her. I was in awe of perfection. I was grateful to Michael for our baby, but I was disconnected from him. I was disconnected from everyone in the room except her.

Michael left for the night and to get Ronan. That night, I spent time with Raela. When she woke up while I was asleep, the nurses took her so I wouldn't be disturbed. Despite it being their job, I felt so loved and supported. At 8 a.m., they brought Raela back swaddled and with a clean diaper. The cafeteria food was amazing. I never wanted to leave. In that hospital room, I was cared for and cherished like I had hoped for since I was a little girl.

Michael brought Ronan into the room. He looked like a giant compared to Raela, even though he was only two years old. We took our first family photo next to the window, with the snowy mountainside in the background. I felt in awe of my life.

That day, I lay in bed recovering with Raela on my chest. At night, the nurses again took Raela. The following day, I was cleared to be discharged but was told that my insurance would cover another day. I told them I wanted to stay another day but that my husband could never know that I was able to be discharged and chose another day. I'm sure they thought I said it in a cute way. They promised me they wouldn't say anything. So, I got another full night's rest and meals brought to me in bed. I never told Michael.

McFly

The week before Christmas when Raela was two months old, we all went to Downtown Salt Lake City to make a donation on behalf of my family in San Diego. There was a vending machine where you could purchase goats, food storage, mosquito nets, and other items for those in developing countries. Although Michael was with us, I alone got Ronan out of his car seat and walked him around to Raela. In the time that I got the baby carrier on, put on the diaper bag, got her out, and shut the door, Michael had gotten out of the car and started to yell. Asking me what was taking so long and to hurry it up. It was winter in Utah as well, so I had to also put the winter jackets on both kids. And I looked at him, but all I said was a simple "sorry." And then we kept walking. His figure is still burned into my memory: his back to us, his phone open, capturing all his attention. He only looked up to make sure he didn't run into something. I believe it was his way of trying to dissociate from the stress, to get through the moment.

I was still grateful to do this because I thought we might get a family photo out of it. Michael never wanted to take family photos. So whatever stress this was going to cause me, for some reason it felt worth it. I managed everything from when we parked to when we got home. Anticipating every move but we got our photo. It was worth it.

A few days later, my aunt invited us over for Christmas Eve dinner. Again, I packed up the kids and got Michael's clothes ready. I told her I would bring dessert—crème brulé, Michael's favorite. Michael started driving, but before we could even leave the neighborhood, he started flicking my face really hard and calling me McFly. Every time he would flick my face, Ronan would laugh. So Michael did it again, relentless and cruel. I asked him to stop, and he refused because it made Ronan laugh. Anger surged through me that he was making our son laugh at me. At a stop sign, I had had enough. I undid my seatbelt and moved from the front seat to the back. As I did, I felt a vice grab tight around my calf. Michael was pulling me back into the front seat by the leg. His grip was tight enough that it was painful.

"Don't you ever do something that dangerous while I'm driving ever again." His yells rattled the car. He turned that car around and drove us home. As we pulled into the garage, I immediately got Raela and Ronan. I could tell Michael was enraged by the look in his eyes and face—the same one I'd learned to recognize right before he was about to assault me. I took the kids upstairs hoping Michael would go to the basement, but I was not so lucky. He followed me into upstairs main bedroom, where he had not slept in since we moved in. I sat in the rocking chair, rocking a crying Raela, while Michael screamed in my face. I was past the point of listening.

Then, the most heartbreaking moment of them all— Ronan started yelling back at his dad. "Don't yell at my mama! Leave her alone!" his tiny voice shrieked. And then his 6-foot-tall dad towered over him, got in his face, and screamed back. Ronan backed up until he was cornered in the closet and shut the door. I got screamed at again before it was all over, and Michael went to the basement.

I texted my aunt that we would not be making it and that I was sorry.

CHRISTMAS DAY

The week before Christmas, James sent Michael $500. I was relieved, thinking we could pay off some credit cards. To my dismay, Michael took the money and said he would go out and get some presents. I know Michael had fun doing this, but my heart sank. We needed the cash. He came home and told me how all the cash register girls thought it was so sweet he was buying things for his family. So when the day came to open the presents, I was nervous.

Michael started the morning by saying "You never want anything, so I just got you a bunch of random crap. But you like random crap, so you will probably have the best Christmas ever." No, I just wanted the money. I pretended to be excited as I unwrapped the presents. He got me some home decor and a bracelet of an elephant because it reminded him of me. Even though at the time, I didn't wear bracelets and he never explained why an elephant reminded me of him. I kept the bracelet to give to

Raela one day. I was afraid to ruin Christmas. Michael saw money in a way I did not. I saw it as a tool. He saw it as something to spend.

2019

123... BREATHE

The first chance I got to get on an airplane and get some help, I took it. I wanted to visit family with the kids and escape Utah's frigid winter. I flew to my parents' house in San Diego, where my sister, Vanessa, was also staying for a while. I remember one night, I woke up and couldn't breathe. This had only happened to me a few times before, and never from a deep sleep. I was terrified. It felt like I couldn't take a full breath, and my throat was closing in on itself. I stood outside of Vanessa's door, afraid to wake her but I knew I had to.

I was scared it wasn't actually anxiety. It felt like a heart attack or an allergic reaction that was made it hard to breathe. Deep down I knew it was anxiety. I told myself over and over again that that's what it was. It was hard to believe though because I couldn't remember a time when I had experienced a panic attack from a deep sleep. I hadn't asked Vanessa for anything in years. There is something about a medical emergency that makes you do things you usually wouldn't. You are forced to rely on someone else to help you.

I creaked open the door and crept up to her bed, shaking. Then shook her gasping that it was hard to breathe. She sat up and took me to the living room where she walked me through breathing. I don't remember much about what happened, my mind was in a haze. What I do remember feeling is that she was sacrificing sleep for me. She gained nothing from this. It was the most vulnerable I had ever been with her. I can't tell you what triggered this episode, but I do know that I got what I needed: a witness, someone to look at me and validate what I was going through. A witness to confirm that I was, in fact, breathing, even as I choked on every inhale. I didn't trust myself at that moment. She let me rely on her and gave me support. We both went back to bed after that.

I know that no matter my relationship with people, or what distance and time would do to our sisterhood, I could look back and have concrete proof of a time when Vanessa sat with me. In that moment of panic and anxiety, she chose to give me mercy and grace.

After a few weeks, Michael decided to fly out to San Diego to see us since I had bought a one-way ticket. I was only going to go back to Utah when he insisted. I bought his plane ticket, but as I stood in front of a friend's house, he sent me dozens of texts demanding that I cancel his flight. He wasn't going to come anymore. He texted dozens of times, trying to get my attention. I don't know what he was upset about, but he did end up getting on the flight. After picking him up and returning to my parents' house, he wanted Mexican food. He then dropped me and the kids off at a park and left. After two hours at the park, he had yet to return and would not answer my calls. I ended up calling my mom and asking her to pick us up instead.

Raela RSV

After returning to Utah, Raela started to get a runny nose. It became so stuffy I could see she was having difficulty breathing. I took her to the emergency room to get suctioned out about twice a day for four days. I went to bring her in again, and I had a feeling they were going to keep her at the hospital. Sure enough, they brought us up to a room. The staff came in and started hooking her up to a multitude of wires all across her tiny form. Her oxygen saturation was low. She took short, rapid, and shallow breaths meaning her attempts to get air were overworked, ineffective, and tiring. I was so grateful to be there because I finally had some help. After we got settled, Michael showed up. After about an hour he took Ronan home.

At this time, I was also suffering from a toothache and begged Michael to make the 10-minute drive to drop my medicine off since the pharmacy at the hospital had already closed. He refused. I started looking for a way to get it delivered instead. Once I finally figured out how, I told Michael never mind, and that's when he said he would bring me some. I wonder if he thought he would look bad in front of the nurses if I had to have Motrin delivered. When he got there he said he understood why I was being such a bitch about it to him. Tooth pain really does hurt.

Raela ended up staying in the hospital for about a week. When it was time to be discharged, Michael's sister, Shawn, offered to come up and help. She brought their Aunt Adrian with her. They cleaned the house for us while Michael stayed in his room. He barely came out to socialize. I was so grateful for their help. Michael criticized me for being an embarrassment as a mother. That our kids kept getting sick because of our filthy house. His family had to come up here to save the children from me.

During this trip, Adrian and Shawn asserted that how Michael treated and talked to me was not okay. They both urged me to leave him. But as strange as it sounds, I wasn't ready to leave him. I wasn't brave enough and I really thought that the love between us, although fragmented, was there.

Traveling Home

After Raela recovered, I planned my next trip to San Diego. That was how I coped. When we moved to South Jordan, Utah, the kids and I would fly to San Diego every two months for a week or so.

I had been in San Diego for a few weeks when one night, Michael called me saying that he missed the kids and I needed to come home. I relented, saying I would look for a flight in the next few days. He got mad, hung up the phone, and then filled out separation papers online. He texted me the documents and said that if I didn't bring the kids home tomorrow, he would leave me. He then texted me a list of girls he had slept with and nude photos of them. He said he did this because I was always in San Diego. I was a terrible wife to him and made him do this. That the kids deserved better than me as their mom. He continued telling me he would be just fine without me because of all these girls. But I would have nothing without him. I believed him.

So I bought plane tickets for the following day and sent him the flight information. The next morning, I woke up, packed my bag, and asked my mom for a ride to the airport. Michael picked us up, but not even an hour later he was at the bar and slept in the next day because he was hungover.

For the next six years, I would get extremely anxious when I heard loud fans, noise machines, or hotel AC units. I didn't realize until 2022 that it was because I associated that sound with leaving Utah on an airplane or returning. It was a feeling of being trapped in an airplane with my kids and either running or returning.

My escapes to San Diego were shadowed by confusion about why I ever flew back to Utah. But it was still my home. It was my children's home. They had their rooms and all of their things. A home that Michael only inhabited late at night. Gone before we woke up and home just an hour before bedtime. A place where we were blessed with random thunderstorms that were the best white noise for naps.

I brought Raela home from the hospital to this house. It was our home through all the colds, ear infections, and doctor visits. It was where Michael started sleeping in the basement while I had the upstairs to myself. I didn't have to be quiet in case Michael heard me. My ensuite bathroom also shared a wall with Ronan's room. Raela slept in my room. We were all together. Close. I could hear every noise my kids made.

When I think of that house, I think of clean laundry piled on my bed. The toys that crept down the hallway from Ronan's room into mine. My rocking chair that I spent hours and hours rocking both children and my kids laying in my bed watching cartoons. I picture walking outside and having instant playdates with all the kids in the neighborhood. A kid ringing the door asking if there was anyone she could play with. Bringing home the porch swing. Friends coming over and having so much room to play. It was my home. I will miss it for the goodness it held. For being a place of refuge.

I felt safe despite the sleeping dragon in the basement. I had shoved all my feelings down around him and it felt like I was living with a terrorist. All so I could enjoy my time in Utah the best I could. Even though he constantly told me he was going to take my children away from me. And if I thought about leaving him and taking the kids, he would find me and kill me. I was at his mercy and I stayed and appeased him to keep my children with me. I was terrified at night, and yet during the day, I loved my life.

I did everything in my power to stay. Guilt burdened me for years about subjecting my children to that. But I truly felt I had no other choice. I thought about leaving repeatedly when I was in San Diego. But each time, I bought plane tickets home, and it was because the monster I knew was less scary than the monster I didn't. I knew what to do when Michael was mad at me when I was his wife. I would not know what to do if I was his ex-wife. So I stayed.

Tired To My Bones

One day, Michael came over with Major G's dog. He had offered to watch him while Major G went on vacation. I had a newborn and a toddler and did not have time for a dog. Michael promised he would walk Jake, but he didn't. I felt so guilty with Jake in the basement all day. This went on for a week. After that week Michael came home and saw that Jake had chewed up a bunch of things in the basement. He found me, exclaiming, "Good news! We get to keep Jake forever!." I fell to the floor sobbing.

Michael looked down at me and said I was the only person in the world that would be upset about getting a dog. He said he was kidding. But I was already a mess. You would think I'd have this reaction because I felt already overwhelmed. The truth is, I did not feel overwhelmed. I loved being a mom. I absolutely loved my home in Utah and staying home with my children. Yes, I was tired. I was tired to my bones. Which I didn't know was possible. That one is more difficult to explain. But I would lie down and still be aware of everything around me.

What made me break down was the thought of managing a dog while managing my husband, our toddler, and our newborn. I wasn't tapped out, but I was a hair away from it.

LETTER I NEVER SENT

March 4th:

I'm sorry that I have to do this over email. And while you are in a different state. I don't know how to talk to you. I know this isn't your fault, but a communication issue with me. The truth is, I'm devastated. I feel like I have been given this role of motherhood and then abandoned. I never see my husband and he comes home every night. It has been a hard adjustment for me turning into a stay-at-home mom. I have lost so many parts of me. The artist, the adventurer, the social, the worker. I love our kids and if having them meant having to give up all of that, then it's worth it. What has been so hard for me is watching you still fulfill all the parts of you that make you whole. All the parts of me are devastated and dismissed because I am supposed to just be a mom now. I feel like I have zero help from you.

We haven't spent one of your days off doing anything as a family. We were in San Diego for a month and then drill weekend, you went to Vegas, then this weekend, and now you are gone for 7 days. I am not trying to make you out to be some villain. What I am saying is that I feel so overlooked. Like hired help. I get minimal interaction from you and have to worry about making you upset or saying the wrong thing and then having to fix it and calm you down. I obsess over organizing and cleaning because I don't want to anger you. I feel like I am living in fear of making you mad. Balancing your days off with keeping the kids quiet so you can sleep until it's time for them to take a nap.

I am absolutely emotionally exhausted from being alone. I know many mothers do this. Mothers who dreamed of doing this when they were kids. That was never me. I never thought I would totally lose myself and become a Groundhog Day person alone and lonely with my husband living in the same house. Maybe I come off as a huge complainer to you. But I know if I don't fix something within me and how we interact as a couple I am going to lose my mind. I want to leave and never come back when I see you lay in bed holding our daughter for 5 min and then handing her back. Or when I ask if you can watch her and you comment "Don't make me feel like I hate her because I don't want to watch her." Or when I call for help with groceries and you yell at me for asking for help. I've got to unload groceries and your screaming daughter from the car. But if I push the issue, you will just recluse further into the basement and tell me to leave you alone.

I've compromised so many of my feelings to just not have you abandon us more. I'm not sure how you think I feel. Constantly surrounded by our children with no help and a husband who actively drinks, stays late at work/the bar/ goes to Vegas. I appreciate that you work so hard. But even when I called you about getting out of the house as a family, I wanted to feel like we mattered to you. Like you could actually go out in public or plan something fun with us and not just with your friends. I get that we are going to the Bahamas, and thank you. But I feel like it's a bandaid for all of the emotional baggage I feel. I can't keep the kids cooped up all weekend and you don't want to get out of bed. So I don't know what to do because I have lost the one thing I never thought I'd have to worry about with you. My best friend. And I can't listen to your advice. I'm sorry for that. But I feel criticized for every conversation or for ignoring you. When I'm breaking every inch of me inside because all I feel is ignored. And if I stop thinking about the kids for 2 seconds the world will go up in flames.

When I asked you not to talk loud so Ronan wouldn't hear you in his room. And then when I was listening to Ronan... you said something and then got mad that I was ignoring you. Then you went off on. How if we had just met that would be the end of our friendship. Well honestly I can see that and how I don't have any friends in Utah right now because I am so hyper-focused on surviving another day I'm sure I ruin the friendships by being spacy and obsessive over my kids. I just don't have any other choice because it's taking 100% of my focus right now to not do something to upset you, or tell you how I feel, and suppress my feelings and needs to take care of our kids. All I want is for help and to relax about not being perfect around you. For you to loosen up about the things I say or do and just let me be an imperfect human with no need to fix me for the next few years while I am taking care of our kids.

Don't Be So Dramatic

Ronan had just started daycare twice a week. At first, it was nice to have Ronan interacting with other children and I didn't have to facilitate it, but Michael promised he would stop drinking so much so we could afford it. He didn't. Ronan did not like going either. It was never easy for either of us at drop-off. Michael said he liked the place because it was filled with young hot college girls and he liked the way the girls looked at him in his uniform when he picked up Ronan. At this point, if it didn't make him angry or explode, I didn't have the energy to care.

Ronan was sick off and on from Christmas 2018 to June 2019. He had ear infections every other week. At one point, and on a rare occasion when Michael went with us, I mentioned to the receptionist that I felt like we were here every week. Michael rolled his eyes in front of the nurse saying don't be so dramatic. I really did feel like we had been there every week for the past few months. Every time we went, the kids were legitimately sick: dehydrated, needing steroid shots, breathing treatments, or having high fevers. I was so upset that when I checked the patient portal when I got home. Sure enough, it averaged out to 1.2 times a week for the past three months. 99% of the time, I made the hour-round trip visit with the kids. It made me feel like Michael was so far removed from the health of his kids, he didn't even notice how much was going on around him.

One day, twenty minutes after I dropped Ronan off at daycare and returned home, the school called, saying Ronan spiked a fever. They gave him some Motrin, but by the time I got there, he wouldn't walk. I called his doctor and made our way there. Then, I called Michael and told him we were going in. When we got to the doctors, they said Ronan was showing signs of his appendix bursting and that they could call for transport by ambulance to the Emergency Room, or I could take him. I looked at him guarding his right side, refusing to walk, spiking a high fever, and was lethargic. I told them I would drive.

As I got onto the freeway, I called Michael again, telling him the new plan. He said he would meet us there. It was about a 45-minute drive from where he was and a 15-minute drive for me. By the time I arrived, I figured Michael was 30 minutes to an hour away. Ronan begged me to hold him as he lay in pain on the bed. I rocked Raela in her car seat with my foot and tried to hold Ronan. An hour went by. I called Michael, no response. I called again. Two hours went by. I texted my neighbor and asked her to ring the doorbell and see if he was okay. At this point, it was still undetermined if Ronan would need surgery. I texted another neighbor who worked ten minutes from the hospital. I was desperate for help. I had been in the hospital for three hours now with a baby and a very sick toddler. When her text came through, she said she could be there in about an hour. I was relieved.

Shortly after this, the nurses took Raela to the nurses' station so I could comfort Ronan alone for a little while. Relief rushed through me, but then Michael finally called back. Apparently, he had fallen asleep. He said he would take an Uber and be there soon, but I knew with the rush hour traffic, he wouldn't. I texted my friend back and told her Michael was on the way. She offered to still come and bring me some food. I knew that if Michael knew I reached out to someone, he would blame me for making him look bad. I thanked her but I was okay. I wasn't okay. I was hungry, exhausted, and felt so alone.

Moving into the 5th hour of being there, Michael finally walks in. I was lying on the bed with both kids as they started the ultrasound. Michael told me to get up so he could lay with Ronan. I asked him to take Raela instead so I could hold Ronan better. He shot me a look, and I knew I was in trouble. I pushed the impending doom aside and held onto Ronan through the ultrasound. When the tech walked out, I remember thinking, "Please keep the door open." Immediately, the door shut.

Michael lost his mind. He pushed me forcefully square on my chest and yelled "What the fu*k is wrong with you!?" He shoved me until I was wedged into the corner of the room. Then he beat against my head over and over again. He was upset at me for undermining him in front of the tech. We didn't show we were a cohesive family; I didn't listen to my husband when he said to move. He said he knew Ronan needed Dad and that I was selfish by just wanting to lie there. The irony. That's when I checked out. The famous thousand-yard stare became my safe space. I stared into the distance and through the tiny rectangular window on the hospital room door.

I hoped someone would walk by and see or hear him with pure disdain. Walk by nurse, I begged silently. Look inside into my hell. Into my children's hell. Open the door, oblivious nurse, to take Ronan's temperature. Involve the police. Walk in so they could not deny the abuse. Take the "he said she said" burden off my shoulders. Nurse, please demand that he leave and get us to safety.

Michael's blow-up was in full view of that window. I hoped he would be caught to distract me from my ringing ears and migraine by his hand. I wouldn't have to testify in court, I thought. The Military would whisk him away like waking up from a bad dream. Something broke the spell. I'm sure it was me profusely apologizing. The song and dance we did best. No one had come in despite Michael's yells and Raela's cries. Could no one see this madhouse?

The doctor came in and reported that Ronan's labs were normal, with no sign of an inflamed appendix. The poor kid had just been so sick, for so long that he exhausted himself. He had yet another ear infection, and his body was not keeping up. I made a follow-up appointment with his doctor and we returned home

The Ideal Situation

Ronan's ear tube surgery was scheduled for the following Monday at 6 a.m. Michael was leaving for a business trip at 5 in the morning the same day. So, I packed up the kids and headed to the surgery center at 4 a.m. alone.

It was going to be easier without Michael. I just hoped that by the time Ronan got out of surgery, I could get Raela to sleep so I could spend some one-on-one time with him before we were discharged. I remember being so tired, not knowing how I could possibly be awake for what felt like two years and counting. Luckily, Raela fell asleep before Ronan came out. I could lay in his bed with him for a little bit. I was so grateful for the timing. A nurse brought me some coffee, which made me feel cared for and supported. I barely remember making it home and up to the master bedroom. I turned on Halloween Curious George, Ronan's current favorite, and fell asleep.

When I woke up, the most interesting post came up on my Facebook feed. Two doors down, my neighbor wrote an exact mirror of my story. Her two-year-old was also sick with ear infections. It was June, but they decided to get her tubes as well, on the same day at the same time. Except, while I headed out that morning alone, she wrote about holding her husband's hand, terrified. Her other daughter stayed the night at her mom's so they could focus on the 2-year-old. The ideal situation. She wrote how terrified she was and how grateful it went smoothly, and that her baby was now resting.

I had no room for such feelings. I was not allowed to feel scared or sad or terrified. I would fall apart if I did. I had to buck up and handle it. That day, the most encouragement I got from Michael was, "I know you got this." This would be the downfall of Michael. The fact that he knew I always "got this." In this way, he had completely made himself void. I needed him for nothing. He was on our ride, getting on and off as he pleased. By the time I did leave, it was more of just not letting him back on the ride again. The ride, the dance, the struggle, the grind that I had mastered on my own. There was nothing to miss, the true tragedy. My life to start living.... by leaving.

THIS IS "MY HOUSE"

One day, Michael got off work and was hungry, and I hadn't had a chance to make dinner. I wanted to suggest that he could have a granola bar while I made a 10-minute pasta, but it wasn't up to me to make that decision. Raela was asleep so he said to take Ronan with me to get take-out from a restaurant. I remember standing in line at the restaurant and feeling my anxiety grow as the line seemed to take too long. According to my calculations, the longer we were gone, the bigger the explosion would greet our return. Raela was about four months old at this time which meant her nap would only be about 30 minutes long. The timer started at the first drop of the eyelids.

When we returned, Michael came up from the basement saying that Raela wouldn't stop crying and what took me so long. As he said that, Ronan slammed the baby gate at the top of the stairs. The unexpected sound startled Michael. In an instant, he punched a hole in the wall. Then marched over to the food and shoved it off the counter, flinging rice, beans, and chicken all over the fridge. He took a step back and swore loudly. Then he walked down to the basement without eating.

I grabbed a fork, scraped the food back into the misshapen takeout container, and scrubbed from the floor to the topside of the fridge. I salvaged one of the boxes and prepared it for Michael. Then I made some pasta for the kids and me. My calculations began again. How long do I let him cool down minus how long until he remembered he was hungry again? Whatever the calculation was, I was right. I presented him with the food and hoped the rice would soak up the vodka. I walked back upstairs, disappointed that today would be a 10-minute dad encounter. Again.

When it was time to put the kids to bed, I asked him if he wanted to say goodnight. He hugged them and told me to come back to the basement after. Shortly awaiting the newfound hurtful phrase. Sometimes, after putting the kids to bed, we would watch movies together. That was nice. It was during one of those nights when we decided on our daughter's name. Raela was a princess warrior. We heard the name in a movie and hoped for that kind of life for her. I knew this would not be one of those nights.

Michael was waiting for me at the bottom of the stairs. *F*ck,* I thought. It's one of these nights. I would be told I need to get my sh*t together. All I do is stay home with the kids and I do nothing all day. "This is my house." he started, "You are just a guest in it. You need to act more grateful because you will be nothing without me."

The next day, I moved a painting over the fist-sized hole in the wall. And life went on.

Gauging Reactions

My mom flew into Utah about every six weeks. At the time, Ronan was really into trains. I had found a train convention, and Michael agreed to go with Ronan and me while my mom watched Raela. About two blocks from the house Michael got angry. In his rage, he hit a cup of carrot juice I was holding, and it spilled all over me and the car. He kept driving like nothing happened. After a few more blocks, he asked, "Do you want to go home and change?" I said, "Yes please." He responded, "We don't have time!" And then kept driving.

When we got to the convention, I had gotten the time wrong. We were there an hour early. Thankfully, a gun show was next door, so we walked around there. Michael had been saying for a few months now that he wanted a rifle. Every time he brought it up, I would pull up our finances and tell him if he cut back on drinking for a few weeks, we could easily buy one. At the show, he found one he wanted. Thankfully he decided not to buy it, but took the guy's card just in case.

When it was time to enter the train show, I walked in, crusted and orange from the carrot juice, but I didn't feel embarrassed. Michael didn't seem to think it was weird either. I spent a lot of time gauging my reactions to how he reacted. If he didn't think it was a big deal, I wasn't going to bring it up.

The train show was Ronan's dream. There were trains set up everywhere including a Thomas the Train ride. Ronan's head spun with excitement. There was a place to make your own personal terrain. I asked Ronan if he wanted to make one, but Michael immediately shut it down. I felt bad because there was so much to see but Michael only wanted to walk around the perimeter. I should have taken Ronan and Raela alone, or gone with my mom. It was easier without him, and I hate to admit that. But I also would have had to manage him if he missed out on an important moment.

When we got to the train ride, Ronan's eyes widened in wonder! There was no line, so he got on and rode around several times. Michael was physically there, but as always, he was on his phone,

149

missing the moment. Again, I had to figure out how to take photos of Michael with us looking engaged. We continued to walk around and raced the trains on the tracks. There was a place to play with hundreds of trains and tracks. I was so excited for Ronan. We could have spent all day there, but shortly after, we had to go at Michael's insistence. All in all, I think Ronan had a great time. That's what mattered.

Zoloft

Michael said that the moment I got pregnant with Raela, I went crazy. For him, that was the beginning of the end of us. We were preparing to move to Easton Pennsylvania as our next Military duty station. Michael told me I needed to get on medication. He said I was driving him crazy because of my fluctuation of organizing and cleaning following exhaustion and messiness. He couldn't understand why the house was ever messy since I didn't work. When I did clean, he said he could never find anything afterwards, and it drove him crazy. So I made an appointment with my OBGYN, and Michael went as far as to come to the appointment with me. Michael, the kids, and I crammed into a small, janitor-sized therapist's office. Everyone's knees were almost touching.

I sat there with my diaper bag packed with a thousand distractions to keep the kids occupied and prevent any frustration with Michael. He rarely spent any time with us as a family, and I knew if I or the kids annoyed him, it would be harder to ask for more time with us. He would use anything he could use as an excuse not to go places with us. I could hear what I'd heard hundreds of times... "It just gives me too much anxiety to go out with them."

"I just want my wife back." It sounded sweet. Everything to blame on postpartum depression. It didn't make sense to me though. I love being a mom. We got out every day and went on adventures. The house was clean and I slept as much as a mother could with a toddler and 11-month-old. I cherished every moment with my kids. Michael wanted his wife back.

Journal Entry November 17th:

> *Hazmat suit required at the gates of my brain. Don't worry. I'm driving to you, and the lane is insane.*
>
> *My heart's not pounding. It's beating to a racing clock. Everything is sped up yet the world has stopped? Louder. Louder! Louder than the semi truck's horn. No one is*

speaking, there is no storm. Except the one in my head. That no one else can hear. The one that gets me labeled as mean, short-tempered, bulldozing the peaceful grassy field.

Check once. Check twice. Like cooking Thanksgiving dinner with just one serving knife. The list of things to do goes on and on. The list of helpful people are away. They are gone. They don't understand how you feel. It's not a "sad feeling." It's a breaking down and smoking up truck that finally yields.

A year of torture. But all the same treasured joy. My baby bundle it's bitter sweet as she grows. The aching and anxiety, and caffeine feeling like a last plea for hope. Hope to not feel like a zombie who awoke. Makeup free, baggy shirts, begging for the next nap then crying to sleep because she's only getting bigger. These moments are passing, fleeting, I hold her close.

So can I take a moment. And express it differently? I passed by the pamphlet with the crying postpartum mom. "Depression" and "worry" these words didn't cross my mind. I'm not "sad" this girl is my world. PPD isn't me... I'm just in the thick of it. But the "thick of it" never ended. Enraged I became as the stress never let up. The "it should be easier now" was met with another cup of empty promises from caffeine. Nothing left. And here she was. Soon sitting, crawling, her first steps to dad. I'm happy I am. But the drowning still has. In my heart. Desperate and pleading to be a better mom... I went in and told them of everything going on. 2 doctors later and the pamphlet lady who wasn't me. Was a clue to the many symptoms of how to get back to feeling ok. I love being a mom but how do I manage my husband.

Cleaning Company

When we heard we were moving to Pennsylvania, we put the house on the market. The problem was, we put it on the market in September when school had just started. Most people move during the summer so their kids can be settled before school starts. We didn't receive any offers on the house. I began to stress about a mortgage and rent. I scheduled the house to get cleaned the day after we moved out. Kristie, the lady who cleaned it, fell in love with the house. She wanted to rent, and her lease would be up that month anyways. She moved in 2 weeks later. It was a miracle. Kristie was a single mom to three daughters who worked hard at a company she built from scratch. She wasn't going anywhere.

Later, her daughter, who had moved out, would announce that she was pregnant. They would move into the basement and bring their little girl home. My home in Utah felt like it continued to be a home. It had the right people living in it.

DRIVING COMPANION

Michael called me and said Isla, a married woman he had known for 15 years, offered to drive with him to Easton, Pennsylvania, where we were moving. He said he needed her help because he couldn't see while driving at night. I didn't feel like I had an option to say no. He said that he wouldn't sleep with her, but at their last stop, he told me they had sex, but he felt gross afterward. Even as he told me, I sat there with my heart in my stomach, I felt like I wasn't allowed to be upset about it. Since I decided to take the kids to San Diego and fly with them to Pennsylvania alone, I left him with the car and no other option. Or so I thought at the time. I didn't want him to say I had to return to Utah and drive the car with the kids. So, I just had to be okay with whatever happened.

That night, we flew into a small airport in Allentown, Pennsylvania. It was pitch black outside and we drove straight to our new home. This was not the first time we rented a place sight unseen, but I was pleasantly surprised at how beautiful the townhome was. We walked in, and I laid the kids in their beds. This was also not the first time Michael sent the movers away without them unpacking, even though it was in their contract with the Military. He knew I would unpack and per his words, he wanted to take a nap. He felt bad sleeping when the movers were working. That is what he told me. So, I laid the babies in the bed and fell asleep. When I woke up, I was excited to go explore. I wanted to stock up the fridge, find the closest park, and see the streets I would be driving for what was supposed to be the next few years.

When the time came to drive around, I fell in love. The streets that would be our main roads were paved through dense forest. The town was first established as a trucker stop between New York and Philadelphia, so they made the roads through the forest. The park down the street from our house was next to a farm that made ice cream from their cows on-site. Even the gas station food from WaWa's was delicious. It was October, so the leaves were turning into vibrant colors in a way I had never experienced before. There was a town square with pumpkins set out. It was magical.

When Michael started his job, he lightened up about us going out without him. I got a membership to the Crayola Factory. It was ten minutes through winding hills and trees and had a huge indoor play area for the kids. I was in heaven and so were they. I'd pack up lunches, explore the parks, and drive over bridges and by lakes. I hope to drive back there someday and take it all in again.

A few weeks into being there, Michael came home one night and put on his dress blues. I was confused. He said he had to go to an event after work. Within seconds I figured it out. "Is it an Army Ball." I said it as a statement instead of a question. He denied it, but offered to have me drop him off so I would have the car because he wasn't sure how long it would go. I told him he could take the car because it was 5 p.m. and I wouldn't go out for the rest of the night. But he insisted I drop him off and he said he would take an Uber home. None of it made sense but still, I packed up the kids and he gave me turn-by-turn directions until we were in front of a hotel.

As soon as I pulled up, I saw men and women dressed in dress blues and ball gowns. I looked over at Michael at first confused and then hurt. He said he didn't want to stress me out about finding a babysitter, then jumped out of the car and walked into the Army Ball alone. Michael was an expert at making unilateral decisions for me. But this one hurt. This one cut differently. We had always gone to Army balls together. From our first one in Missouri to the last one we went to together in Utah. They were my favorite memories with him. If I had not seen the ladies in ball gowns, I don't think he would have told me it was an Army Ball.

Despite the hurt from the Army Ball, I went home with the kids and continued to unpack, cook, clean, and be with our babies. I was hurt but I was fine. I could still do what I loved, which was being a mom. I didn't know how to be a wife anymore.

Even after all that had transpired, from October to December, Michael and I were the most solid we had ever been as a couple, especially as parents. His work was a few short miles away, the kids were slept a bit better, and we started going to the gym 2-3 days a week together. We had a good rhythm and were excited to be in a new place. It felt fresh. To say we ate a lot of gas station food sounds funny, but you have to try it! Wawa's was perfect after a workout dinner. We mostly went to church socially, but I still believed in God. I think Michael did too. He never talked like he didn't. The Mormon church gave us a sense of community and friends. They also had a good influence on us.

2020
AND THEN. COVID

Overnight, the world shut down. Michael came home and said he was going to start working from home. Wow, I thought. We get to be a super family! Of course, he would have to work, but we got to have him around!

It is forever imprinted in my mind when he came downstairs at 8 a.m. and opened a beer. I did not dare say a word. To say my husband died of Covid is a fair statement. He died of the effects of the shutdown. From the lack of accountability needed to check a few emails a day while everyone tried to figure out how to successfully work from home. Morning beers grew into all-night benders that resulted in sleeping nearly all day. Michael started staying up all night, checking his emails in the morning, and then going to bed. I was in charge of keeping the kids out in the backyard or in the house quiet while he did this. Sometimes he would fall asleep on the couch in the living room, so I'd have to sneak the kids to the basement or the upstairs without waking him.

The weather was warming up, and our backyard was first a patio and then a vast grassy area shared by all our neighbors. When our bubbles began showing up in the neighbor's window, Annie, a retired schoolteacher would sit with us outside.

Crooked Glasses

One day, Michael wanted to go to the gym at work. Since we only had one car and I needed to pick up my medication, I asked him if we could come along. It was a great idea because there was an indoor basketball court where the kids could run around, and we had been so cooped up because of the lockdown. I thought it would also be nice for them to see his new office. Michael went to work out, and I secretly hoped that he would take a while so we could play for as long as possible. The kids ran around thrilled. When Michael opened the basketball court door, we were apparently being too loud. He came up to me and hit my head so hard that my glasses flew off my face and onto the ground. One of the screws came out, and I could not find it. I had broken glasses again. Without my glasses and blurry-eyed, I packed up, and we all left. On the drive to the pharmacy, Michael had the kids chanting, "Time to get mommy her crazy pills, crazy pills, crazy pills." Michael entered the store to get my prescription and a glasses repair kit. I stayed in the car with the kids, and when we got home, he watched me take my medicine like he always did, and then I fixed my glasses. They could not be fixed perfectly because the frame was too bent, so I just walked around with crooked glasses, and that just had to be okay.

March Easter

On Easter, our neighbor Annie offered to take family pictures of us. Ecstatic, I dressed Ronan in a button-up shirt and Raela in a flowery dress. When Michael came downstairs, I told him of the opportunity that had presented itself a few moments before! Furiously, he told me I always spring things on him. He stormed back upstairs, and the kids and I didn't see him for the rest of the day. I went back outside, set up the Easter egg hunt, and took photos of just the kids.

> *The following year, Michael posted on Facebook that "Easter kinda fuc*ked me up. It's usually thinking about my son that*

161

spirals me. But this holiday had me thinking about my little girl. Not seeing her pick up eggs is the strangest trigger I've ever had." My jaw dropped. I stood up and set my phone down. I had to walk away. Another year had passed since Easter in Pennsylvania. I thought back at this moment as tears filled my eyes in despair that he had missed every Easter with Raela.

DROPS OF HOPE

As I saw Michael start to go deeper and deeper into drinking, I began to panic. I had spent the past six months every two weeks racing to Sam's Club with the kids and loading up groceries before he spent the money on alcohol or chewing tobacco. Michael never spent more than we had, but he would drain the account of whatever was in it every time there was money. I stress-bought and meal-prepped to ensure food was in the house. All while trying to balance not spending too much because Michael needed a thousand dollars more to buy his drinks and tobacco.

I secretly researched foods that might help with his depression and mood swings, and to lower his sex drive. Then, I began cooking everything possible from scratch with the cleanest ingredients Sam's Club had to offer. I paused before serving to Michael to pray to the cosmos. I prayed to anything that might listen. I could see the end of this tunnel, and it shook me to my core. This felt like my last chance to positively influence him while we lived together. The final drops of hope from the well that was running dry.

On a walk around the block, I called Michael's sister, Tammy. I told her how bad it was getting, how he was really starting to scare me. She urged me to leave. I responded that I could be the nanny. Michael was done with me, but I could cook, clean, and cater to him. I could make it work if it meant my babies were with me and I could manage Michael enough to do that. I remember Tammy supported me as much as she could, that she understood why I needed to stay.

Michael would admit later that he felt me pull away and enter this role I created. That's why he woke me up one night and tried to put another baby in me. Because of that night, I went into the doctor's office to refill my Zoloft and refused to leave without an IUD.

According to Michael, my decision to get on birth control was just another way to show him that I didn't want to be with him anymore. He wasn't wrong. Michael had been talking about having a 3rd baby and trying without my consent. When I came home from the appointment, I was bleeding and in a lot of pain. Michael tried several times without my permission because he read that there was still a chance to get pregnant, especially in the first week after placement. He got me pregnant. Twice. The pregnancy didn't stay with the IUD. I had two miscarriages. I begged him to stop, but he refused, saying I had the IUD, so he was going to be fine. But later, he admitted that he hoped I'd get pregnant so that I would stay. I don't remember what I thought when the thin positive line came up. When I got my period, he tried again. I remember screaming for him to stop as he held me down. However, he had done this plenty of times. This time, he physically harmed and choked me throughout. When he finished, and I was crying, he said, "Oh, I thought you were role-playing." We have never role-played like that.

Last Birthday with Michael

With the lockdown in place and my husband's mental state on a seesaw, I made myself some cupcakes—yellow cupcakes with chocolate frosting. Michael came downstairs with a request for dinner on my birthday. I didn't get to choose. I packed up the kids and went to the grocery store. As I walked out the door, he said, "I forgot a card. If you pick one up, I'll sign it." I had no idea how much that card would later traumatize me. In the grocery store, I got what I needed for my birthday dinner. With Raela in the shopping cart and Ronan running down the aisle and back, my hand reached for the card. The outside of the card read "Happy Birthday to an awesome person," and the inside said, "You should save this card. You can send it to me on my birthday!" Cool, I thought. He could sign it, I'd give it back to him on his birthday after I signed it, and we could do this for years to come. I didn't know that I was actually buying the last card we would ever have.

I walked into the house and handed him the card. He set it down on the counter. He just had to sign it. I made dinner, and we had the cupcakes I made. He did not sign the card. It stayed on the counter where he left it for a year and a half.

May

I want to remind the reader why I am writing about my experience with Michael. I am not actually telling you about my late husband, or about anyone else other than myself. I am informing you of what I experienced. To explain the reasons why I made the decisions I made, when I made them. Michael battled dragons bigger and deeper than I will ever know. He did not feel safe to talk about them, even to me. I never knew the boy beneath all of his reactions to whatever happened to him. I only ever got glimpses of his soul.

I sense there is goodness that comes from explaining when his coping skills shifted to become life-threatening to those closest to him and his life taken from him. In that explanation, I envision empathy for myself and him. I wish I had realized sooner that my attempts to carry him through his unresolved trauma did not raise either of us but drowned us both. Every time he chose reaction, instead of recovering, I found myself in the middle of his Capua's Arena (a Roman Colosseum where gladiators fought to the death leaving only one victorious in the early years of the arena).

This is my attempt to bring light to the impact of PTSD and addiction and transform tragedy by the example of my own personal self-discovery, healing, and closure. I hope to offer a voice to the often silent struggles of those who live with or love someone suffering with PTSD and addiction. I still cared for him and know that if he had the tools to do better, I know that he would have.

Over the next month, I fell into a deeper level of hyper fixation regarding Michael's moods. Before, I could appease him by anticipating if he was hungry or tired or what would annoy him. I was losing that gauge though. With the amount of drinking he was doing; I could not keep up. I put away more and more of myself until I was almost a complete robot around him. It still wasn't enough. We lived together with completely different lives. He still slept all day and had his own bedroom. The times in our relationship when we shared a bed were out of pure necessity. If we had a spare room or a couch, he was on it. At the beginning of our relationship, I would tell him how much it hurt. It made me feel like an afterthought when night after night, month after month, year after year he would "be so tired" he would fall asleep somewhere else. I stopped feeling that way when I got pregnant with Raela.

Every night, I would put Raela to bed, then Ronan, and then go check on Michael who would wake up at 5 p.m. I would put a plate on his nightstand for breakfast. Then at lunchtime, I would replace the empty breakfast tray with his lunch. Then, I would do this for dinner. The only time he would be awake was to eat, for an entire month. I'm sure he was up throughout the day to check his emails, but this was when our interaction would start. He then would eat dinner; I'd put the kids to bed and then I would come in and massage him until he permitted me to go to bed.

I kept peanut butter crackers under my pillow in my room and knew the steps to take to not make a sound when going to the bathroom. Michael rarely woke me up anymore, but if he knew I was awake, he would have me come in and massage him. So my solution was, if I were hungry in the night, I would chew up a peanut butter cracker, then take my water and swallow it as quietly and quickly as possible. It took me years to be able to eat those crackers again.

Michael knew I was checked out. He knew I was trying to survive this season. But I was not trying to leave him. I had no intention of leaving him. But I also could not do what I had done for years: run away to San Diego while he calmed down. The world was shut down.

It's difficult to admit that Raela reacted differently when it was just me compared to when her dad was around. She followed directions and interacted with me, but when both Michael and I were present, Raela very clearly dissociated. Whenever Raela felt Mama get anxious, she would trip over her own feet, walk into walls, or fall over for no apparent reason. One of the many times when Michael was screaming at me, I stood on the stairs, at eye level since he was two steps below me. I'm not sure what I did or what he yelled, but there was a hand in my face and words screamed. Raela did not move out of my arms or cry. She just stared straight ahead, silent. I started to think that maybe she was developmentally delayed. This was an easier assumption than admitting that my one-year-old had learned to disconnect herself out of necessity.

When Michael switched from video games that were just slightly violent to highly volatile, alarm bells blared in my head. He had asked me a few times to water down his vodka to help pace himself, but it wasn't helping. At this point, he was drinking an entire handle of vodka (39 shots), 2 bottles of wine, and a six-pack of beers a day. I stood in my kitchen googling: alcohol and violence.

However, it feels more concrete to talk about how he hurt me. What's blurrier is what exactly was going on with his mental health because that was not my journey. Everything that he did was a symptom. Of what, I can only speculate. It was his cry out for help that I was unable to decode. I vowed, "in sickness and health." I tried with "in sickness." I can't speak for him, but I hope he tried, too. We were a product of not knowing better, of acting in fear. Of trying to get through to the next day instead of sounding all the alarms, putting ego and fear aside, and taking any help we could get. I continued to look at him as a symptom. I tried to get through to the next day. I was running out of strategy. He was running towards me.

There were days when I would sit on the couch with the kids, and I didn't know if he would turn the corner on the stairs and charge at me, tackle me, or take my phone away for the rest of the day. I didn't know if it was a day when he would break the bathroom door in half to throw me on the ground while the kids were in the bathtub. I didn't know if I would be getting dressed after a shower, and he'd come in to "get his" or scream, shove me, and whack my head until I was shoved in the closet. With his final "eff you," he'd slam the closet door shut and tell me not to come out. Of course, when I heard the guest bedroom door shut, I would come out and continue to care for the children. I can't remember what I would do that upset him. I just remember that any time I woke him up from being too loud, I'd end up with a migraine and bruises.

THE MONTH WE SEPARATED

June 20th, 2021 (future post):

> *I was asked. To sit in Traffic. Hostile. Maybe, a little. But life moves on the streets. While I sit. Unable to move. Stuck in the moment after his fatal peril. Left with the broken pieces of my heart. Packed away, stuffed*

into a suitcase with buckles about to break. Neatly thrown into the trunk.

What was once my sanctuary, is now a war zone. Blank stare. Induced dementia. Survival stare. I gaze at the wall, unable to convince myself that I am safe in my own home. A sanctuary. Now I see that it's blown up from the inside. I see myself standing there. An outsider to my own experience. I become "she." And she gazes right past me.

My gaze draws downward. How did I get here? I'd been here all along. Just in denial. The pain of my hair used as a way to physically control me. The bald spot on my head has removed a chunk of hair from my scalp by his grip. Strains floated in the air for all time and space to witness. To the ground this time I go. Bruised arm and stabbing stomach pains. All conceived by this man's hands and feet as they plowed through me like a baseball bat that just kept swinging.

He made his choice and that was to attempt to kill me over the course of four days. As the first of June began, I would have thirteen days until I had no other choice but to find a way out, over the span of four days to escape the house that was our home. The thought would consume me. When he first saw me 8.5 years ago, when we first met, why couldn't he have just kept walking? Walked straight past me and on with his life. So on with mine, I needed to go.

June 12th

I sat with Ronan on the porch swing. This had become our favorite way to fall asleep. I rocked him as he watched the fireflies until he drifted to sleep. After a few moments on the swing with him asleep, I started thinking about carrying him to bed. But my mind was distracted that night. There was a horrific domestic violence attack a block away from our home in Utah earlier that day. The dad shot his two kids and then himself. His wife got off her shift from the hospital and found her whole family.

I remembered then that my friend Candice had reached out to check in with me a couple of days before. With the stress of the last few months, it was hard for me to keep in contact with people. With the news, I texted her back. She told me that she used to work for a domestic violence advocacy agency in Utah. One in four women in the United States are victims of domestic violence, and the statistic was one in three in Utah. She had just called out my statistics. There was no more trying to convince myself that it was something else. One in four. That conversation was monumental in my decision to leave. To break the cycle for my children.

I called my mom on the porch and asked if she could be on the next flight to Pennsylvania and drive back to San Diego with me and the kids. My heart sank with her response. I must have caught my mom off guard, and she did not have a response to my request. After a few moments, I said goodnight without explanation and tried to stop my spinning head. But I had lit the match that would start the fire by telling my mom to pick me up. I had no excuse to back down since my mom was now involved. With that failed idea, I had to think up a new plan. Looking back, I could have just got in the car and left. But I feared Michael would follow me. I know he would have been so angry he would have found me no matter what. I knew I had to have him voluntarily let us go.

June 13th

It was my son's 4th birthday, and I was locked out of the house in the backyard of my own volition. I had undermined Michael's parenting by telling him to stop pestering Ronan and calling him names on his birthday. I heard his footsteps behind me. Fu*k. I had done it again. An explosion of cuss words fired behind me as I set the food down and turned to face my nightmare. I stepped back, intuitively clearing some distance between us. In response, I got a McDonald's McMuffin launched at me, and when that missed, exploding all over the kitchen, I was shoved forcefully to the ground. It was a more fool-proof way to get his anger out—a release of rage from inside his body and into mine. In a break of self-preservation, I raced to the back door, feeling his giant hand barely graze against my leg as he attempted to grab me back.

I was locked outside, again. At least he has time to calm down without being able to hurt me further, I thought. Ten minutes later, the door opened. Michael spat, "June 29th, bitch" before slamming and relocking the door. June 29th was the day set by the military to resume traveling during the pandemic. It was also the expiration date Michael gave me for my time in the townhome. He was reminding me that I had until June 29th to prove I was worthy to live in the townhome with him. If I didn't, I would be forced to move out of the house. I convinced myself he at least gave me up until the 29th because he loved me.

I walked around to the front of the townhome and asked Ronan to open the front door. "Not until bad Mama says she's sorry," Michael taunted. With too much to do today and guests on their way in a few hours, I began. It was always the same: a chorus of "I'm sorry," followed by "like you mean it." It repeats a second, third, and fourth verse. A deeper and deeper apology.

Michael unlocked the door, and I rushed to get everything done. I reached for my coffee mug. It felt full, but all I got was a mouthful of water. He had purposefully dumped out my coffee and replaced it with water. I threw it away. By the time the party started, the house was clean, the food set out, and ready to welcome the guests. I didn't have time to be upset. All evidence of the morning had disappeared, but I knew life could not go on like this.

June 15th

On June 15th, I sat on the couch and typed the driving directions to San Diego. I put Ronan to bed and walked to Michael's doorway. I looked at Michael lying in bed, and something in me broke. I screamed. Not in terror. But a fractured, shattering sound that revealed all the confusion, pain, and frustration bottled in me. I shook like an earthquake as the noise left my body. Michael pointed to the cracked open window, "Bro, the neighbors are going to hear you," and returned to his phone. I took a step back and walked away.

I stood in the kitchen making tea, my mind completely blank as I stared out the window. When I came to, still stirring the tea bag, I realized I had traveled so far in my mind it was like I had dementia. I was no longer home inside my body. I was merely a vessel to care for the children and an embodiment of all of Michael's triggers.

Still stirring the tea bag, I heard his footsteps coming up the stairs. Whack! For the 3rd time in the last few days, he turned the corner and bashed my head, then gripped my hair to throw me to the ground. But this time was different. There was hatred in his eyes. One look and I was immediately out of my body. I watched from a bird's eye view as his foot rammed into my stomach, then arms that covered my stomach, next, my head. I felt a sense of peace come over me as I curled up, that this would all be over soon. I thought I was dying. And then, as the final blow hit my head, he stopped. Michael stepped back, his eyes completely glossed over with something unreadable, "I almost murdered you." I froze. Michael took another step back and then walked blankly back up the stairs. He did not come out of his room the rest of the night.

June 16th

On the 16th, I went out to my car during nap time and made a life-changing phone call. I called Amy. We had become friends in San Diego while Michael was deployed. I stumbled through the small talk pleasantries and then blurted out, "Can I come to stay with you for a few days?" She must have been so confused, but she replied that I could, of course, even though they had moved from Carlsbad to Tennessee. When she asked if I was okay, for the very first time, I admitted aloud that my husband was an alcoholic, and it was no longer safe to be with him; I had to leave. I then told her not to contact me. I would let her know when I started the drive.

After our phone call, I began secretly packing. Clothes went into a container, important documents were hidden under the driver's seat, and the kids' favorite toys were stuffed in the car's crevices. I tried to think of everything we needed.

I still didn't have a fully formed plan to get out. But that night, I walked into his room again and sat on the bed uninvited. Michael listened as I poured out my broken heart with compassion and honesty. I told him our relationship was not sustainable and we were going down a catastrophic road. I didn't know what to do or how to help him. I had lost my faith in God. I told him I loved him, but we needed some space. Then I asked him if I could take the kids to San Diego until things settled down and we got back on our feet.

Miraculously, Michael received it well. He understood and agreed to let me take the kids. I felt like I'd breathed fresh air after being held underwater. But as I made to leave, he asked for a kiss. I felt like he didn't understand what I had just said, or the severity of the situation. I pulled back from him in a split reaction. Michael's face soured. He told me I ruined the best moment that we had had in a long time. I couldn't even treat him like a husband.

Despite that, Michael agreed to let us leave on Friday. It was Monday. After he was upset about the kiss, I knew I needed to leave immediately. We had to go in the morning.

June 17th

The next morning, I woke up and packed the car. Since Michael knew we were leaving, I didn't have to pack secretly anymore. When I tried to get back into the house, Michael locked me out. Again. Through the screen window, he said I wasn't allowed to leave today since it was only Tuesday. He told Ronan to call me "bad mommy, crazy mommy." Then he said I could only take Raela to San Diego, but not Ronan. It was all the more apparent that I needed to leave immediately. Somehow with both kids.

Michael continued, telling Ronan to give Raela one more hug because he would never see her again because Mama was taking her away forever. Quickly, I said, "Ronan, let's get ice cream." Michael got upset that I could try to trick Ronan into coming with me and told him to call me a naughty mommy. He told Ronan if Mommy tries to kidnap you, yell, "Help, help, help!"

I managed to get back into the house, but my nerves were fried. I had messed everything up, I thought and ruined our chances at a safe exit; surly Michael wouldn't let us leave now. I heard Michael talking to someone on the phone in his room. I could hear him saying terrible things about me to whoever was on the line.

My body tensed in preparation as Michael came downstairs. But all he said was, "You're going to drive to Virginia." He had been on the phone with my mom. Somehow, she convinced Michael to let me take the kids to Virginia, where my Aunt Susan happened to be on the route back to San Diego. I would meet up with her, and he trusted my aunt enough to drive the rest of the way. We were allowed to leave. My mom had gotten us out of the house; she said exactly what he needed to hear in the way he needed to hear it. Something I was incapable of doing in that dire moment. It was a miracle.

As I prepared to leave, I found myself in the kitchen with Michael. I thanked him and told him this wasn't the end, we just needed to find solid ground. When Michael asked me how long we would be gone, I replied, "Maybe six months?" I said that, but I knew we wouldn't be back. This was the end. As if he read my mind, Michaels lit up with fury, "I thought this was only going to be a few weeks!" Anxiety rocketed through me as I thought of a way to calm him. With kindness and compassion, I hugged him and gave him a kiss. I said, "Michael, I just said a number, I don't know. Let's take this a day at a time." It seemed to settle him.

With the kids buckled into the car, Michael gave them one last hug. Remembering that I left Raela's baby blanket in the house, he went to get it, and I followed him back into the house one last time. As he handed it to me, my eyes locked with his. This was the man I married. The man I loved for all these years. He was letting us go. I gripped the blanket tightly and turned to walk out the door.

As I turned my back to Michael, I heard a voice, clear as day, "Don't look back." I could feel his eyes burn against my back. I knew if I turned back, he would snap out of whatever trance he was in that loved me enough to let me leave. Heartbreak flooded my heart with every step towards the door.

I stepped past the threshold of our house — the house that almost killed me — and into the fresh outside air. I got into the car, put it into reverse, and drove off, never looking back.

TORRENTIAL RAIN

I merged onto the main road and drove west. I passed Allentown and kept going. Soon, I could see signs for Virginia, but I knew I wouldn't stop there. My aunt already had a flight back home if I did not meet with her. My goal was Tennessee, twelve hours away.

In Virginia, rain started pouring like a fire hose on my windshield. Everyone was going ten miles an hour, and the wipers were futile. Going under the overpasses and bridges terrified my already unnerved body because the rain pounding the windshield would suddenly stop, complete silence, and then start again. I was terrified of driving but not as scared as spending another night under the same roof as Michael.

181

A metaphorical (and literal) sea parted as I drove through the torrential rain. Just as God led Moses and the Israelites out of Egyptian captivity, so did He make a way for me to escape from Michael. It was the miracle God provided even though I did not actively believe in an all-loving Creator. God saw me even though I was deliberately opposed to him. I was so angry with God for so long. Looking back, I believe God gave me miracles all the time. It would take me a while to return to faith in God to acknowledge and hold sacred all that he granted me.

At some point during the drive, I texted Michael and told him I was driving to Tennessee to stay with Amy. Like Pharaoh allowing the Israelites to leave Egypt, Michael also let me continue my journey. Two little souls looked out their windows as we pressed on through the thick rain. We made it to West Virginia and continued West. Pennsylvania grew further away behind us. This is it; we start over from here. I was dizzy just from the gravity of my decision.

It was 11 at night, nine hours in, when Michael called to check in. He was calm at first, but I could hear him slowly get angry as I explained it was ten total hours to Tennessee. I didn't say that it was twelve hours to Amy's house. I had hoped to get there that night. Michael screamed at me, saying it was too late to drive with the kids and that we needed to pull over.

I thought I could still make it, but I didn't want him to jump in the car and find us while we were sleeping, so I agreed to stop and get a hotel.

I will forever cherish that decision. When I woke up the next morning, it was just me and my children sharing a king-sized bed in a random city on the border of Tennessee. I took a breath and realized then that I had done it. I got us out safely. Surely, it had been Divine Intervention. Before leaving, I took a quick photo of me and the kids and promised them we would be okay.

Fresh Baked Cookies

I was finally at Amy's house. The car went into park and my body moved towards the front door on autopilot. I had not been able to eat since before I called her. When I am stressed, food is the first thing to go. As I walked into Amy's house, she pulled out a batch of freshly baked cookies. I inhaled nearly all of them. The aroma of chocolate chip cookies filled her house. A smell that breaks down my defenses to this day. It was my first breath of safety, and it humbled me.

Amy greeted me as though we were traveling through town. She treated me like a human. Not like I had crash-landed in her home after not talking to her for a few years. Not like I was running from domestic violence. She didn't look at my children with pity or at me with shame. She showed nothing but kindness when my son screamed profanities at me that he learned from his father. They did not ask if I was okay, probably because they could tell that all the pieces of my broken heart were in my pocket, and I could not remove my armor until it was okay to be out of survival mode. Instead, they took my kids to collect the eggs from the chickens. They played with my kids in the backyard and the blow-up pool at her parents' house. They brought over toys and showed me that I was not alone.

Later, I went out to the car to clean it, and she put the kids on the front lawn with a blanket and some toys. She gave me a moment to exhale, organize the car, and in doing so, organize my thoughts as well. I spent the next few days waiting for my mom to arrive. She was flying into Nashville to drive the rest of the way to San Diego with us. I had made 1/3 of the drive by myself. Although I asked her to fly into Pennsylvania, I think it happened like it was supposed to. I got some of my power back at that first hotel. Although I feel like I have been rescued by many, I took the steps forward and drove when no one was going to get me or give me an excuse like I had hoped for before.

My mom was to fly in at night, and that morning, I came downstairs tired and still in pajama shorts and a t-shirt. I had forgotten to get into jeans and a jacket. When I walked into the kitchen, the room got quiet. I wasn't sure what was wrong. Amy stirred the eggs and then looked down at the ground. Quietly, she asked, "Are those from him?" Startled, I grabbed my arms. My arms and thighs were covered in bruises. How could I have just come down in such a peaceful trance that I had not covered up? Just as quietly, I confirmed what was obvious. She finished the eggs and moved the conversation along. She didn't push any conversation, but that moment made us both realize that while we could pretend I was on vacation, the truth was evident. I was homeless and ran away with some clothes, birth certificates, and Peppa Pigs.

That night, I made the 90-minute round trip to pick up my mom. Come morning, I was all packed up, and we headed out. Vacation was over. We had 24 more hours of driving. I took a photo in the bathroom mirror on the way out. I wore a shirt that said "dreamer." A dreamer I was. I dreamed of a whole and full life in front of me. A life of recovery, and with the end of survival mode. One with security, vulnerability, creativity, and peace.

That day we drove out of Tennessee, through Arkansas, and to Oklahoma—ten hours in the car. The following day was through Texas, through New Mexico, and into Arizona—eight more hours. The last day was another eight hours in the car.

When we got to New Mexico, I planned to stay the night with my Aunt Susan at her house. When we arrived at my aunt's house, she had made an entire Thanksgiving dinner. I accepted this as her way to show her love for us. Everyone ate so well.

It was still early afternoon, but I was slowly growing anxious about the drive. I asked my mom if we could get back on the road. I had let my mom drive maybe an hour or so, but other than that, I did all of the driving. It was my way of feeling in control.

For the entire few days, Ronan and Raela stared out the windows watching the scenery go by. There was no screen time. They didn't ask for it. Even at four and eighteen months, they knew. They knew we had to get to San Diego. They stared out the window for days, strapped in a car seat, and let Mama and Grandma handle it.

After we left my aunt's house, we spent the night in a town next to Winslow, Arizona. In the morning, we drove to the famous "Standin on a corner in Winslow Arizona" corner. My mom was a huge Eagles fan, and I grew up listening to their music. Years ago, my mom told me that when she got anxious, she would say

"Take it easy." I decided to adopt that phrase. As a present, I got us both license plate covers that said "Take it easy" on them. My mom made that drive with me, and I am so thankful for it. Maybe she didn't show up exactly as I imagined or thought I needed, but in the end, God was in control and the way everything happened gave me great peace. I felt his mercy.

Home

As we came out over the pass on the 8-freeway heading west, I knew I was home. There were now thirty minutes left in the drive. We had done it—all four of us. I was still angry with God, so I did not acknowledge Him, but I felt spiritually drawn to the feeling that angels watched over the car and carried us across the country. At that moment, the kids started screaming. It was like they knew we were at the end of our journey. On June 26th, we were home in San Diego.

Misfired

One night, I told Michael I was going to bed. The kids and I had left Easton about three weeks prior. Michael would go between making sure we were okay to fits of rage. I understand this transition was hard, it was a lot to ask of both of us. But I could not see any other way. I was trying to find solid ground and I knew there was no coming back from our last encounter. But he was still their dad. I also wanted to make sure I didn't set him off. I made sure he was able to talk to them whenever he wanted to. I don't think I realized what torture it was for him to see the kids on video without seeing them in person.

I thought that if I could create an atmosphere where he could be his best through a screen or whenever he wanted to visit, the kids could have a pleasant experience with their dad. I also focused on getting my life back and attempting to draw boundaries. I was drained. It was a night when Michael was texting me a lot, which was fine. But when I told him I was going to bed, he got upset. He texted me repeatedly, so I silenced his text notifications and slept.

I fell asleep instantly. From a deep sleep, I awoke to my phone ringing. "I just tried to shoot myself, but the gun misfired." I panicked and exclaimed, "What!" I ran as fast as I could down the hall and shook my dad awake. I muted myself, explaining the situation to him, dazed and bewildered. You have to call 911 no matter what when someone says they are a threat to themselves or others. While back on the phone with Michael, I texted my friend, Tanya, a 911 dispatcher, begging for help. She coached me through what to say and what to do and got me the dispatch number in Easton. My dad called Easton while I talked to Michael until I heard the doorbell ring through the phone.

"What the fu*k did you do, Mariah?" I couldn't explain anything before the phone hung up. I didn't hear back from Michael until the next day. When he finally contacted us, he said that the police were awesome, and they invited him to a BBQ next week. He had told them how he was going through a messy divorce and that this was a tactic I was using to win custody. He actually wasn't mad at me. He said, "I handled it, and the police saw through your bullshit." I let it go and didn't bring it up again. He wasn't mad at me, and that was all that mattered.

That night traumatized me, though. I had tried to tell him I needed to sleep, and whether he was drunk and lying or the gun actually misfired, I would never know. He always found a way to pull me in whenever I drew a boundary. He had my attention. This wasn't new. It started with him calling me a bitch and telling me I'd never make it without him. Then came the holes in the wall and the bruises on the arms. Next, it was pillows over my face, broken down doors, ripping out chunks of my hair, trying to end me. Every time I tried to walk away; he ensured I couldn't.

The Dragon's Reign

Every stroke of the hairbrush was a brutal reminder of his control over me. My hands trembled and my breath raced. My chest tightened just thinking of how he used my hair to control me physically. His dragon reigned over me, attaching itself to my head. But this hair wasn't made for guiding; he was no longer allowed to hurt me that way. Yet his imprints of subduing me covered the strands. Every shower was a reminder. Finally, I decided to make sure once and for all he would never touch those locks again. I stepped out of the shower and handed my mom the clippers and a picture. I grabbed a section and said all of this. She shaved the back of my head into a triangle. Saying goodbye to that was easy. I had the bonus of looking trendy. But my reasoning was for freedom.

I loved to cook, so I started filming. I made videos and posted them online with the melancholy desire that if I died, my kids would have something left of me. They were online, and I prayed it would heal my children to have a reminder of their mother. I was desperate not to disappear. So, I made cooking videos. People seemed to love them, and it was my way of coping.

I also found morbid comfort at red lights, wondering what it would feel like to just roll into the intersection or hit the median on the freeway. Every time I drove, my prayer was, just make it quick. The same thought haunted me every time I laid down to go to bed. If he takes his gun and shoots me from the bedroom window, just let me not wake up for it. I found a strange sense of calm in the hope that there was a possibility I could not be awake for my murder. I could implore mercy, at the very least.

I wish I had known these were coping mechanisms. I found comfort in knowing it could all be over in an instant. I was confused and discouraged that I had these thoughts even though I knew I was free. Had I trusted the God of the universe, I would have put my faith in God instead of trying to control what was humanly uncontrollable. I did not want to die. I wanted to live. I wanted to live so big and loud and free.

They Needed Snacks

Moving back in with my parents was my only option. One I was grateful for. It was a safer alternative because I wasn't in danger of any physical harm. However, it wouldn't be until a year and a half later that I realized I was just surviving. I hadn't found a place or space to heal. My parents provided four safe walls, but they were their four walls. I had to make myself fit comfortably in their life. That was my rent, so to speak.

My mom has a hard time bending over physically. So, she would kick things across the room to my section of the house and out of the common spaces. When I told her that it was upsetting me because it reminded me of when Michael would throw things at me, she said there wasn't anything she could do about it. So, I stayed on edge as my body reacted as it did with Michael. My soul removed itself so far away from my body that I became just my flesh. This made me capable of parenting and showing up for my children the best I could. My children did not need a parent who was scared, crying, and reliving her trauma daily. They needed snacks, a ride to the park to run around, books read to them, and hugs. I learned what my parents' rules were usually by breaking them. They were vocal about boundaries in their house. It was hard to feel relaxed and at home. When I tried to re-sleep train Raela, I was told it was too upsetting to hear her cry, so I was not allowed to train her in their house. This further depleted my spirit because I felt no hope for a whole night's sleep for me.

I learned not to react when things were kicked across the room. I did what was frustrating to someone trying to confront another: shut down. I checked out. I closed my ears when they spoke to me. It was hard living with them and their rules. But my kids and I were safe, and we had a temporary home. I told myself I could heal later.

I Exhaled

Michael came to visit the kids in September. I arranged a hotel on the Military base on Coronado and politely requested that he not drink. The first day went better than I thought. I picked him up from the airport, dropped him off at the hotel, and then brought the kids to meet him after nap time to spend time at the beach.

The next morning, we played on the beach in peace. While walking Michael back to his hotel room, he asked if I would hold him for a minute when we returned. I felt pressured to keep the peace. I didn't think I had a choice. What would happen if I refused? I did so many things in the name of peace. Michael knew I was uncomfortable. I don't know how he enjoyed cuddling my stiff body. He tried to kiss me, but in an instant, I stood up and announced it was time to go.

After nap time, I came back with the kids and my mom. When we got to the hotel pool, I smelled beer on Michael's breath. He saw that it upset me, but I stayed silent. While swimming, Michael pretended to chase me in the water with Ronan on his back. I freaked out, and I asked him to stop. I was shaken to my core. It brought back all the times he'd chased me around the house.

While back at the hotel, I found an Airbnb for him for the next day since he had to check out. He blew up at me and said he was staying with me or would find somewhere else, but he refused to stay at an Airbnb. I reminded him that because of Covid, my dad did not feel comfortable with him in the house.

Later that night he asked me to book the Airbnb. It was in a good neighborhood next to a grocery store. I thought it was perfect. When we arrived the next day, the house was filthy. A bowl of wet cat food and bugs crawling in and out of it were displayed in the hallway. The floor was sticky, and hundreds of dead bees were glued to rocks. In the backyard lived a tortoise; the kids were thrilled at the reptile. The pool had so many leaves in it you could barely see the water.

Thankfully, his room was the cleanest part of the house. It looked fine to spend the night. Michael asked to take me to dinner to thank me for coordinating the trip. I wasn't opposed to the idea. We had so many obstacles on that trip already, and Michael did seem to be flexible, even if his first reaction was to yell. While waiting for a table, Michael put his arm around me and said, "Are you mad I wasn't this awesome when we were together? I've changed. We can be such a power couple now." I told him no and became scared that I was sending him mixed messages. I wanted us to work as two people who had children together. I loved him deeply and for a very long time. But 'us together' was over.

The following morning, Michael contacted me to pick him up. When I arrived, he said he was not going back and would get a hotel. A rash covered his back. I gripped the steering wheel so hard it felt like I would break it in half. My mom he said could stay with us and appreciated that he tried the Airbnb. He said thank you and that he could feel the tension in the car. I knew the Airbnb was unsuitable for staying, but I felt I had to diffuse the situation. Offering for him to stay two nights with us was the only way I knew how at that moment.

That night, when Michael went to shower, God sent a gift. Michael had left his phone open, and I saw it when I went into the room to grab something. I never knew his password. Even though he always had to know mine. When I left him, it was the first time that he did not have free reign over my phone. His phone lay open right in front of me.

But this seemed like a message from the universe. A reminder and solidified proof that no matter what he said about wanting to be a family, he still pursued other women. That's just my justification for looking through his phone. He was texting a girl named Tiffany. He said he was dealing with his toxic ex but was so glad to be with his kids. Tiffany was supportive of him. I felt like I saw what I needed to and clicked the phone off. Michael got out of the shower, and I put the kids to bed.

Maybe Michael noticed the shift in my demeanor. After putting Raela to bed, I went into the guest room where Michael was. Ronan had fallen asleep on the ground next to Michael's bed. When I walked in, Michael stood up and started pacing. Frantically I mentally ran through our day. Where was the breach? What was the problem? I grabbed Michael by the arms and asked him what he needed. When we lived together, I had chewing tobacco and liquor hidden in places for moments like this. If I didn't have any hidden that meant I would be taking the kids to the liquor store. I can't tell you how embarrassing it was or how many times I stood in a liquor store with a baby on my hip and a toddler running around as I bought chew tobacco and bottles of vodka.

With my hands on Michael's arms, he kissed me. I pulled back in fear. My body, mind, and spirit knew what was about to happen and I braced for it. He pushed me onto the bed. I whispered for him to stop, but with Ronan two feet away and afraid he would wake up, I went silent. I had already told Michael to stop, and he took off my pants instead. When he finished with my body, he lay next to me and thanked me. He said, "If you could have just been this awesome and supportive when we were together, I wouldn't have drank so much." He told me he was freaking out and wanted to drink but he was much better now. Then he fell asleep. That was the last time we slept together.

Michael left the next morning. I exhaled.

No Small Talk

Life goes on. No matter how hard this was, the kids came first. Survival mode was still in the driver's seat. The children knew that if we went to the park, we had to listen the first time and leave the park nicely when it was time to go. I had no energy. None. I had the ability to get dressed, pack snacks, grab the sunscreen, and sit.

I could barely move. I did what I had to make it to the park and then sat on the stairs of the playground. My thighs had been in constant pain since June. It was where I carried all of my stress. I had debilitating pain in my thighs, hips, and lower back. I would say that I was depressed, but in a way that is rarely recognized. I was scared and feared my life would end any moment while also being relieved that this could end, and the nightmare would be over.

It took all of my energy to shower. When I did, four to five days had gone by. I'd shower sitting down. Sitting took all the energy I had for anything, anywhere. My legs hurt constantly. I knew I couldn't live like this, so I took steps forward, beginning with chair yoga. My heart hurt. My anxiety was through the roof. I continued my obsession with cooking. My room was a constant mess, an outward reflection of my inward mental state, and I felt like I couldn't keep up. But as difficult as it was, I got out of the house every day. I felt like I had to. On Wednesdays, I got "fancy coffee" at the coffee shop down the street to motivate myself. It was better than my instant coffee at home.

I found myself at the park again. Staring blankly as the kids played. A voice piped up next to me. "Hi there I'm Kelly. I've seen you around. How are you? " "I'm Mariah. I'm going through a terrible divorce, and

I'm not okay." That was my response. I had nothing to give the chipper and kind mom who approached me. It was all I could do to sit there while the kids played. Her daughter sat next to Raela, and they played with the sand toys. We talked about God and how I wasn't interested because God and I were at a tug of war recently. She said "I've been there. For quite a few years actually." And that was it. No niceties. No small talk. Kelly met me where I was.

KITE STRING

One afternoon, while lying on the ground in the toy room, I reminded myself that Michael and I were connected through all of our history of the last 10 years. There was no denying that. But that connection was covered in grief. I knew we would always be connected, but I needed to become my own person again. When I think back to this, I thought I needed to become who I was before I met Michael. But now I know that even before then I did not know myself. I knew how to be happy and survive. I knew how to make friends. But it is also true that when I finally found myself, I was no longer the "girl I knew before him." But I also wasn't the girl after that either.

While lying on the ground looking at the ceiling fan in a trance, I felt as light as a kite. My string that connected me to Michael flew away. Just drifted off, through the roof, and into the sky towards the abyss of the universe. It was me letting go of control. I knew I still had to keep Michael on my radar, but I wanted to start my own life. One where I was a main character. Where I became a singular person. It wasn't earth-shaking or a megaphone announcement. It just was.

Looking for Fairy Tales

I had already let the kite string go. I knew back in June 2020, we had to be over. There was no coming back from the attempts he made to take my life. But that didn't mean I hadn't loved him for the last nine years or that I didn't love him now.

I texted Michael one night. I told him I wasn't his person anymore. I told him I was devastated about how bad things had become. It was my first text saying I knew he suffered from mental illness. That he had since before I met him. I asked him if he ever loved me. I think he thought I was trying to reconcile our relationship. Through therapy, I know now that I was trying to subconsciously wrap my head around how all of this happened. I was tearing everything apart to understand how we got here. So I could avoid ever being in a relationship like this again, for both of our sakes.

Michael was looking for fairy tales, that's what he told me. We thought we knew what love was, but love is where are in when God is with you. We were two spirits reacting to our human fears in a void of God. For me, it presented as fawning to Michael. For Michael, it was severe domestic abuse.

I knew I was with a man with firm convictions in what was right and wrong. And although his addictions dragged me through the mud, I could count on him doing the right thing. Even when financially poor, spiritually broken, and, later, psychologically shattered, he would do the right thing. But the danger was in the lack of boundaries; we only knew how to have fun with each other. Then when it was volatile, I ducked my head, ran for cover, then crawled out when the smoke cleared. Michael liked me for that. But he did not respect me for it.

I did not know how to walk away. I was terrified, too. His words echoed in me that he would take our children from me and leave me destitute. I did not put my faith in God. Neither of us did. Instead of trusting in God's provision, we chose to live in fear. I wish I had left sooner. But after Ronan was born and then Raela. There was too much at risk to leave after that, until I did.

Michael hurt me so incredibly deeply, but I had to exhaust every resource before I gave in and ran out the door for my life. I had to know it was undoubtedly over. That the tide wouldn't change. That Jesus wouldn't find us and save this. Yes, I wish Jesus would have, and I know He could have saved Michael. But when it got to the breaking point, history showed me that the violence only worsened. And even so, had he done a 180, I knew Michael's propensity to hurt me. The boxing match had to be called. Both losers, an all-around loss.

In this text exchange, Michael admitted that he knew he pushed me into situations sexually that were not okay. That he violated my body without my permission over and over again. That he never should have kept demanding things from me that diseased me spiritually. This text exchange was a gift from God. Michael said he never felt like I was good enough for him. So he escaped into the beds of other women because he knew when we had our first kiss that it was something special. He was trying to sabotage our connection before I abandoned him first.

He knew I would be a good mother to his children, so he got me pregnant. I felt that he made himself brave enough to have a potentially fulfilling family life because he knew I would be a good mom. A good legacy holder. It was his way of coping which I came to understand years later. He was coping with the gap between the man he *was* and the man he *wanted* to be. Not realizing they could have been simultaneous. It wasn't the next move, the next promotion, or the next lay. It was the here and now. It is the here and now.

He told me of all the stress on his shoulders. About the impermanence of his job in Utah. How buying a house terrified him. The amount of stress he was under and this unearthing feeling that the next paycheck would be his last. How I wish he would have known that was the fear of man talking to him. That comfort and peace do not come by notches in the bedpost or drinking games alone. They come in spreadsheets, budgets, and speaking out loud your fears to denounce them. I was crippled in the house, gaslit, and towered over by a man trying his absolute best to "make it." When he already had.

When he texted me all of this, it brought us together, but not in the way he thought. It gave me closure. It validated me that the stress I felt was indeed from him. I wasn't making it up in my head or going crazy.

He told me how when he shut down during Covid and slept and drank every day away, he always thought "I just need a day to reset." Days turned into weeks then months. He said he realized now that I didn't have the luxury of a day off. He said when he meets God, and God asks what happened, he will say "We had three bad months that broke her. But it revealed a lot of deeper issues." When I agreed that it was the three months, but especially three days that broke me, Michael lost it.

He told me I hadn't listened to anything he had said. He took back everything, saying he only said what he did in hopes of giving the kids their family back. That he tried to get me back to give the kids what they deserved- a mom and a dad. He ranted on about this boyfriend he thought I had, but never did. How I never listen and round and round the carousel. Except I wasn't riding anymore. I had changed the script and gotten off the pony.

We could have had a healthy conversation; he could have fought for the kids. Had the conversation not turned reactionary, we could have both healed and sat in our disappointment for a future we hoped for that didn't end up being. That's why this thief turned destructive. That's why his dragon lashed out. The dragon protects the gold. His dragon did that, and he never left the castle to realize there was plenty of love to go around for everyone. In relationships, everyone has dragons. You are just supposed to fight the one inside of you with your partner together. Our downfall was we were both fighting Michael's dragon while mine slept.

2021

Zoloft No More

Michael said that he would allow us to get divorced if I stopped taking my medication for a month. I later realized that the checklist for his agreement to sign divorce papers was unending. At first, I was insulted by his demand. He was the one that made me get on it in the first place. But despite that, I started to think I was ready. I hated the way the medication made me feel, but it undeniably helped me survive. It also prolonged the abuse; disassociation is a powerful tool. I wish I had known how it affected my alarms that things were wrong. The antidepressants made it so I could check out and get through the grind. I was unable to give the appropriate reaction to what was happening.

    I decided that with the help of my doctor, I would taper off. Michael wanted me to quit cold turkey, but when I tried that, I got extremely sick. So, my doctor prescribed me a lower dose, and over the course of about six weeks, I slowly weaned off of the medication.

It. was. brutal.

The vertigo was bad enough, but add two years of suppressed emotions. Every feeling it helped me suppress was now surfacing. That's how trauma works. Even if you don't feel it, it stays in your body. I only got better when I felt it and released it. It was the only way for it to leave my body. I thought I had terrible nightmares before, but now I woke up on the bathroom floor with the door wide open. I was sleepwalking constantly. I gained about 40 pounds and still had no energy.

I took it one day at a time. I am grateful for detoxing from Zoloft at the time that I did. I needed a clear mind for the decisions I would have to make and it was the best time to unpack my baggage and address it. It was like waking up from a long sleep. It was time for me to step out of the life I survived, into one where I thrive. It would still take years to get there. But every suppressed emotion came out of me in those years, like the emotions came flooding out of my body and I was powerless to control when they did. But I released them.

Concussion

Michael started dating a girl named Marie. When he told me, I was so relieved. He had moved on. I thought he was starting his new life, one I hoped he could honor.

In mid-February, Michael called and informed me that Michael's cousin, Jake, had physically attacked his girlfriend Rebecca. From what Michael told me, Jake moved into our townhome in Pennsylvania—the same townhome where I ran for my life. In the same bathroom where Michael had broken the door in half while I hid with his kids in the bathtub, Jake now also attacked Rebecca. Now, in that same bathroom, Michael went and pulled Jake off of her.

Michael called me saying he had broken up a domestic violence assault. That he was so sorry for what he did to me. He got it now. He understood how scared I must have been. I believed him. His voice rattled and shook as he described ripping Jake off of Rebecca and then Jake throwing Michael into the bathtub in his rage. He left blood from the side of his head everywhere and an instant bruise. He asked me to call Marie, who had been there, to make sure she was safe. Michael gave me her number and I texted her making sure she was okay. I made sure she had a hotel and told her to turn off her location services. I told her to tell Rebecca to do the same. They assured me they were safe. Michael sent me a picture of a huge bruise behind his ear and his uneven pupils. I begged him to go to the hospital. He did not go that night.

Eventually, Marie called Michael which ended my role as the middleman. Michael went to the hotel. He texted me updates and profusely apologized. That seemed to be the end of that. In the next few days, I again asked Michael to get checked out at the hospital. He said he needed to come and see the kids. I told him I would help him book a flight, but I needed him to get checked out first. So he did. He went to the hospital and was diagnosed with an acute concussion.

Hiking

In mid-February, I reached out to Steve, an old friend I knew as a teenager. I needed friends-people who could help me find myself again. The moment I saw him on the hiking trail. Standing in front of my car, our eyes met, and it felt like he saw into the depths of my soul. Like he truly looked at me instead of through me.

When he invited me on a hike, I left Raela with my mom, but Ronan came with me. I was just meeting up with an old friend, so it didn't feel weird at all. Until

I saw him. It was like the floodgates of my feelings had opened and poured out of me. We were kids when I saw him last, and I couldn't stop thinking of all the past memories. I learned later that when you expect one thing—like seeing an old friend—, you might get something completely different, a grown man who seemed to be full of confidence. My brain dumped a ton of dopamine into me. It wasn't that I met my knight in shining armor; it was that I got a pleasant surprise. I was not used to those.

Steve was kind and funny and way cuter than I remember. He felt honest and sincere. He carried himself confidently, and it felt like he didn't have a care in the world. He stood tall. But I should have known. Anyone can appear strong for a few hours. I practically wrote that script myself the way I carry myself. I am not saying Steve was being fake or a bad person—I just put him on a pedestal. I saw the surface level of what he was offering. I knew this man had been in love with me (he admitted this) for ten years, and that made me feel safe. It's easy to be in love with someone you haven't seen in 10 years because you romanticize it. You don't actually know them.

When I got home, he texted me nonstop, making me feel like he was devoting all his time to me. After our hike, he went beach camping with his family and sent pictures—his dad barbecuing, his lovely mom, his whole family together. He even sent me a picture of his tent. It felt like I was just short of being there. He made me feel certain.

First Date

A few days later, he asked me on an official date. I jumped right into the deep end with no hesitation. On February 18th, I put the kids to bed and met Steve at his uncle's house which he was house-sitting for. I sat in my car moments before going inside thinking, *was I really going to go on a date with Steve? The nerd?* But he was no longer a nerd, and we were no longer kids. So, I walked in. He said he was tired, and I cowered inwardly. I suggested that we could just stay in, instead of going for a walk on the beach. But he shook his head and said no way, get in the car. I felt so special. Even though he was tired, he was going to take me out.

We walked along the beach and the cold water slipping over my feet made me feel alive. As the waves crashed on shore, I found myself walking deeper and deeper into the water. I felt like I orchestrated a second life for myself. I was in disbelief that a year prior I had a completely different life. I had a chance to be happy with a man. Maybe Michael had a chance to be happy too. I could be safe. Steve grabbed my hand, and I felt my hand melt into his. When we reached the pier, he grabbed the small of my back and leaned in to kiss me. "No way Steve!" I said out loud. It was my first date. He played it off and later said I was giving him all the signs. I'm sure I was, but I was still incredibly nervous and not ready.

When Steve asked me out, it was the first time since leaving that taking a shower didn't expend all my energy. I easily hopped right in and put makeup on. It was the first time in a very long time that I was excited for something, just for me. Steve wanted to spend alone time with me. I was so happy about that. But looking back, this was the start of our trauma bond. I allowed him to make me feel important. It wasn't fair to give him that power because my self-worth needed to come from within. I firmly believe that you cannot run away from relationship triggers and expect them to be resolved. Working through relationship triggers requires being in a relationship. But Steve welcomed all of my horrid past and held me while I cried and cried. But he didn't offer to tell me any of his, even when I asked. Steve became my comfort. He told me repeatedly to let him comfort me. I think I became Steve's drug, boosting his self-esteem as a man who could 'fix and save me.' It was never something I asked him to do, but when he offered, it was very easy to accept and let him be my knight in shining armor. His self-esteem should have come from within himself. We would both be taking addictive hits off each other for years.

On the drive back from the beach, Steve was so nervous he ran a red light. I screamed. He said, "Oh my! I'm so sorry, you distracted me." But as I turned to look at him, it was the face of a boy on a date for the first time in his parent's car. It was the face of innocence. Of what felt like a magical new beginning. There was so much excitement in the air, and it was pure.

I was up all-night thinking about how alive the cold sand and water made me feel. How real it was to be locked in his arms. The feel of his hand in mine, and not being terrified. *Could he believe how terrified I was of someone I married? Did he think I was a fool? Why can't I stop thinking about how sincere the night was? Did I really distract him? Am I really that interesting? What is his story? Why does it involve me?*

Steve courted me resolutely and all-consuming. I felt like he asked so much about me that it left no room for him. That pattern continued. But whenever I would ask, he would say, "I'm not sure, I just live a very boring life." Well, I did not. I had wished for it to be boring. Over time, I stopped asking as much about

213

his day. He worked a lot, and when he didn't work, I was his priority.

We continued like this for three weeks, living in a fairy tale. Then, Steve went on vacation with his family to Brian Head, Utah, and texted me a picture of a girl playing pool, smiling right into the camera. I asked who that was and he said it was his cousin. I thought it was weird and the smile was strange for a cousin, but I didn't question it.

BATTALION AGREEMENT

The day after my first date with Steve, Michael said his battalion commander, Lt. Dun, wanted to call me. He said he was acting up, and they could tell he was depressed. Michael asked to visit his kids. I told Michael from the beginning that he was always welcome to visit the kids and that I would make sure it happened. This time it made me nervous because he had just had a concussion. His battalion was there to protect me, they said. For the first time, it seemed like there was hope that they would hear me, that they were finally seeing what I had been telling them all along. In December, I called his commander CW and said, "I'm not going to say anything to trigger an investigation or get Michael in trouble, but I did not leave Pennsylvania because I missed San Diego. I am not on vacation out here. He needs help. Help him." CW wanted me to write him an email. I was afraid to do anything besides call because I didn't feel I could risk getting him in trouble at work. But with what seemed like support, I could open up to them.

OUR LAST HUG

On Sunday night, I picked Michael up from the airport and had to open the car windows because he reeked. I wasn't sure what the smell was, so I said we should get him some new clothes on Monday. I dropped Michael off at the Airbnb. We established that he was to stay in the Airbnb and was not allowed at my parent's residence for his visit from February 21st to 27th.

The following day, I picked him up, bought some fabric odor eliminator, and went to the park. Michael started sweating profusely and overheating after about 45 minutes. I took him back to his room. He called again in the evening to be picked up.

When I picked him up, I handed him some papers that he needed to fill out for the divorce. He was supposed to fill these out before coming to San Diego, but he pushed it off because of the concussion. We got dinner and headed back to the Airbnb to eat it. He had changed his clothes into new ones. This was when I realized the smell was from him, not his clothes. It was his body metabolizing the alcohol. I would later find out that he had liver failure.

When I arrived home, Michael began texting me, saying that he would not fill out the paperwork unless I admitted to having a boyfriend. He said he asked Ronan and that our 4-year-old confirmed that I had a boyfriend. I was furious that he dragged the kids into this drama and responded, "I would feel better if we came up with a plan for the paperwork before we see you again."

At this point, I didn't care about signing the papers, I just asked him for a plan. He took this as a demand that he sign. I didn't hear from him until the next day. The papers were now a bargaining chip.

On Tuesday, I called Michael three different times, but he wouldn't pick up. Ronan asked to see his dad all morning. Finally, at 1:30, I got a hold of him. We made plans to pick him up for dinner. Michael then texted my mom and dad saying I was keeping the kids from him.

Two hours later, Michael texted me, "I don't want to see you tonight. Let's start fresh in the morning." I responded, saying that it would make Ronan sad because he had been looking forward to seeing him all day. Michael relented. We decided on food, and then Michael said he was catching up on work and that 5 p.m. would be better. I picked him up then and we got takeout. Because it was so late, I decided that we would eat in the Airbnb, even though I wasn't comfortable with it.

We got to the Airbnb and I sat on the bed. Michael inched closer to me and said, "I know you still love me. Are you mad because you wish I could have been this awesome before, and now want me back?" I asked him to stop and he said, "Only if you kiss me." I refused. Then he said, "Fine, just on the cheek." I again said no. It felt like things were escalating, so I insisted that it was time to go.

At the car, I buckled the kids, turned and looked at him standing on the sidewalk. Even through the terror and trauma, I loved him. I reached my hands out and hugged him. My heart broke because I no longer felt any sense of his soul. It felt trapped too deep for me to even get a glimpse at. That was the last hug we ever shared.

When I got home, he called me. I answered and said he made me very uncomfortable and was crossing boundaries. He apologized but he just felt a connection between us. I said thank you, and that I'd call him in the morning to pick him up. I was still feeling very violated and texted that I was concerned about the way he was acting and that I thought he should go to the ER again.

The conversation got heated. I said I wanted him to go home to Easton. Back at the Airbnb he said he had never planned to divorce me, ever. Over text, I begged him to divorce me. The last text I sent him said that I would call him at 9 a.m. tomorrow and we'd pick him up if here were awake.

We didn't see him at all on Tuesday because he never answered my calls. On Wednesday morning, I continued to call him, but he didn't respond until 10 a.m., when he texted saying that we needed to regroup. I said we would see him after nap time if that was something he wanted. He then said he was legally allowed to see his kids and I needed to drop them off with him. I responded by saying we were going to head to the park and if he wanted to go, we would pick him up. I was not going back in the Air BnB.

I contacted Michael's battalion commander, Lt. Dun, and informed him how the last few days were going. I said that I was starting to get uncomfortable with how Michael was acting and that he was threatening to call the police if I didn't let him see the kids. Even though I was trying to get a hold of Michael all day to make plans to see the kids. Lt. Dun told me to focus on the kids and make the trip about them. He assured me that he was there to help if I needed it.

At 2 p.m., I texted Michael that we could get dinner and then go to the park so he could spend time with the kids. When I arrived two hours later, he was very shocked about the plan. He insisted that I had only just texted him about the plan, which was false. I didn't push it. We just got food and then went to the park. Michael threw a frisbee around for the kids to chase. Soon after, my mom showed up and discreetly told me that he reeked of alcohol.

After a few throws, the kids wanted Michael to run with them to get the Frisbee. Michael started sweating profusely and said he needed to go to the bathroom at his Airbnb. This was strange and shocking to me because Michael had always prioritized physical fitness. He worked out almost every day and was always the strongest man I knew. He would have never been winded from something like this a couple of years ago.

On Thursday morning, we all went to take Ronan to his gymnastics class. Michael kept asking me to see if his pupils were uneven from his concussion. I repeatedly told him that both pupils were pinpointed because of the sun, which made it difficult to determine. He went on to say how he felt like his concussion was making him fuzzy and forgetful and how he didn't feel good. This was what I had been telling him for days.

That night, while trying to get Ronan to bed, Michael called and asked me to stay on the phone even if we weren't talking. I said I would call him back later because Ronan was using my phone as an audiobook to help him sleep. I asked him to, in the meantime, write down ten things he was thankful for. Forty-five minutes later, I asked him if he was feeling better. He asked again if I was going to call him back. Anxiety slithered through me. He was asking for more attention than I was willing to give him. I texted him that I couldn't be that person anymore. He started to insult me, so I asked him to leave me alone. He kept texting me hurtful things, so I muted my notifications from him and went to bed. I missed the text at 11 p.m. informing me he was outside my house.

Sometime in the night, I walked to the bathroom to see my parents standing in their bedroom. My mom clutched her phone murmuring, "It's horrifying." I looked down the hall at her and asked, "What is?" She assured me that it was just something on the news. They didn't tell me that they were watching Michael outside of their house, pacing. My parents had been extremely uncomfortable with him outside, but Michael insisted that he just wanted to be near the kids. My dad gave him a pillow and sleeping bag to sleep outside; he didn't know what else to do. At 3:30 a.m., the doorbell camera recorded him leaving.

The next morning, I woke up after a full night's rest. I saw his text and was confused, thinking he had just come to the house that morning. He didn't respond, but we had plans to go to the pool. When we picked him up, Michael again appeared to have gotten no sleep and smelled horrible. I tried to focus on the kids and make it a fun time. It was difficult when the kids refused to be in the car with him unless he was doused with fabric cleaner, and all the windows were opened. Michael was very irritable and snapped at me, yelling, "I'M HIS PARENT, TOO!". When the mention of lunch was brought up, I asked, "What would you like?" His response was "NOT TO EAT WITH YOU!"

That night, he started to text my mom. He asked her why he had to lose his family. He was having a mental breakdown.

At 6:30 p.m., he called to ask what the plan was for the evening. I told him we were all ready and could pack up the kids to get ice cream, but he said it was too late and we should see each other tomorrow. I decided to hide my alerts from him since we wouldn't see him that night.

8 p.m., I texted him to confirm our plans for SeaWorld the next day.

9:28 p.m., he texted me that he was going to take his life when he got back to Easton. I had my texts hidden so I didn't see it.

9:48 p.m., he said, "I'm doing it right now, Never forget your worth." When I saw the text, I called 911.

The next hour was harrowing. *Had he convinced the paramedics and police I was crazy just like before?* I sat in my room shaking. If he had been released, he would be on his way over here. Angry. I felt an urgency to get out of the house. Here, I was a sitting duck. I called 9-11 back and they connected me to the police officer who responded to Michael.

I was told that he had been taken to the hospital but that was all they could tell me due to privacy laws. In pure desperation, I told the officer how scared I was. I pleaded that I knew the privacy laws, but I needed to know if I needed to wake up my children and go to a hotel. If he was released from the hospital he would come after me. The officer, in full grace, responded not to worry; he would not be released tonight but in three days. That was the officer's way of telling me that he was placed on a 72-hour hold without outright disclosing it.

What that officer did for me, I cannot repay. Michael was safe. I was safe. And I could sleep knowing both of those things. There are moments in life where when I knew he couldn't show up, I would sleep so deep it felt coma-like. I didn't have to listen for noise outside my window or wait for him to call me repeatedly. When he would video call the kids at night, I would hang up the phone and immediately fall asleep, knowing that if he left the townhome in Easton right that second, drove to the airport, went through security, got on a plane, and took an Uber, it would take him at least 7 hours. On those nights, I slept well for 7 hours and woke up immediately concerned about where he was. I did this for over a year.

One night in Easton, I was filling my car with gas when the lady beside me said, "California plates, huh?" I responded, "San Diego... As far away from my hometown as I can get!" I was joking, but after making the drive back home and all the distance between Michael and I, it felt like strange foreshadowing. I was reminded one night while he was in the hospital of that conversation and how I was very far away from him. It helped me sleep at night. The days we didn't hear from him were when I slept terribly. And we didn't speak much.

I texted Lt. Dun and gave him an update. At 3 a.m., Michael texted me, saying that he was admitted to the hospital. Lt. Dun inquired if this was the first time that Michael had threatened his life. I informed him that in July 2020, Michael called me saying he tried to shoot himself, but the gun misfired.

In the morning, Michael informed me that he was being checked into the "psych ward." I went to the Airbnb to get Michael's things. I found an empty bottle of Vodka and some beer bottle caps. In his bags were 3 medications, a testosterone enhancer, and some pre-workout.

Afterwards, I called his sister, June. On the 3rd ring, she picked up. "Hey Mariah, how are you?" I let everything out. "June, I'm so sorry to tell you this. Michael is in the psychiatric unit. He will be there for a few days. He threatened to end his life. I had to call 911. They took him by ambulance. He's at Balboa." Silence. I knew I had disclosed a huge disaster.

"Mariah, who's Michael?" Terrified and second guessing-myself and reality, I said "Your brother. My husband. Michael." It was then June realized I had dialed the wrong June. This was June from my high school. She met me with compassion and held space for me and told me she hoped I was okay. I thanked her and hung up.

I was so grateful to June for giving me a trial run before I called the right June. I could feel my heart pulsing hard in my chest. I called June, Michael's sister. She didn't pick up, so I texted her. There was no better way to say what I had to say. But I got the text out and transferred the tragedy to her.

While Michael was in the psychiatric unit, I'd call him once a day to see if he needed anything. One night, when I was putting Ronan to bed, Michael called. Angrily, he questioned, "Who was that man that answered the phone?" I didn't know what he was talking about. It was only me and Ronan. Michael was convinced I had a boyfriend and that he had answered the phone. I hung up. He called me back and said that he was being released in the morning and that I needed to pick him up. I was baffled because it was Monday, and he was supposed to be there until Wednesday. Also, he was supposed to have a Military escort pick him up, not me. Once again, I let Michael frazzle me.

I texted Lt. Dun. I was terrified they would let him loose and that he would be at my door in the morning. I knew Michael was mad at me. I tried so hard to make sure he was taken care of and that even if it was so painful, be present to facilitate him spending time with his children. It doesn't seem like it should make sense. But the level of known danger I was in, was better than the danger I didn't know.

A year and a half later I would be going to our 10-year high school reunion. I thanked June in person for being so kind to me. Not only was her response kind and so that was nice. But when I was scared and terrified being met with kindness gave me strength. That was a gift she gave me.

Journal Entry March 3rd, 2021:

Today, Major G picked up Michael and then had the police there so Michael could pick up his things that I had from the AirBnb. I am so incredibly mad that it had to come to this. He has put me through so much. But the hardest part was sticking to my guns that his kids are not safe or in a healthy environment around him. Now that is some twisted stuff to put on me. I will always do right by my children. But what really took a toll on me was having to make the decision every day that the kids are better off without their dad. And I know it is because of Michael's choices. But watching the hurt in his eyes and his action. Yet still having to stay strong. And not fully having the support of the Army. How did I survive that? And it still hurts. Major G has always felt like a kindred soul. He is going through a divorce right now.

His husband cheated on him. And Michael was planning on having him move in with him.

You hurt me so much, and yet were consoling Major G? Acting like you sympathized with him? You acted worse than his ex. And you saw how much it hurt him. I wish I could have given Major G a hug today. This must have been brutal for him. I am so grateful for him though. I feel that even though it took almost a year, I am finally validated. Like everyone sees that I was not out to cause trouble. That all I want is peace. The kids have done so good through all of this. I am really proud that I have given them enough safety and love, that when they saw their dad and when Michael left, everything was fine. Again. Its laced with sadness. Because Michael is so far gone. I can tell the kids know too. My heart is just wounded but also starting to heal. I love hard.

I can't believe how I power through things. Today was hard. I mean crippling. I don't even know where to start. The last time I texted Major G it was a plea to get Michael help. And I said no need to text back for 2 reasons. First I didn't want to create more drama, or to drag him into anything. But also, I didn't feel like I could validate myself. Like everything I was saying could be seen as a "scorn ex." And that broke my heart because I felt like no one saw what I saw and no one knew how bad it was. So I was stuck in a really weird place where I knew how bad it was, but if I spoke up too much I would just be seen as a problem. And that really did take a toll on me. It really wounded me.

3/4/21 "Woe is me" keeps the torture endless. Broken. An endless void for hatred to consume. The only way through is to understand it. Naïveté no longer has a seat at the table. It has been forced out in the name of healing and self-forgiveness. Stand in the fire and let it burn. Then declare exactly what it is. I am broken. I have been burned. And evil thrown your way will not define you. I will heal.

3/8/21 I filed a restraining order today. I'm so angry that Michael pushed it to this point. It's like he is trying to see the depths of hell I can withstand. And I keep on thinking about why I stayed with him so long. He calculated it. Every time he would break up with me it would "confirm" how much I loved him. How I needed him to feel whole. And how my life was a "mess" without him. And then he would take me back and build me up. Like I was a charity. So every time I thought of leaving him, I would remember the heartache. So I would stay. Because I didn't know that life got better. It seemed to only get worse. It was a mind game. And so I did whatever I could to not lose him. He made me file a restraining order because he sent naked photos of me to my mom and said if I didn't text him back he was sending them to my dad and putting them on the internet.

    3/9/21 What am I owed? Nothing from you. Nothing from anyone. Every second with my kids. Every chance to breathe. These are all pages that would have been blank if I hadn't escaped. Who is to say that I did? The amount of internal work I have to do to make sure I don't get upset from a trigger from Michael stresses me out beyond belief. Holding my walls up is exhausting. I want a safe place to leave my horror at the door. The universe has taken away from me everything I thought I absolutely needed. Everything that was actually bleeding me out. And I have progressed to here. And damn I have a ways to go. It's terrifying. How much more awful could happen? What else can I be stripped of? Here I am. Well aware of how my life can be stripped before me. With Michael I looked into the abyss of evil. The dragon in him. We all have one. But I saw his up close. I stared at the dragon and thought, "How is this possible?" Now I have to hold Michael responsible to ensure my safety. But thou shalt not judge. Stand before a JUDGE and submit evidence proving the evil that was done to me by Michael.

    03/10/21 I don't know where to start. I don't know how to stop Michael from harming me. I have to live my life grateful for every moment. Thankful for every breath. Because he could fly out here and kill me. I am forced to live in the moment. I have to be completely authentic. It's brutal because I have to be extremely mindful of how I feel and why. I have to live in my truth. And accept if that's not acceptable with people. It has nothing to do with compromise. It's about not falling into patterns of pleasing. Out of fear of losing.

3/14/21 I wish that I could wish Michael the best. He just demanded so much of my time. Then threatened me if I didn't give it to him. I didn't have a moment to think without him trying to push his agenda on me. I wish him better. But only because I want him to leave me alone. I was tormented for so long. I have so much anxiety over "non-issues." Like when people yell. Or get upset. I'm right back there again. I can't believe that I am at a stage in my life where I am grateful for every second I'm alive. And I feel like I can never have another bad day again. But that's also really sad for me. To just have to be eternally grateful to be alive.

"WELLNESS CHECK"

It felt like Michael always looked for ways to show that he had control over me. One night, as I was putting the kids to bed, he texted, demanding to talk to them. I told him we could video call in the morning because the kids were asleep. He kept calling incessantly, so I stopped answering. He said if he didn't see his kids, he would call the police for a wellness check. I sent him an email copy of the restraining order. The restraining order had been granted, but I was waiting for him to be served in Easton.

I was lying in Ronan's bed when I saw the lights flash outside the window. There they were. I grabbed the paperwork and invited them in. One of the officers had been there a few days before when Michael picked up his things. The officer wrote down the incident numbers so I could use them for court. His partner said he would call Michael and tell him to knock it off. They put in the system that they don't need to come out if he called another wellness check. Ronan ended up waking up, and they gave him a sticker. Then the officer went outside and called Michael.

> *03/19/21 I have such armor around my heart. I want it to drop. And be free. I hate even saying that I have insecurities from my last "relationship." It doesn't feel like a relationship. It feels like I am unshackling myself from my captor.*

03/21/21 The hardest part of panic attacks is I feel like there is nothing I can do about them except ride the wave. I just want the pain to stop. And have good moments that stay. But there is so much hurt.

03/27/21 It's so frustrating that I have a good day, then lay my head down to go to bed and instantly have a panic attack. I just laid in bed thrashing around. Pictures of horror running through my head. I think that when I actually slept I never got rest. The only way for me to survive was to exit my body.

03/31/21 I really feel like I'm struggling. I don't know what I need. Well. I need to be divorced and have a job. I need to be in a place where I will be okay if Steve doesn't want me in his life. Because right now I feel like it will crush me. It's giving me such anxiety. I think living here isn't healthy for me. But I have no choice. I have no job. My money is going to lawyers. I'm not getting child support. I can't afford childcare and to get a job.

Nightmares

Journal Entry 04/3/21

There is nothing to be scared of except that he is someone who can change his mind. I don't believe this is real. Safety? Having my life back? The possibility of getting my own place? All while I could still be in Pennsylvania. Or living in a coma. I've made it clear to Steve that I've been through hell. And I can't even believe the hell I've been through. As hard as it was to suck up my ego and move back in with my parents... man. I acknowledge that I am not entitled to anything. Even happiness. Anyone who says you are. I don't think they know that you cannot be happy by the help of someone else. It has to come from within. Part of me is grateful for this. Because I know I will always have myself. The other part knows how much damn work that is. Constant. Work. Constant checks and balances.

04/06/21 I'm so exhausted. My tank is empty. That doesn't mean I get to stop. It just means there is more emotional weight on my chest. And that I have to keep moving forward. There is no one I can count on except myself. I'm exhausted. I have all this hurt in my heart. Michael is so mentally ill. How can I say I love Steve if it would possibly bring him into the nonsense of Michael? I feel like my happiness is running out. Like I'm holding onto what could be the last happy moment. When I have tried my best to just give love to everyone. But I have to keep my sanity intact. I'm just sad. All the damn time. And no one gives a damn. Or if I think they do, I don't want it. I don't want to trust because it scares the life out of me.

I just want to feel my body again. Instead of carrying all the sadness above myself to get through the day. I'm angry that I was conned. That Michael is not the only one with this mental illness and that so many other victims are out there suffering. There is no advice that I want to hear. There is nothing that I want to say. I just want peace. I do everything in the name of peace. Yet I have someone constantly attacking me. Restraining order or not. He's a bully. He just won't leave me alone. Here Kelly told me I don't carry myself like someone who has been through so much trauma. Well I don't know how to answer that. I don't think I'm brave. I think I don't have a moment to breathe. I don't have any options. That's life's cruel joke. Nothing is consistent. The only thing the same is that things change. Life's lesson is that no one deserves anything. Everything can change in an instant. People change. People hurt. And Michael believes his delusions. What's more scary than that?

04/08/21 I have been so emotional today. Crippling anxiety to being okay. Back to anxious. I'm disappointed. I'm frustrated. Steve is pretty hard to read. He said he's an open book. I don't think that's true.

4/11/21 I feel like I am really coming to grasp my anxiety. I feel like I am really leaning into who I am. I am embracing how I feel. I still am insecure about who I am to people. I think Steve likes me. But how or is he going to tell his parents about me? Do I want to meet his parents? There is a lot that I feel like I would be dragging Steve into. I know that his parents will see it this way as well. I don't understand him or know his thought process. And that scares me. Especially since he says he's an open book.

Last night I had a nightmare where I was standing and started getting yelled at. The yelling was so loud. Then Michael started to pull me by my shoe. I got away but I was still facing him. He got my sock off and kept yelling, trying to get my shorts off. I woke up terrified. It put me right back at the broken place I was when I left. I felt like I had time traveled. Steve told me that I should try and think of the gratitude moments. I thought of how I'm grateful to be in San Diego instead of back in PA being tortured.

I used to leave my body around Michael. Like I was a robot. Or like someone was ringing the doorbell but I couldn't answer. I thought when I left, I had to leave before the person I used to be was completely gone. She was alone in a huge room. Cornered in the fetal position. I could barely see her. Just an outline of a rag doll in the corner. I was gone. Michael used me as a punching bag spiritually and physically. I will never understand Michael. I know he has a mental illness. But looking back at Ronan's 4th birthday and the 3 days after. How could he not have had one lucid moment? It's because he knew he could use fear to control me. And he knew that in his lucid moments, I was nothing to him. I need to remember and acknowledge this. It was about control for him. I am working to become free from him. But it does leave me in such a sad situation.

I had therapy today. I think I am finally hitting the anger phase. I have not had a voice for so long. And I feel that I still don't. But I am slowly finding it. I've had moments lately where I really feel it hard that I am a single mom. That Michael is so far removed from the ability to parent. I gave everything I could. I gave Michael every avenue to just not be slimy. I just wish he would disappear. He can send me my money and be on his way. Leave us the fu*k alone. The tone of his voice asking for sympathy when he was trying to get people to be "on his side."

There are no sides, you dumb ass. Nothing has to do with sides. You broke me. You dismissed your children. Put me in this position. FOR WHAT. To add to your made up story?

I hoisted you up so you could look like a man. I carried the family so you could live in fairy tale land. You spat on anything that could help me grow. Anything that would clear the fog from what you were doing to me. The drama around you, created by you. To distract me from how you treated me. In therapy today, I remembered something really important. You were always an asshole. And I don't know what I saw. How did I not see it before? I don't want to give myself excuses. I want to know. What did I see? Michael told me that he just treated me like sh*t because he never thought that I would actually leave. So what was the point in treating me nicely at all? What was the point? I wouldn't have left if he didn't get that violent. Who the fu*k was that girl? I can only liken it to being in a cult. Brainwashed.

*He had no accountability in Pennsylvania because of the lock down. He drank so much that something switched in his brain. He became a different person. Well. I think he just lost the good part in him. It became all bad. All evil. And transparent. He lost his charm. There was nothing left of him. There is nothing left of him. So what do I do with that shit? He conned me into being with him. So I could make him look normal. I was just a cover. Fu*k him.*

*Why do you think I can handle this? Fu*k being a single mom. Fu*k the system. Fu*k. Make all this pain worth it. Fu*k. Fu*k. Fu*k. Fu*k. Fu*k. Fu*k.*

First Breakup

Three weeks after our first date, I showed Steve some martial arts moves in the backyard. I took martial arts as a kid, and it was always something I wanted to continue as I became an adult. My martial arts moves moved to wrestling on the living room floor. I pinned him down and gazed right into his eyes. He told me to kiss him. But it had been three weeks, and I was still scared to give him my heart. When I said no, he wanted to compromise with a kiss on the cheek. So I did. And then I gave him a real kiss.

Later that day, I cried in his arms because I was so scared to love again. I told him he had to be so careful with my heart. That I couldn't put myself together from this if it fell apart. The further in love I got and let him in, the more it would hurt. I begged him to be careful. It's amazing what the mind is afraid of and seems to manifest. It is a way to show us that our fears will all have to be faced. We feel we cannot do it but will be forced to do it anyway.

When I saw Steve after a few days, he appeared happy to see me. He picked me up, and we had a fantastic time goofing off. At the end of the night, we pulled up to my house and the car became still as the engine turned off. In a split second, the mood changed. The air became frigid. Steve stared straight ahead like a robot, then bowed his head and cried. Then he said what I thought was unthinkable: we needed to break up.

That girl in the photo, who he said was his cousin, was his girlfriend of four years. They had just broken up, but their families were close friends, so she went on the trip with them. He said she was his best friend, and they never got closure. He planned to fly out there to see if they should pursue their relationship or move on. I know how much my situation scared him. I know how easy old love must have felt with his ex. I know that what we experienced with Michael in the psychiatric unit for three weeks was terrifying. Steve knew as well as I did that Michael would most likely go after him. Michael was already obsessing over me about having a boyfriend.

At the time, I felt oddly relieved. Steve had history with this girl, and doing the "right" thing by wrapping that up. This thief was a more romantic version than him just running away from my train wreck. He was setting up a future for us, I hoped. I wasn't worried about her. I did not realize at the time that Steve would put in 100% of himself to manifest his fantasies: his one true and actual soulmate, only then to have regret over breaking up with the previous girlfriend. I was everything he left his last girlfriend for.

Steve told me that from the beginning of his last relationship, they both agreed it was just for fun and knew it would never work out because she was in the Military. I think he felt comfortable with the lack of commitment. When she eventually moved, making her officially no longer an option, he was forced to confront his shattered ego. That is, until I came into his life, boosting his ego and offering a distraction from his pain. But I believed in our connection. I know it was real. Just like Michael, Zane, and now Steve. It was just a question of whether we would let our fears, ego, or cowardliness get in the way.

Journal Entry 4/22/21:

I'm not really sure why I was asked to endure so much pain. Love opened and then shattered over and over again. All I have ever been is honest. Tried with everything inside me to stay true to myself. Now I'm asked to respond to something that has no guide book. I'm stuck with a restraining order against my husband and a boy who chose to start dating me and then chose to extract himself so abruptly it traumatized me. What Steve did to me was so awful. Up until the very moment he dropped me off on the date he denied any problems. I in fact asked him a few times because I could tell he was upset and he always denied it. Refused to acknowledge anything. I couldn't ever imagine a scenario like that. I am so tired of being the aftermath of people's decisions. Having to react to Michael's decisions. And then to Steve's. Did Steve think I was just telling *him the Sunday news over coffee in the morning when I spoke and cried and shook in his arms? How can he ask me to handle what he did to me? Both of them. Why would you ever ask anyone to do that? What kind of mind fu*k is all of this. I'm really trying hard to not have Steve's actions be actions that hurt me. But damn I'm hurt.*

What high road is he taking that he cut me out. Complete cold turkey after giving me all of his attention. Love bombing me until I was all the way deep and leaning on him. Trauma bonded. Why would he take me out that night and be so charming knowing he was going to break up with me. How could he sit there? Looking across the table from me as I told him I wasn't doing so great. That I was still in survival mode. Steve devastated me. I allowed him in. I was a dreamer. I believed there was still good out there. I gave good everywhere I went. He was unkind to me.

He asked me the questions that opened my heart. I put trust in him and that was my mistake. I am a broken human. I am broken. And honestly no one gives a shit. They do.

But they don't. Everyone has their own problems to deal with. But when I make a commitment to be someone's friend, I care. I thought that was the point of asking someone if they are okay. Or getting into the deepness of their heart. I'm done with the mind effing. I'm done with waiting. But that's the worst part of life. There is nothing to do but to wait. I can't force Steve to be with me. I can't beg. Well maybe I can. But I don't want pity. I want him to get his head out of his ass. Look himself in the mirror and be a man.

I feel like I am becoming a toxic person. I'm so fucking sad. I wait for the end of the day just so I can sleep. I was doing just fine before Steve came around. Just fine. Not great. But fine. Then he blazed through my insecurities. Did I allow him to have too much of me? What is the point of dating someone if you can't give them what you have to give. I lost a friend. Because he wanted to be a fu*king idiot. I did not sign up for any of this. I am not saying I am a victim. I'm saying what I have been asked to go through is so painful. My sincerity ran so *deep. I gave you validation of being a man to help a woman in crisis. To knight in shining armor me. I wasn't offering that. I was offering you my heart. You are riding the coattails of my confidence. Of my love. Get the eff out of your bubble.*

After three weeks, I figured he had to have decided whether to stay with me or his ex. I texted him, "I miss you." Immediately, he replied that he missed me too and asked to call me. He talked of having a big family with me and wanted to take me out on his next day off. He told me that he was sitting on his balcony roof in downtown San Diego, so delighted to talk to me. I felt I got him back. I was worth it. From there, we went full steam ahead. He asked me when he could meet the kids. We talked about how hard it was to say goodbye every time. He told me about the house he was going to buy. We talked about marriage.

Martial Arts

Martial arts was great for my confidence. It's where I turned off my mind and got in tune with my body. It felt like a dance. I remembered the forms from childhood, and when I punched and struck a punching bag, it became therapeutic. I started classes again with my instructor from high school. One day, we were learning hand grabs, and it was my partner's turn to grab me. I took a deep breath. I was anxious, but I thought I could keep myself grounded. Then Sifu, the instructor, spoke. "If a normal person grabs you, you can break away and run. The problem is when you involve someone who is drunk or on drugs or mentally ill." My chest felt like someone had dropped a ton of bricks on it, squeezing air out of my lungs. I felt my sluggish body try to go with the movements as I struggled to run from sudden flashbacks.

Shove

My partner shoved me back as we practiced our forms, but it wasn't my partner in front of me anymore. Michael stood above me as I was pushed to the floor.

I blinked away the thoughts as we were called to sit and meditate. My eyes burned. I needed to get out of there. Class was dismissed, and I walked out without a word. As I pulled into the driveway, I needed to switch back into mom mode, but my mind was still trapped back in the class. Every adult was a predator. *How could I be so stupid and surround myself with people who could easily attack me?* Those who were more advanced than me. What was I thinking? I sat frozen in my car. I looked at the gate my dad had installed. My dad. He would never grab me. Neither would my brothers, David and Dustin. I went through a list of men who would never harm me. There were many.

I snuck into the shower in the bathroom. It was my safe place. I closed my eyes as water poured over my face. I felt calmed then, again. Shove. I saw him every time I closed my eyes to blink. I felt him. He invaded and corroded my body and thoughts. I felt the sting of the hits. Fu*k. *Get out, go away,* I scream at him in my mind. *You are not welcome here.* I step out, and my body moves, but I am not connected to it. I must get through this alone. I can't rely on others to get me through my trauma. I am fine. I will be fine. I always am.

I put the kids to bed robotically. Shutdown. I fell asleep instantly. It was how I coped when things were too overwhelming.

Screaming in my ear, chased by Michael. He's got me by the leg and is starting to cut off my foot. Moving slowly up to my calf. I'm screaming. Shaking uncontrollably. My arms are going to be ripped out of the sockets. I'm trying to pull myself away from him.

Ronan. Ronan woke me up by taking his whole body and laying on top of me. Like a weighted blanket, my nervous system and muscles began to relax with the pressure on top of me. I thank him. I'm so sorry and mortified he had to witness that. I instantly fell back asleep.

But Ronan cannot protect me from my nightmares: **Michael. He's trying to break in every door. I hear the thuds on the back door and run to close it tight. Triple check it's locked. He's attacking the bathroom door next. I race to meet him and I see his shadow from the security light. I stand there freezing.** Only to wake up. It was a dream. I woke up standing by the bathroom door that leads outside. It's the one I just dreamed of Michael breaking down. It's wide open. I quickly shut the door and walked back to my room. On the way back, I saw that I had opened the other door I dreamed about—the one where Michael was trying to get through. It had all been a dream. I had opened the doors while sleepwalking. I knew Michael was not in the house. If he was, I pleaded that he'd kill me while I was asleep. That was the only way I coaxed myself back to sleep.

Can I be 30 yet?

I went to my Aunt Autumn's house a week after my birthday. She asked me how old I was. I said, "Well, twenty-nine, but I'm just going to start telling people I'm thirty." I was exhausted. Deeply exhausted. I had filed a restraining order against Michael, and we had pending divorce papers that needed to be signed. I knew the next few months would be absolutely horrible for everyone. I was fighting a dragon two hundred times bigger than me. A dragon that I did not actively sign up for. I was waiting until I was thirty. I wanted this year to go as quickly as possible. She responded that I'll miss my twenties and to soak it up. Sure, that's usually true. Had I known what would happen a few months later, I would have wished even harder to get my twenties over with.

Julie, Michael's mom, started calling me every Sunday. I hadn't spoken to her since before I left Pennsylvania. She wanted updates on the kids. She understood why I left and just wanted me and the kids to be okay. Every Sunday, I could expect her phone call. It was a relationship we needed to build in the coming months. I'm so grateful for those phone calls where we spent a few minutes checking in with each other.

Journal Entry 5/26/21

Sometimes it's so painstakingly obvious that I'm a single mom. I love being a mom so much. But it's so lonely. And I can't just decide to go to the beach or drive to the store and wander around by myself. My life is not mine. And Michael. He promised to do this with me. My whole life has changed. Over and over again. With each curveball. With each slam to the ground. I'm responsible for 2 children. And now I'm responsible for whoever comes in and out of their life. That includes their dad. I have to look at Raela and know that there is a man out there who actively has to be removed from her life.

I protect my kids from so much. Every day. Every decision I make has to embody their safety, well-being, and happiness. My life is not my own. My world is on a timeline. I'm "type A" because I have no other choice. It is a trauma response. Every damn thing I do is a trauma response. It's not about happiness for me. It's about survival for my children. I am their vessel. I love every ounce of them.

I love them so much my bones hurt. The sadness that I feel is like the deepness of the ocean. Maybe that's why I understand the sea and her coldness. I'm connected to pain. It has to steer me. Because if I hold onto the pain. I will recognize it when I feel it again. I can use the feeling as a guide. And stay the eff away. Every part of my body has been violated. Every part of my soul was exposed. And still, compared to what I've been through, others have been through so much worse. But I also know I've been through so much worse than others. That it's not normal to lay in bed and hope that if my partner kills me, I don't wake up through it. That death could overcome my life with a passive last breath. That was how I got through it. Knowing there was nothing I could do to control my own destiny. Because my "partner" wanted me dead.

Why do I have to feel all the pain that he is going through? Why do I have to look at my son and daughter and know they are not getting the best of their dad? Yet, I have to grieve that he chose something over them. Drugs. Drinking. Sex addiction. Violence.

It's going to devastate them someday. Mommy, why did you choose him as my daddy? I don't know my babies. Why is every outside force besides us three a threat? Because Mommy can't predict the world around her. I was never supposed to guard you from the outside world. That was your dad's job. That was the agreement. I protected our home. Then your dad became a terrorist. A threat from the inside. And I held my end of the deal up. By removing him from our life. So now I'm left to defend both inside and outside our sanctuary. And the truth is, I have to miss out on so much because I just don't know how to judge the outside forces.

So we stick to the parks. To our friends. Not much more is manageable. So much of this revolves around my PTSD. So much around not being chosen first. About being everyone's second thought. Because I don't get to live a passive life. It's constantly forced and intentional. Everything is a threat. I give all of myself constantly. I just want someone who isn't my kids or family to embrace me. To hold and treasure me.

Like I treasure everyone around me. I see the light in everyone. The most stressful part about protecting my kids is knowing at any moment he could come and kill me.

Mandated Rehab

In May 2021, Michael was admitted into rehab and the doctor told him he was in liver failure. His next drink could be his last. He spent 29 days and then was released. Knowing he was there helped me sleep at night. I thought he was finally getting the help he needed.

Mouths To Feed

I secured a position as a Covid Compliance Officer for the San Diego Padres Media Department. I was nervous about starting work, but I had no other choice. I had no money. Child support might come in, but it would take months, and I had lawyer fees to pay and mouths to feed.

It was time for a court date to decide on child support and alimony. That video conference is engraved in my memory. Looking at myself reflected on the screen, I felt soulless. I did not recognize my face. I swore in, and so did Michael. The judge awarded child support and gave me a small amount for alimony. She said I needed to focus on getting my life together to support myself. I needed to devise a plan, but in the meantime, she would give me some alimony. My heart sank. I felt the tremble in my throat as I forced myself to speak. I glanced down at the computer keyboard, then back up at the judge.

"Ma'am. I got a job. I just have to wait a few weeks to start because that is when the job offered me to start. But I have it in place." Fear flooded through my veins. *Was I talking back? Was I allowed to say this?* I did not want to be reprimanded. *I just corrected the judge. Why didn't I just agree? Nod my head and say, "Yes, ma'am."* My entire body felt underwater. The judge looked at me. There was a pause, like the weight of the world held on a single breath.

"I commend you." She said, "I commend you for getting a job and taking control of your life. I am awarding you the full alimony amount." My entire body dropped to the center of the universe at that moment. The court was no longer in session, and the video conference ended. I was still in a deep abyss. *What?* She commended me; I had done the right thing. The validation this judge gave me in her approval and confidence carried me for a very long time. It was a defining moment that proved I was on the right path. I stood a little taller on her back until I could do it on my own.

QUESTION OF THE DAY

My first day of work after five years as a stay-at-home mom was simultaneously daunting and exciting. I drove there for the first time, nervous about where to park, what to say, and where to be. But I did it. And then I did it again.

On the third day of commuting, I cried. I cried the next day, too. I had a quiet ride without children, sandwiched between two places where I had to pull it together. My body recognized that those 20 minutes were my chance to let go of pent up emotions. Without consciously searching, I found my place to release some of my heart's heaviness to the cadence of the maps app. My car served as the lone audience of my tears and sobs. I then parked, fixed my mascara, and walked in with a smile.

I honestly was happy to be there. The smile was genuine, but the confidence was not. Every shift, I received negative comments from the employees I cleared of Covid symptoms. Comments like "hope you brought a book" or "enjoy watching movies all day" trickled in. Rude, maybe jealous-filled comments. Day after day of being overlooked, it started to hit a nerve. I had just left my marriage. I had been a stay-at-home mom for five years. I was alone, isolated, and had been told for years that I was getting a free ride from my husband. Even though I knew I played a critical role in raising my children, it did not erase my insecurity.

One day, while sitting at my desk, I wondered how to reframe the hurt that they were unknowingly doing to me into something that didn't sting. I came up with a "question of the day." This meant that while doing my check-in, I would ask them a question. Some were as simple as "bear or rhino?" with no other prompts. Or "If you had 10 seconds to decide where to go on vacation, where would you go?" It was a way to engage for a moment and build a connection. And it worked! People loved the question of the day. It turned into an entire office buzz. Everyone wanted to know everyone's answers. I'd finally become a part of the team.

I was proud of myself for taking something that hurt and finding a solution, even if it was a minimal and debatably forced interaction. I even included the security guards at the front of the building. The questions were a bridge to get to know people more deeply. Friends were made, and follow-up questions were asked. It felt good. This went on for a few months. The question of the day turned into them pausing to ask me about my day and I would do the same in return. That progressed to learning about their families and so on. I had successfully turned something that was hurting my soul into a bonding experience.

Then, one day, one of the staff members pulled me aside. He said I was invading people's privacy by asking them for information they were not willingly offering. That this was pulling people's energy without their permission. He quoted a philosopher whom I do not remember. I tried not to let it phase me, but it did. As I drove home that day, and over the next few days, I tried to create another way to keep the bridge of communication open in my isolating job while still being responsive to my feedback. I settled on asking people "question of the day or a fun fact." I gave them the option to just listen to me for 30 seconds while I spouted off a fun fact.

I could have got even more feedback from the staff members. But I also had an agenda. I have no problem admitting that. So, thank you to the Padre's media team. To those who participated or at least indulged me for a minute or so. It did heal me. The comment the staff member made, however, stayed with me. He made me aware of something that I would have felt better about being ignorant of. It is now extremely difficult for me to ask people about themselves. I swung to the other end of the spectrum. It stunted me. It is part of the reason I chose to publish my book. I hope to invite others in. I'm here, I'll listen. My book is my space in the world that you are welcome to walk into or out of.

Journal Entry 6/3/21:

I don't know how I feel.

NOT GOING TO BE UNDONE

One day, I called Steve after work to vent about an incident with a rude coworker. We talked as I drove. When Steve asked where I was headed, I explained that I was going to an addiction recovery meeting to support Kelly and bring her food because she didn't have time to stop on the way. Steve responded, "Mariah, this world doesn't deserve you. You are too good for this world." I was speechless. Well, that was nice of him to say, I thought. It was a bit dramatic for someone just picking up food for a friend.

It made me uncomfortable. I was doing whatever I could to help my friend. I was trying to be nice and make her life easier. My reaction did not match his compliment. It was like I was defending what I was doing and justifying my existence.

In the meeting, a man stood up. He explained that he had not been present in his marriage because he drank excessively and, for so long, tried to drown out his wife's nagging. I knew this guy. I knew the nag. I was the nag. It was the cries of desperation for a husband to choose his health and family, and well, if it worked for him, even Jesus. I watched this man and thought about all the runs to the liquor store. How I hid chewing tobacco around the house just in case. High enough for the kids not to reach, creative enough for the monster of addiction not to find. I sat in terror in a house with a man like him. I tried to gently tame the destructive dragon within.

I looked at this man with disgust. *So you are here. Now what?* Then he said it. "I finally realized her nagging was a cry for help. She was begging me to change to save myself and my family." He was not wrong. That *is* what we implored. I continued to analyze this man who so closely mirrored my husband.

Why, then, was he here? To taunt me? To make me question if the man who towered over me mentally and physically could change? And what did it matter? He'd kill me the first chance he got anyways. So what was this predator doing in this class? Are they all predators? Is this just a place for people to co-sign each other's lies? That's not why Kelly and I were there.

Afterward, Kelly and I sat in my car silently. We both shared the same ideas about the man in the class and that we were both triggered. Something slimy and cold and unwanted squirmed through my thoughts. *Was I too pushy? Did I force Kelly here when she didn't want to? Did I force us into this situation where we had to encounter a man like our abusers?*

Once these thoughts started, it always snowballed straight back to him. Wa*s Michael right? Am I too pushy and needy, and ask to hang out too much? Do I fear missing out so much that I ask too much of people? Is this why I have no friends and will never be successful without Michael?* It was the narrative he fed me for years. That was the reason I was a stay-at-home mom. That was why Michael supported me, and I needed his paycheck, so he said. He told me everything in the house, including the kids, was his. I would be nothing without him.

"Kelly... Steve told me that I am too good for this world. I need your honest opinion."

"He's right." she replied without skipping a beat. We talked for a long time after. She told me how grateful she was for my friendship. She knew I would be there for her at any moment, just as she would be for me. Kelly loved me the way that I am. But the way that I am was once used as a weapon against me. I had to suppress myself because I did not know how to decipher reality. That is why what Steve said struck me so deeply. It had been so long since someone saw me and didn't ask to cover all the parts that made me, me.

The next few weeks were rough. My depression hit me hard and brought me into another wave of lows. I could also start to feel the tendrils of Steve backing out of our relationship again. Even after he insisted that he was all in and wanted to meet the kids, I could feel it. I was confused about why he wouldn't want to be with a woman who was "too good for this world." I didn't know what I was doing wrong or why I wasn't enough for him. I held onto my conversation with Kelly. Knowing the years of being gaslit by Michael would not be undone in a single conversation. But her confirming that I am not a pushy person and am lovable was something I reminded myself of during that time. Unfortunately, it was simultaneous with Steve saying nothing was wrong, when I could feel that something was.

Let The Truth Be Told

A. Around July 2021, Michael's Company Commander, CW, told him he was under inspection for early Release from Active Duty (REFRAD). This meant his job would not continue. Michael spent the next three months desperately trying to get the REFRAD removed. He struggled to get to work and to complete his assignments. He labored to do day-to-day tasks. He was in a mental health crisis.

I got an email on the 11th detailing that Michael would settle in court if I dropped the domestic charges. He also agreed to give me full legal and physical custody as long as I dropped the restraining order charges. I read the email in my friend's driveway after a day at the beach with the kids. I walked up the stairs and fell apart on her couch.

It was strange knowing he would settle. Like after fighting this invisible tornado, I was finally fighting fair instead of nice. I suppose Michael finally understood that. What he did could put him in prison and on the sex offender list, so he decided to settle. I had been hoping for a year that he would come to his senses. I didn't know if he did, and it was terrifying.

It was a surprising turn of events, but something kept bothering me. I was depressed and anxious and I didn't know why. I was so relieved that I got the settlement letter returned, but I felt heartbroken. It took a few days, but I finally figured it out.

On a Sunday after work, I went to Miriam's house, a friend I made at a mom's group. Ronan and her son Oren had been friends since they were six weeks old. Miriam told me she grew up without her dad. They just recently had lunch with him. He had other kids and a whole different life that didn't include her. My heart broke for her. And for Ronan and Raela. Getting full custody was the best of a devastating situation.

Miriam's husband, Mark, came and sat with us on the sunset deck. He said that he grew up without a dad as well. It left his mother in pieces. I felt like there were so many parallels between him and Ronan. His mom had to relive it when Mark would tell strangers about their family situation. When we first left, Ronan would tell everyone that we had to leave because "my dad was mean to my mom and would hurt her." I couldn't tell Ronan that it wasn't true. That was gaslighting and diminishing his experience. I just had to learn to let the truth be told.

Journal Entry July 14th:

I feel strongly about giving my kids a "home base" aside from my parents house. I want them to have their own room and backyard. To leave crafts on the table and have some dishes in the sink. For them to wake up and go into their living room and watch some TV or go play in the backyard for a bit. I want them to know that their mom gave them a home. That no matter what, they will have their room. I want to paint their rooms and decorate with them. I want to invite people and their friends over. I feel like I am in limbo.

Two days later I felt better, but not great. I still didn't fully understand why I felt this way about the settlement offer. I knew it was partly because I felt like I was letting a predator run loose. I felt like Michael should have to tell the court all the things he did and be held accountable. But he could lie, and then what would happen? I racked my brain, plagued with fear, knowing the wise choice was to settle. I would get child support if I did. That's money for the kids, car payments, and savings. It made sense. I felt like I had no one to talk to or get advice from and had no hope.

September 2021

I learned much later that in the first week of September, CW told Michael that even after rehab and not being able to keep up with his workload, he did not have to worry about his job or the REFRAD. CW had gone back and forth with him about his retention in the Army. At this time, he was close to being written up.

One day, Michael missed a day of work. He would have missed every day of work, but most days, the office would send runners to his house to wake him up for work, drive him, watch him sit at his desk with reduced responsibilities, and then drive him home at night. This was their solution. On this missed day of work, Michael's team changed the format of a document that Michael managed without notifying him. CW wrote up Michael for something he didn't have knowledge of. Michael asked for six days of leave to regroup because he was so upset about the write-up. CW granted it.

On the day that Michael asked for leave, he sent me a photo of his head and face bleeding. He called me and told me he was in a fight outside of a grocery store, which I had a hard time believing was true. Amped up and frantic, he said he saved a kid from being jumped. With no idea what was going on and the phone call completely unexpected, I told him he needed to go to the store and get the security footage. That he could not show up to work like that. I was afraid he had another concussion.

I asked him to do a phone call with the kids instead of video because I was worried the kids would be scared of the blood all over his face. He told me he would tell his work and get the security footage. He ended up not calling the kids later. I never fully found out what happened. Witnesses from a Military report said he came back to work refreshed and ready to start again. He thanked those who stepped up in his absence. We never talked about it again.

Run and Hug Him

Journal Entry September 10th:

> Michael and I are finally drawing up a settlement agreement. I just wanted the kids to not feel totally abandoned. I wanted Michael to give his all, twice a week on a video call if that is all he can handle. I want so bad to not be "proud of him" when he calls. How fu*ked up is that. This man tormented me. I'm terrified of him. I'm scared to have "won." I'm scared that my

trauma is too deep. Too embedded into my mind.

A man two nights ago rang the doorbell at 9pm at night. I RAN to the door thinking it was Michael. I looked through the stained glass. Saw a tall man with Black hair. I thought for sure it was Michael. I took one breath and thought. Ok if it is him and he has a gun pointed at me RUN AND HUG HIM. Tell him thank you, I missed you and can we be a family again. Just diffuse and confuse him until we can get to safety again. I opened the door and it was someone from my parents' church. I tried to go back to bed but sat up in my bed and felt my heart pounding instead.

I Don't Want It

Because my job as a Covid Compliance Officer was seasonal, I was excited to have the opportunity of an interview for the local fire department. On the day of the interview, however, I stressed about what passing or failing would mean. I could have a career and support myself. On the drive, I thought of all the people who imparted their wisdom to me. All of my mentors who taught me drills, how to put out dumpster fires, allowed me to make calls in times of crises. I pulled 200-pound firefighters out of buildings for search and rescue drills. I sat in the Fire Engine driving down the streets of San Diego on numerous ride-alongs.

As a teen, I spent years building relationships with firefighters. I knew the firefighters who responded to my classmate, William. These firefighters helped me turn the pain of losing him into productive ways to help others. I thought about how walking into any station felt like a breath of fresh air, like I was home. Like I belonged when I was there.

And for a teenager, that's the greatest gift they could have given me. I was protected there. I loved learning everything and the physical challenges thrilled me. But most of all, the feeling of a family kept me coming back.

I felt confident as my interview progressed. They asked questions, and I answered. I had already passed the written test. The finish line stood across the table in the hands of these three men with a pen. At the end of the interview, they asked me if there was anything else I would like to add. I told them I was a single mom of two and wanted to make them proud of me when they saw me in my uniform. I wanted to provide for my family and to make myself proud for finally achieving this after working so long for it. I stood up misty-eyed and shook their hands.

Strangely enough, it was at that moment I decided I didn't want the position. Despite all the joy I experienced through the years, something deep within me recognized that this was not where I was meant to be. I said thank you and walked out the door. After hundreds of hours of learning, ride-alongs, academies, internships, and interview prep, that was the end.

I'd appreciate the space here to apologize to all my mentors because I didn't follow through. But I would also like to say thank you. Because of you all, I received years of excitement, personal and professional growth, and saw a side of San Diego I would have never seen otherwise. I grew in compassion for those going through tragedy. I believe it made me a better person. It has taken me far too long to stand tall. And part of that process was the interview. But more importantly, it was thanks to the firefighters who always answered my call.

A few weeks later I got an email stating that I had been pushed through to the next phase. I shut my laptop and went to make breakfast. I never followed up.

October

Right before the USR briefing—a conference to report a unit's deployment readiness. CW told Michael that his time in the military would be terminated when he returned from Delaware. CW's higher-ups did not approve this decision. CW did not have the authority to do this, but he did it anyway. He told someone at the unit to start the paperwork. Someone saw Michael leaving CW's office and described him as "more upset than I have ever seen him."

The next day, he attended this briefing in Delaware, where they discussed personal wartime readiness. Michael had dedicated his entire life to being wartime-ready, serving for 14 years and deploying multiple times. It was hostile behavior for CW to send him to this briefing. It was emotionally viscous to make him present numbers and figures of all those ready to deploy all while thinking he would never be able to do that again because of the unapproved, but seemingly authorized, REFRAD. This information was given to me directly from the Army's official investigation.

October 4th

I sat out front with the kids and watched the thunderstorm. It went on and on like nothing I had ever seen, forever imprinted in my head. Lightning lit up the sky over and over again and I sat in awe of it all. After the kids went to bed, I drove to Steve's house for a few hours. I loved this man so incredibly deeply. He walked through every moment with me. Michael will never know that Steve held me up. He will never know of the struggle and turmoil I put Steve through as I constantly responded and reacted to PTSD triggers. I went days without showering before I met Steve. Peace and calm came when I was with him. The universe gave me Steve, even if just for a short while. I knew Michael would never let me be free. Michael assured me of that so many times.

In a quiet whisper, amidst the loudness of the thunder and lightning, I spoke the words that still haunt me. "I will never be safe while Michael is alive." It was the first time I spoke those words to him, right in the thick of the storm. Michael destroyed me, every ounce of me.

This was the last night before my whole world upended upon itself.

October 5th

I took off my gloves and gown and threw them in the trash. I had just Covid tested 20 elementary school kids in the school library. I was five days into my new job with a school district. I pulled out my phone to see a missed call from the Delaware State Police Department. I stepped outside and called them back.

"Victims unit," I heard on the other line. I stated my name. She stated hers. "Your husband, Michael Parke, attempted suicide," Her voice echoed through the phone. "So where is he? The ICU?" I said callously. I'd been down this road before. I was not prepared for her next words.

"No, ma'am. The Medical Examiner's Office." My legs gave out, and I dropped to my knees in front of the elementary school library, unable to hold my body up any longer. I hung up, and the detective called me again. "Ma'am, why don't you call me back when you have had a chance to gather yourself." I could not respond, not one word could form.

With no floor beneath me, I tried to walk back in. Staring at the door, I froze. My boss is inside and can help me. Can I walk in there? Someone, please come get me. I dropped to my knees again. I couldn't move; my legs no longer obeyed me. My boss walked out, oblivious, and I blurted something that sounded incomprehensible even to me, but he seemed to understand what I meant. Every alarm in my head went off as my spirit left my body. He brought me over to sit down. This was a man I'd only known for five days, a virtual stranger. He took my phone and called the detective back. I have no idea what was said.

My coworkers appeared by my side now, seemingly out of thin air, surrounding every side of me. A cold water bottle was pressed into my hand. Where did the water come from? The world had stopped. I need to go home now. Where were the van keys? I just had them; I drove us here! Frantically, I emptied everything out of my diaper bag that I repurposed for work. I searched for what felt like an eternity for them. Everywhere but the side pocket. Where are the keys? Get me out of here! My coworker drove me home in my car. As she drove down the freeway, I watched myself from above my body like a horror movie.

I texted my mom, "Come home now." She responded, "Who me? Why? When? Now?" I could not handle that. I called my brother, David. He didn't answer. I called again. My brother answered the second time. "What's wrong? No one calls twice." I knew he ignored the first one because he was busy at work. That was fine. He knew a second phone call meant something was wrong. The first weight of the million pounds on my shoulders felt lifted. I said "Come home now. Emergency." He hung up and rushed home.

I have a hard time believing my life was "that bad." I have confided in people that I wish I had made all of this up. That this was just a psychotic break I had. Knowing this world can be this terrifying based on my own human experiences, I would rather it just be made up. But my brother's response told me that he had been worried about me. Just one "call twice", and he was on his way home.

In the living room, I broke the news to my mom. My brother walked in soon after. I told it again. We all stood frozen at the words I had just unleashed. I sat with my coworker while she waited for my boss to pick her up. The world had stopped spinning. So, we did fuse beads. When the world froze, I took a fuse bead and asked her to please make one with me.

I went to the bathroom and sighed with relief. I am finally safe. Why am I relieved? I'm terrified. I'm relieved. I feel free. Instantly, those intrusive thoughts of accidentally hitting the median while driving and rolling off a cliff, or of Michael shooting me in my sleep and having it all over quickly, were gone. Those thoughts left me and never returned.

My life had been a constant battle, fighting and preparing for whatever crisis could fly out of this tornado named Ruin. I always anticipated anything that might come my way. When I close my eyes and think of that moment, I picture my younger self standing at the base, waiting. A sword duct taped to my hands, ready to slice anything flying out of it in half. Only this time, the tornado had stopped mid-spin. I stood there in a fighting stance, sword still in hand.

In that bathroom, I stared metaphorically at all the stuff that had been flying around, now desolation on the ground. Everything that was airborne was now shattered on the floor. Nothing to fight, nothing to save. Just therein Michael's wake. Left for the living.

About a year later I would get through panic attacks by closing my eyes, visualizing the sword, and intentionally setting it down. Over and over again. Reminding myself that the storm was over and the grieving had begun.

It's almost always true for me that the state of my house and my appearance reflect my mental state, time and time again. When the doorbell rang and it was time for my coworker to go, I looked around at my living space. A desperate cry for help. A physical manifestation that I am in over my head. I shut the door and think what do I do now?

Lt. Dun will be my guide. I will call him. I think he will have navigation for me. I have to tell him Michael is gone. How do I do that over the phone? Maybe they are looking for him since he should be at work.

The line trilled "Hello." He knew. Lt. Dun told me no one there was no plan to inform Michael's parents or siblings. It was up to me. I sat there as the only civilian who knew. That time and place will forever scar my memory. I sat with my life-altering knowledge. Responsible for unleashing the news of trauma and unimaginable heartbreak.

"In sickness and health. Till death do you part." The marriage vows I took brought me here. I was the real-life representation of everyone's nightmare. Mariah, standing here as the widow. No. Matter. What. Nothing changes that fact. I tried to hold onto the moment before I knew I had to call his mom.

Jarred back into reality, I remembered how fast things travel on the internet. Social media and texting. She has to hear this from me, not the internet. I had to call immediately. It was time to open the gates of hell.

The line rang, ominous to only myself. "Hi Julie. Are you with Greg?" When she affirmed that Greg was present, I told her and hung up. She had started screaming. A little later, Tammy, his sister, called me. I hadn't spoken to Tammy in months, but within seconds she called just to confirm the truth. The truth that I had to confirm. Her brother had died. "Is it true? Is he gone?" "Yes," I replied. She hung up.

I walked back out to the couch and sat down. My dad had come home while I was in the other room. My dad fell backward onto the couch and sobbed. My brother stayed next to me. We sat side by side on the couch for the next three hours. We both stared at the wall as I repeated to him, "he's an asshole."

I remember picking Raela up from preschool. Her little hands touched my arms with tender embrace. This was my baby girl whose father had just died. Next, I picked up Ronan from after school care and it was the same. His world had changed forever as he ran to put his oversized backpack on his tiny body. My little kindergartener ran to Mommy. How long can I shelter him? Echoes of Julie's cries, Tammy's voice for the first time in months, and the "No. He's at the Medical Examiner's office" tear apart my heart as I take step after step.

I fed my babies as my heart screamed. I changed them into pajamas as vertigo threatened to overtake me. At bedtime, I laid them both in my bed with me. But I could not sleep. I played the "Oh Brother Where Art Thou" soundtrack as my body turned into its own airplane, imagining myself lying on a grassy field in the countryside. It's now morning. Sleep had not become me.

The next day, Esther, my friend since high school, came over. I physically could not walk. She cleaned my room and put my laundry away. We ate donuts. I alerted the world by making a Facebook group. I knew it was going to traumatize everyone, but I had to. I clicked to make the group live. I was the wife. This was the father of my children. No one was going to do this for me.

I told my work I needed to return. Being alone when a minute felt like a day, was torture. After only one day off of work, I was back. I took the elevator and walked slowly. I could not stand for more than a minute. My coworkers carried me mentally. My boss handed me a card with the money I had missed from not working the day before. The next day, I showed up and still could barely walk. For two weeks, I struggled to take more than five steps at a time. I exhausted myself going from one room to the next.

The LDS church brought meals to us. I was completely checked out as they set the food down. The strange thing is, although I never would have imagined Michael would die by suicide, I occasionally had thoughts as if preparing myself for it. For months prior, I knew if I showed up and there were two cars in front of my house, then I would know the relief society, the women of the Mormon church, was there because he took his life. I occasionally thought that if I turned the corner onto my street, and saw a cop car, I would know why. Three days before he died, I had told my mom that if Michael died before Raela turned three, she would be the one to get Raela through it. He died six days before she turned three. I had no idea how I knew and did not know at the same time.

Friday was the first day a representative from the Military showed up at my door. It had been three days. Dress blues. One Army Major. Major Waynes. We sat at the dining room table: the Major, mom, dad, David, and me. She told me this was her first case.

In the same breath that she explained that a substantial amount of money would be transferred into my bank account, she asked me to pick out his coffin. She flipped the page in her binder that had printed-out photos to choose from. She then followed with, "Where are we to bury him?" Michael and I had not discussed this before. I had no idea. In one conversation, I went from $500 in my bank account to more than I could make in years. All it took was a "sign here" from an official representative of the United States Army.

When it became time for her to go, I could not muster the strength to pull my body out of the chair. I sat there lightheaded and dizzy as the world seemed to move all around me. My family walked her out.

It was now three days before my daughter turned three. Sunday afternoon came around and my brother David texted me to say that the cake was ready. He had put together a birthday party for Raela without being asked to. I sat there as children played, pictures were taken, and the cake was cut. It was the normal my children needed. I still hadn't told them their dad had died. Life was happening *to* me and I could not have been more grateful. All I had to do was sit there because they handled everything without being asked.

As someone who has been through tragedy, I've experienced the frustration of being asked "Is there anything I can do to help?" and "How are you holding up?" Here is my answer: do not ask what you can do; think of two to three ideas of things you can do to help such as a meal, walking the dog, or baking a treat. Then, offer one of those things. If that person needs it, all they have to do is say yes, thank you. Second. I was not holding up. Those around me were holding me up.

For the next two weeks, I'd drop Ronan off at school and my mom would take Raela to daycare. Then I'd get off work, pick up Raela, and then pick up Ronan. Day after day. I'd lay in bed every night with my kids beside me, still listening to the soundtrack to "O Brother, Where Art Thou?" Until the sun rose, and it was time to jump back on the carousel.

My kids ran circles around me while I made dinner. I watched them run carefree, still unaware that their dad had died, knowing this world of innocence had a deadline.

I clocked two weeks of radio silence from the Army. I was to wait for their instruction. When I finally had a date to drive to Las Vegas for the funeral, David stopped me in the driveway. He said he would be able to make it to Las Vegas. I was shocked. I figured I would take the kids and go alone. It hadn't crossed my mind that others would take time off to go. That people would stop their busy schedules to support me and honor him. I thought this was something only I did. For so long, I had been in the "grin and bear it" or "tie your bootstraps and go" mode that it didn't occur to me that this is the time people came together. My brother showed up with the energy that I needed.

At this time, I knew I had to do what I had been avoiding. I sat my babies down and read them the book The Invisible String (Karst, 2000). I finished the book and while holding each of their hands, I told them. At first, they did not understand. They asked a few questions and then ran off and played. Over the next week or so, they would ask questions sporadically. That was until we drove to Las Vegas for the funeral where they witnessed firsthand what I meant.

We drove to Las Vegas and checked into the hotel. My children enjoyed the pool. They were oblivious to the disparity that mucked down and consumed all the air of this trip. We drove to the LDS church, exited the car, and walked in as the immediate family. Before the services started, someone ushered us into a side room where the bishop spoke to us. I can't remember what he said, but I remember being in that room with all of his family. People I hadn't seen in years. People who I spent years with. We all gathered for the person who brought us together in the first place.

After the services, my friend Carie greeted me with a hug. A few days before we drove to Las Vegas, she had asked me how I was doing. I told her how worried I was about a few women who contacted me, especially one in particular: Isla. She was the one who drove from Utah to Pennsylvania with Michael. She was the one whose texts I had read, with Michael saying, "Hey babe, how's your day? I love you," and she responded, "Love you too! Took the kids bowling today." She was the one who made me feel less like Michael's wife and more like his nanny.

Isla had texted me, saying that this was all my fault. She wanted to know what happened. What happened is between Michael and God, not me. I know they are sorting it out even as I type this. I had also told Carie about another woman, one of Michael's affairs, who had RSVP'ed. Throughout our marriage, Michael had promised me that they were just friends. But after Michael and I split up, he sent me the nude pictures and explicit texts they sent each other. I felt like I was walking into a storm. When I shared this with Carie, she told me to relax at the services, assuring me she would be there to make sure no one said anything they shouldn't to me.

Carie drove with her husband from San Diego to Las Vegas to support me. I felt so loved. Her actions made me look at life through a different lens. She had packed her bags, drove all that way, got a hotel, and dressed to go to the services of someone she never met, to sit and support me. Then she drove home. She didn't ask anything of me. All to make me feel safe. She gave me the chance to be in the moment with my children. The women I was worried about never showed up. At least, we didn't see them, and they didn't sign the guest book.

When I walked outside, I saw that some of Michael's friends had stayed behind. They were hanging around a motorcycle and the kids started climbing all over it. Standing there with some Military friends was one of the last moments I felt part of the Military family. After six years of Military family life, I now feel like an outsider.

At the park for the celebration of life, I was surrounded by people I knew yet consumed by loneliness. I must have looked so strange because I was sure Michael was going to pop out of the bushes and yell, "Surprise! You guys miss me or what? Gotcha!" It got to the point where I was looking around and behind the bushes for him. Denial can be a strange thing. But I was certain of it. The kids played at the park. His family had brought a football and Skyler, his cousin, said "Michael made us promise when we were kids that at his funeral we would play football." So, football was played.

Michael's friends, V and Abe, who I considered my friends as well, walked up. The celebration was almost over and Michael had not jumped out of the bushes. They agreed that they thought he was going to do the same thing. We sat there in disappointment. I told them how scared I was that one of these women would confront me. They asked "Who is Isla? She contacted us as well. We are here for you, Michael's wife and his kids. We have your back." And just like that, I realized I had more people looking out for me than I thought. People I didn't even know did that for me.

When we returned to the hotel, I was restless. It has always been my stress reaction. My brother David had a list of fun things to do in Vegas, and he let me choose what we'd do. I knew I didn't want to sit around the hotel room, and the kids would be antsy if I tried anyway. It was exactly what I needed for my sanity: a distraction from reality for a few hours to rest my racing mind.

My parents, David, his family, and mine ended up at the Rainforest Cafe. While waiting for dinner, I found myself transported to a place of thunder and lightning storms, just like the night before he died. It felt like a portal to hell had opened with the lightning and we had fallen through a black hole. After that, we walked around the M&M factory and to the fountain show. We all fell into our beds that night exhausted. Exhaustion was a gift, and falling asleep easily was a gift. David also ensured I got my coffee and breakfast, driving me to get some in the morning.

A few days later, Michael was finally set to arrive in Las Vegas. The Medical Examiner's office had taken him to an office in Delaware, but because there weren't Military personnel to process him, they transported him to Maryland. This floored me. The horrific images of cargo for a human was unbearable. Not to mention the extra time it took for him to be moved. When we finally got word that he was to be flown from Maryland to Las Vegas, I was mortified. It had been over two weeks—seventeen days for him to be laid to rest.

On October 20th, I still hadn't written a Eulogy for the Military Services. How was I expected to do that? Taylor Swift's "Long Live" circled on repeat through my headphones. I must have listened to it over 100 times. When we got back to the hotel, I pulled out my laptop and wrote it all out.

Journal Entry October 21st, 2021:

> *I wished him a better love life. He deserved to have a long, beautiful life. He deserved to be loved. He deserved to be whole. I think*

he felt God was the only one who could make him that way. That his body was too broken to do that in this life. So he robbed everyone who knew him of peace. He robbed himself of a full life. I wanted to be safe. I wanted peace. I wanted him to get the help he needed. The help I begged his commanders and his Army friends to give him. I thought the Army had the power to help him. To care for their soldiers. I thought they prided themselves on being a family.

Airport Tarmac

The causality officer drove me to the airport. We waited on the staff side to be ushered onto the Tarmac to meet the plane. After hearing about all the moving and the time it took to get him here, my heart sank when there was a flight delay. I remember telling Tammy that my soul was not in my body and hadn't been for weeks. I could feel my soul hovering about a foot away from my body. I'm not sure when I came back in, but it was gradual and over two and a half years.

When it was time to meet him, with thin clouds in the sky and the sun beaming down, we were ushered on and pulled up to the airplane. Everyone on the plane watched out the windows as the airport personnel entered the cargo area and put a flag over his casket. I could feel their gaze on us. *What did they say on the plane that informed everyone to look? Who on the plane was affected, trapped, with nowhere to go as they witnessed bringing Michael home to his family out that window?* It was all too much. I wish I could have been fully present in that moment, but I honor that my body protected my heart. People told me how well I handled everything, but it was because only my body was there.

Michael went into the back of the hearse, and his family and I followed in the van. Although he was being driven right in front of us, it was hard to believe it. When we returned to the airport parking lot, his family went home, and the two officers drove me to the funeral home. Sitting in the front seat, having an officer drive me and another in the back seat felt surreal. I felt like the main event and that horrified me. The officer in the back had flown in to make sure Michael was positioned correctly in the casket. That his pins and uniform were perfect. What a horrible and absolutely necessary job.

Our Final Goodbye

They told me to wait outside so the Army officials could position him and touch up his makeup before I saw him. My stomach turned after hearing that and knowing I would soon be seeing him and having to accept reality. I paced twenty feet from Michael, yet lightyears away in my mind. Eventually, I sat on the sidewalk, deflated as I dug deep again to find some peace in my heart. I wanted to get into the mindset to do this, to truly take in this moment instead of running away in my mind. *Remember this moment*, I thought. *It's the beginning of the end of your denial.* The moon illuminated the sky and I was humbled once again by the universe.

The door opened and hands motioned for me to come inside. My feet walk me in. An open casket lay twenty feet in front of me. I took another step forward. Nineteen feet away.

"Ma'am, would you like some privacy? We can go, or we can stay."

Why was I the one here? Why was it just me in a room with him and two officers standing behind me?

"Stay," I whispered. My hands trembled.

I reached the end of the room and gazed at Michael. Unable to speak at first, I looked at him from top to bottom. The hands that hurt me, right there. The arms that hugged me, right there. *This is your last chance, Mariah, to forgive him face to face.* Knowing this, I said something I did not mean.

"I forgive you. For trying to kill me, Michael, I forgive you"

I tried my very best not to be angry. I tried with all my strength to forgive him, hoping to forgive myself.

The two men who stood behind me heard my words but remained silent as we drove the thirty minutes home. The air had been sucked out of the car as we sped down the freeway, gazing at the millions of stars in the vast universe. All three of us had just witnessed a Military man lying forever asleep. The dirty, taboo, secret of the United States Military: to have the strongest Military in the world, lives on U.S. soil go unnoticed, and left to figure out their mental health alone. It is the disease of every great organization, like an open sore on a body. Everyone can see it, but the body marches forward because until you need an amputation, the mission is to keep the vast majority on the frontlines, protecting our freedom.

Meanwhile, women and children are in homes, caught in the crossfire of the service members they love who are affected by PTSD. While the four walls of our nations are protected, the four walls of their homes are invaded. It is past time for an amputation.

Graveside

Again, I walked in with his children. Little hands that I was responsible for, I had filled their life with funerals, grief, and devastation. Words struggled to form in my mouth, and I hated it, and myself, with every fiber of my being. We sat down in the front row of the funeral hall. The director spoke and then turned the time over to me. I stood, not tall, but I stood, walked towards the podium, unfolded my paper, and began:

> *"Thank you, everyone, for coming out here today to honor and respect Michael Joseph Parke. As I stand here, I am humbled by how short life is. Graced by the surrounding love of friends, family, and those who have helped bring Michael home.*
>
> *Michael was a lot of things: a corpsman, a soldier, a spiritual believer, a husband, a dad. But most of all, and transcending through all of these "titles," a friend. From day one, Michael was a friend to all. He*

always knew exactly how to make someone smile. And not in a "come easy way." He was thoughtful. He saw people to their core and knew, with those eyes of his, just how to brighten someone's day. He had the gift of knowing what to say. Always.

In his childhood, a few stories stand out. The first was the "golden boy." And however many thousand times I heard this phrase, I knew what it really meant. Michael was the one everyone wanted to play with, talk with, or just be with. He helped people come together from all walks of life.

Another one of my favorite stories is when Michael was about five or so, he was at his Anyu and Papa's house. His Papa walked in, and seeing his toy soldiers lined up in two lines, his Papa asked him what he was doing. Normally, it would be a war zone. He looked up at his Papa and said, "They are doing the pre-planning meeting." It was then that his Papa knew he was going to join the Military.

To me, that experience showed a thoughtful, quiet moment of a little boy who was more aware of life than most his age. As a history major, I feel he always looked to the patterns to learn from others' examples. As a spiritual person, I feel he always looked to the "gut feelings" he always had. As a dad, he was sometimes crippled by fear of making sure the kids were safe. Because he loved his kids so much.

I'd like to take a minute to talk about those two beautiful children. Ronan. You have your dad's love for others. You know when someone needs a hug. Just like your dad. When you start to go on about teams and competition, athletics, or when you come up with fun games to play, I stop and think of your dad.

When I see you sitting at the table doing your homework, I remember how your dad told me how much he loved school too. He loved learning. I think of all the things your dad liked to do, it was learning he liked the most. In the early years of getting to know Michael, I would be taken aback by some of the things he did. He and his brother Robert were always sharing soundtracks to movies.

I had never thought to look those up—except, to his dismay, the Evita soundtrack! It made me realize that when we were watching a movie, he was four levels deep, focused on the beauty of the music.

Your dad also loved "Josh Jarbo," and if you look up his YouTube videos, there is a distinct opening sound. Oh, how in the middle of the night when I heard that I wanted to chuck the phone across the room. But it is another example of how Michael was always looking beneath the surface. He researched these movies before and after watching them not to see if it was worth it to watch, but to get all the backstories. I mean, we watched some pretty terrible movies. But it was always more than just if a movie would entertain him. It was always about if it could make him think.

Ronan. Keep sitting at the table. Keep thinking. Keep asking me "why" a million thousand times because it is keeping your dad with us. And I will try to remember that, too, and be just a smidge more patient.

Raela. Wow. My word for you is spitfire. Please raise your hand if you would describe Michael as that. When you came into this world, you took it by storm. So did your Dad when he was born. Never afraid to speak your truth. You get that from your dad. I learned that from him.

Raela, the way you get excited about things. That was your dad to a T. In fact, I know that through his excitement, he got people excited about things that they weren't initially excited about. He had a way of rallying. When I see you get excited about going somewhere or excited to read books. The learning mostly, but making Mama stop everything so you can learn. It reminds me of your dad because even if I was hesitant at first, you make everything fun.

I woke up yesterday morning with a song stuck in my head. And I feel Michael shaking his head at me. But I'm going for it. Here it comes. Bring it on Taylor Swift. Don't worry, I'm not going to sing it...(I read the whole song, but these are the lyrics that stood out the most.)

"And the cynics were outraged... Screaming, "This is absurd!."... 'Cause for a moment a band of thieves... In ripped-up jeans got to rule the world... Long live all the mountains we moved... I had the time of my life-fighting dragons with you... I was screaming long live that look on your face... And bring on all the pretenders... One day, we will be remembered... Long live the walls we crashed through. I had the time of my life, with you"

Michael, you will be remembered. As Ronan says it best, there is an invisible string connecting us all. The string starts at my heart and connects to everyone we love. Ronan knows, and we would like to share with you that the invisible string reaches all the way up to Heaven where Michael is. Please join me in tugging on our invisible string to Michael. God be with you till we meet again."

The twenty-one gun salute began. They folded the flag and handed it to me, the wife. Then they handed flags to Ronan and Raela. The director of the funeral home drove Michael, myself, and the children to Michael's final resting place. In the hearse, the funeral director said I was so strong, and he didn't know how I did that so eloquently. I didn't know then, but now I know it was the grace of God.

Watching my children place lilies on their daddy's casket put me in a state of unimaginable heartbreak. There are no words for the world you live in after that moment. The amount of daily anxiety I had to acknowledge and hand over to God felt insurmountable. Watching that and then placing dirt after he was lowered in makes me nauseated every time.

We drove home to San Diego after that. Life needed to go on, and I felt in charge of ensuring that for myself and my children. The question was, how? That following Monday, I went back to work.

Opening a Time Capsule

My parents hosted Thanksgiving dinner at their house. It had been forty-five days since Michael died. As my extended family trickled in, it hit me that I was no longer the eight-year-old girl running around at Thanksgiving. I'm not the girl who brought her boyfriend while visiting from Las Vegas. I'm not married with a baby and a husband who's deployed or going through a divorce with two children. I am the forty-five-day new widow with a massive identity crisis and all the iterations of my being boiling over. The other family members filter in and I get consumed with green beans for Raela and ham for Ronan.

Three days later, we shipped all of our things from the townhome in Pennsylvania to San Diego. I thought back to how I drove off that terrifying day and left it all behind. I drove off in my car with no hope of seeing any of my belongings again. Now, I didn't want my things, not this way. Now more than ever, it felt like "just things."

I thought of Michael. He brought nothing with him when he died. Everything he had left in the hotel room was exactly where he left it. His phone which he never let anyone look at, left behind. I felt the gravity of how he wouldn't throw away his trash ever again, wouldn't buy another thing, he dressed himself for the last time. How lonely he must have felt. He did all of it alone. All of his things were touched for the last time by him.

My neighbor in Pennsylvania sent me videos and pictures of every room of our townhome. It was a biohazard. There was food piled up on his desk, holes punched in the walls, two doors broken in half, and black mold in the toilets. Mail had piled up and trash bags filled the garage. Alcohol of all sorts, probably over a hundred bottles, littered his room and truck. Everything kid-related had been moved to the basement. How is it that his coworkers sent runners to his house and no one said anything? There were urine stains on the wall.

The moving coordinator for the military started cc'ing me with updates through email. They sent the emails to Michael's email. "Dear Michael Parke," it read. When I opened that email I was shocked. How insensitive! Emailing him? He will never open his email again. I responded asking them not to email or address him. They didn't stop. Every correspondence was addressed this way and sent to his email. Each time was another horrific reminder that he was gone.

The day the moving truck came, I sat on the house's front steps. They were apologetic for running late. What did it matter if they were a few hours late? Unloading the boxes was like opening a time capsule. There were things I didn't remember we had until the seal of the cardboard box was breached. All of the things I used to raise my babies. All of his shirts I washed hundreds of times over the past ten years. What did any of it matter? They were merely the vessels and tools we used to get through life. A thing that harbored most of my babies' sleep. How often did I stare down at my beautiful children as they fell asleep in it?

It was a reminder that I didn't need any of it. I got by before this moment, and I could have gotten by without the materials as well. There was something sacred about it. I was blessed with these tools. I had memories attached to them. I could hold something and say, "Yes. This all was real." There is a kindness in that, and an inability to deny that I had made a full life with Michael. The proof just landed at my doorstep.

My Body Said No More

My work carried me through every day as I searched for some normalcy. I sat in a corner and put the droppers on the test. I was not very helpful or capable. My coworkers did the rest. It was a tremendous miracle I got to be around people. I can never repay the kindness and grace they gave me. And they never asked me to.

A week before the school I worked for went on winter break, I spoke to my bosses. Even as the words spilled from my mouth, they knew. I told them that I would forever be indebted to them for this opportunity. I had felt like part of a family and the love every day was an extreme kindness. I had come to the end of my denial phase. I had only been distracting myself from reality. It worked until my body said no more. I was going in every day and although it was helping, my body was also screaming at me that the band aid was coming off. I was being forced to look at this tragedy. It was time to process. My body did its best to protect me from what was unbearable to acknowledge.

I gave them a week's notice. I knew I could not come back. They carried me long enough. It was time to focus on healing.

BACK AT IT

Despite my intention to heal and slow down, it was only a matter of time before I sought more work as a distraction. Just a week after leaving the school district, I got a message from my sister-in-law, Sophie. There was a new event medical company looking for EMTs that sounded amazing. Most of my time working as an EMT had mainly been for events. I emailed the owner, Kacey, and then waited anxiously. A few days later, the phone rang. Kacey wanted to know if I could come in to work a soccer game in a few hours. Panic and thrill shuddered through me.

Off I drove to Pechanga Arena. Memories flooded my mind as I parked the car and walked up the steps. Fifteen years ago, I saw my first band, The

Cure, there. Twelve years ago, I saw Taylor Swift. Walking in as a potential employee was surreal.

As I entered the medical room, Kacey introduced herself and showed me around. She asked me about my experience as an EMT and then gave me a shirt. While glancing at my resume, she noticed that the last place I worked at was in Las Vegas,

"What brought you back to San Diego?" she asked sincerely.

I paused and said, "My husband and I were going through a divorce, so I moved back home."

"Oh, that happens," she said compassionately. My eyes scanned the room as the walls seemed to close in around me and my chest tightened. What I said was true, but it omitted the other half of everything. I stood there awkwardly, silent.

"Okay," she said, breaking the silence. "Why did you leave your last job?" Nothing could stop the immediate flooding of words that came out of me. I was completely transparent.

"I left my previous job because five days into starting there, I found out at work that my husband had died. I worked for a few months after that but resigned because I needed time to focus on healing and spending time with my children. So, it might be a little confusing if you call them and ask about me."

I was more worried it would be hurtful for them to find out that I was off to another job two weeks after resigning.

Another pause. Then a weak, "So did I pass my interview?" I was ready to show myself the door. Kacey met me with grace and told me she understood. She then asked if I would like a tour of the arena. Relief filled me and I exhaled the breath I hadn't realized I was holding in.

Over the next few months, I learned that Kacey had bought the business six days after Michael's death. She bought it on Raela's birthday. She was just starting to build her clientele and physical events when I walked in on that Sunday afternoon in December. We would spend the next few months doing a makeover of the inventory, gear bags, and protocol book. I was just a pair of hands as I watched her transform this company that had been dormant since Covid into a thriving and exciting business. As I took pride in being part of this company and watching it grow, so did I hope I could move on and thrive in the same way.

2022

Heart Grow Fonder

Walking back into my parents' house was a reality check. I was a survivor finding refuge. But a refugee at the mercy and rules of my parents. My life could never be mine alone without keys to my own home or my own dishes soaking in the sink from the night before because I was too tired. I met up with a friend I met at a park a year ago, Robyn. I vented that living with my parents bruised my ego. She posed a question that changed my perspective. She offered me a question of grace.

"Is it your ego or your mental health?" It had never occurred to me that there was an alternative view, but the answer was obvious. I was allowed to do things for my mental health. It wasn't my ego. It was my mental health. And probably my parents' mental health as well.

I spent most of the following week preparing to move out of my parents' house, and into a house my grandmother owned. When the prior renter moved out, I was astounded. She had basically packed a suitcase and walked out. My dad, brother, and I worked together to haul out trash, carpet, tile, and anything else she left behind.

Moving out gave me the ability to make my mom my friend again. She would tell me what shows to watch and we would go to bakeries together. After not living with my parents for a decade, and then having to crash land at their place, I think that everyone started breathing easier when distance could make the heart grow fonder.

I was now in my house with my kids and a bed. The first night I slept in the house, the kids laid on my bed with me. I woke up in the morning grateful for our little but mighty family. At this time, I knew I could move out of survival mode. I had four walls to hibernate, recover, and emerge whole again.

Michael's Birthday

Michael's birthday is St Patrick's Day. The reminders start early; with every shamrock and leprechaun displayed, I was reminded of his birthday and that he also has a death day. We shared ten birthdays besides the year prior due to the restraining order. And now, this one where I can't contact him because he is unreachable from the great beyond. Even with brewing anxiety, the fear of idleness led me to take the kids to a place Michael and I both enjoyed. I had a picture of him at the restaurant, so I printed it out with "Happy Birthday Dad!" I handed the photo over to the kids and walked in. The feeling of eyes on me sent prickles of anxiety over my skin. But I knew I had to swallow that feeling. I could do this for them once a year.

We were seated, and the picture was placed on the table. The kids got whatever they wanted as I'm sure Michael would have insisted. At the end of dinner, we ordered cake and sang Happy Birthday quietly. I knew, at the very least, I wasn't causing harm to them. I hoped I was doing what was best for them. At the end of the meal, the manager came over. He told us that the meal was on the house. I didn't know what to do or say. Initially, I felt we were drawing too much attention, and I hated it. I never wanted to go back to the restaurant. But the following year, the kids wanted to come back again. And the next year and the next year after that. I knew we had found our tradition.

Army Presents Their Investigation

In what I learned to recognize as "typical Army fashion," I was given a binder that neatly summed up Michael's existence, at least in their eyes. After I looked through it and highlighted at least 100 spelling errors and wrong information, they flew a chaplain and colonel out to my front door to present their official document. I sat with my brother David, awaiting their direction. They flipped through their slides and asked me if I had any questions or comments. Yes. Yes, I did. I prepared a statement of my comments, actually. This is what I read to them:

My husband, Michael Parke, is described in this report as:

Quoted from the investigation of his death report: "Experiencing significant stressors: divorce, separation from children, finances, alcohol abuse, mental health issues, passing of his grandma, work performance, and negative relationship with his company commander. Together, they presented a picture of an officer who was struggling psychologically and emotionally."

When you think of the Captain Parke that was at the 76th in Utah, is this what you think of? At the 76th, he was described as the "number one officer, best in the division, among the most technically sound I have ever served with."

He came to the 130th and got this rating "hit the ground running" "consistently executed to or above standard"

He arrived at the 130th with the same behavior as the 76th. Can you tell me how no one believed me when he did a complete 180? How he and I both got dismissed when his ability to perform did not match the "number 1 officer in the division?"

Everyone in the 76th knew him. They knew me. So when Captain Parke started presenting as "struggling," when his wife of six years, together ten reached out after leaving months prior, SHE was ignored. When I called CW in 2020, I had already left. I tried everything I could to save Michael from losing his career. I made it clear to CW that I was begging for his help but wasn't going to say any trigger words to start an official investigation. This pattern for me was consistent. I left silently. I only reached out when Michael told me he was planning on moving to LA. It wasn't until December 2020 that I filed for divorce. I tried to give him time, to keep him on the upswing as best I could. It was only when I felt things spiraling that I reached out.

I was the one who convinced Michael to tell his commander about the concussion because I was afraid for his health. I convinced him because he was afraid he was going to get in trouble. That is the kind of mental health care CW put in place for Michael.

When Michael came to visit, it was clear by this investigation that everyone was concerned that if he was denied visitation to San Diego he would deteriorate further. I was contacted by Lt. Dun. He wanted to make sure I was okay with it. I was put in the same position as Lt. Dun. Deny it and watch Michael deteriorate further. Or have him visit and feel again like he wasn't getting the treatment he needed the entire time. The Michael I knew was gone. The Michael that was showing up at 130th was not the one that arrived. And yet the only care he got was when he was placed in a psychiatric unit.

I was put in an uncomfortable and unsafe position. The Army failed Michael and me. The only two options were to deny or have him come visit. Where was the intervention that "if he's so upset maybe he needs medical/mental health attention." The position I was put in was to be the crazy ex-wife and "deny him from seeing his kids." And I felt this way because of how I was already dismissed by CW. So I was forced to try to manage his visit. I felt like Lt.

Dun listened and we came up with a plan. However, when Michael was visiting things went very south.

I was not made aware of until this report that Michael was not doing his morning check-ins or his assigned work. These should have been red flags that he was not doing well. That he was not able to manage even that. I was put in the line of fire and left in the dark. I was upfront and the Army gladly took the information I provided. But I extremely disagree that they were transparent if relevant information that involved sending a mentally incapable Army Captain to my and my children's doorstep. I also know that with the information they shared, they did not intervene when it was clear that through Michael's actions, he was begging for it.

When Michael arrived, and as I stated in my email to CW, he reeked of alcohol. There is no way that the flight did that to him. He was presenting like this at work. Nothing was said or done. Myself and his kids, four and two years old, could not be in the car with him without having the windows down. In the report, it said runners were constantly sent to the house to pick him up for work.

Upon the request of CW, I emailed him a breakdown of the trip. Again, CW was eager to get information, but not eager to work with me. I was taken at less than face value. I was given no guidance. I was left in the dark. And with the power of the Army, I feel like I was pressured to do as he said. I had very little information on how he bullied Michael. I would have never sent "ammo" to CW had I known how he treated him. After Michael came and picked up his things from my parents' house, Major G escorted him to the airport. I found out through Michael's phone that he was not escorted back to Pennsylvania, as he had been promised. He had a flight delay and Major G left him on the promise that he would get on the next flight. Not hours after being released to his command (not back out into the public) from the hospital for attempting to take his life. Just prior to going into the hospital he was extremely hostile, stalked me outside of my house, and sent naked photos of me to my mom.

    I believe CW was out to get Michael kicked out. I know that it was extremely hostile behavior to tell him he was being retained. And in that meeting finding out that CW didn't even have the authority to do that. Then, have him sign a counseling statement that he wasn't going to be retained after all. Then directly after signing, sending him to the Quarterly USR where the assessment of wartime readiness, personal readiness, unit training proficiency, etc. are discussed. Sending Captain Parke who served over 13 years, a month shy of 14, with ribbons such as "Global

War on Terrorism Expeditionary Medal, 4 deployment ribbons, and Army Commendation medal" to that training—where everything discussed was what he would no longer be able to participate in—was malicious.

He worked and dedicated his entire career to the Military. There is no way CW approved him going without having to consider how this would affect his mental health. He did not show any compassion or tact in the timing of the counseling statement. And given the nature of the statement, it should have been presented with compassion and with tools to navigate his next steps. CW was made aware, shown in the counseling statements he wrote up himself, that this was emotionally destroying, life-altering, information.

CW's response to Captain Parke committing suicide was nothing less than a memo. He texted in WhatsApp "Captain Parke killed himself." Then said he was not going to be available because he was in an all-day meeting. His delivery and inability to acknowledge that his actions permanently traumatize the recipients is gut-wrenching. CW was heard chuckling when talking about it and consistently referred to Michael as "killing himself." I know there is annual training as to how to appropriately address this. "Killing himself" is extremely crass and insensitive.

The very bare minimum was done. He was sent to twenty-nine days of rehab. CW even said he needed longer but he did not push. He was "ignored." SUDCC said he had impaired abilities. Why was he denied the Warrior Transition Unit? Why was it considered compassionate that his command worked with him when he couldn't make it into work? Why wasn't that taken as what it is? What he was going through disabled him.

I can tell by the statements who was being interviewed. Given the amount of time he was in service and the people who were interviewed, it shows the bare minimum was done. He was seen as a lovable person by all except CW. He loved being in the Army and when he was told he wasn't being retained, he called me. Listen to this voice memo. This was mid-September when he was fighting with everything to keep the career that he dedicated his life to. I learned from this report that this was the day he was told he missed suspense because the requirements were changed. Michael was on leave. He didn't know. And yet it was sent to the battalion commander. All while in the throes of trying to get retained. Michael then requested and was granted leave to gather his thoughts. He came back "refreshed" and thanked this captain for taking the reins. Why is this counseling statement not in the report?

I am pretty sure that these next statements are coming from PR: Captain Parke was complaining that CW changed his mind because he put in for leave. This would be around September 30. "He was very upset, and I couldn't remember a time when he was that upset." Major G stated that Michael came forward begging for help "in a situation like this a leader should have stopped everything they were doing to assist him. Often SM don't come forward with the assistance they need. In this case, Michael did."

I found out that Michael passed by a phone call from the Delaware State Police. I was five days into my new job and I got a phone call. When I get home, I call Lt. Dun and he says he knows. And that no one is going to tell his parents, I have to. I had to call his mom and tell her. I was given no tools. He told me I was the person who had to or they wouldn't know. In an age where everything gets out, I knew I needed to call her before she found out from someone else. I was right to think that since now I know CW already put it in a group chat.

It took three days for Major Williams to show up. All the evidence points to CW not acting appropriately to get me assistance. I was unable to walk for two weeks. My coworkers carried me through work. I could not be alone. I was left with no information and no Army contact for three days.

When she arrived, I handled everything the best I could. I made decisions that still the thought of making horrifies me. Picking which coffin to bury my husband in. Where to bury him. Then as I awaited details on the services, Michael moved from the hotel to the Delaware Medical Examiner's office, then to Maryland I think because "The person who was supposed to process him wasn't there." Why did you move his body again? That image gives me nightmares to this day. It took over two weeks for me to lay him to rest.

I am disabled from all of this. A recent medical diagnosis is that the trauma since October has left scars so deep, I will never be the same. Scars the Army so callously gave me. When his belongings were being sent from Pennsylvania, they kept addressing Michael and sending messages to his email. How would you like to get cc'd on an email that's being sent to your spouse's email that will never be opened because he is dead? Over and over again.

Yesterday I worked a medical event on the Miramar flight line. How would you like to arrive thinking "The last time I was on a flight line it was to bring my husband to his final resting place." I am doing the best I can to move through this pain. But so much of it was avoidable. His death was avoidable.

CW called me about a week after he died, looking for Michael's cousin's number. He kept saying, "We think Michael is still living with Jake," I said, "What are you talking about? Michael is living with Jake?" "Yes." "Michael is ALIVE!" "No."

I was told that I had to get Michael his uniform to get laid to rest in. Lt. Dun helped me. We built his rack. I bought the pins. Everything. Completely stressed because Michael earned every inch of that uniform. All to find out it was already being taken care of.

Instead, those pins were placed on my son Ronan's dress jacket. How fun would that have been for Michael to see? Now it's another thing he will never experience.

I am left navigating our entirely new life. Moving my children and myself through inexplicable and preventable trauma. Michael gave all of himself to the Military. When he moved to Pennsylvania, the Army took everything."

The Killers Concert

I have always liked the Killers but was particularly drawn to their recent album. I could write a list of all the ways they have healed me. Their song "Blowback" directly describes what mentally traumatic blowback is. The moments you take in before taking back your life. To "Spaceman" that explains what it feels to me to have an identity crisis. "Caution" hits the nerve of starting over, which I have done over and over again. "Run for Cover" which helped me process running for my physical life.

Music, to me, is microdosing PTSD. Music pulls feelings out of me slowly and at my pace to address and relive until I can come to peace with the events that took place. After his passing, I have felt Michael around only a few times through the years. When he would come to me in my dreams, they were nightmares. But on this particular afternoon, with my heart out, "My Own Soul's Warning" came on. I was listening to their newest album in my car in preparation for the concert I was to work at in a few weeks. The night before Michael died, the sky filled with thunderclouds, a wild amount of rain, and lightning. In that moment, Michael's soul sat in the seat next to me. It was a truly humbling and sacred moment as I felt Michael confirming his feelings the night before he died through the lyrics in this song. He was saying he was sorry and understood what he did in his life and the afterlife. *Brandon Flowers was singing about his life, and I was reflecting on my late husband's.* That was my first thought as my eyes shifted to the passenger seat.

I had not been very open to the idea of Michael visiting me after he died. It hurt too much, not to mention that I was still in denial. My body, mind, and spirit could not handle him visiting. I was pretty sure he loved me and was furious with me. That had been the pattern of our entire relationship after all. But there, at that moment, he asked me to listen. So, I listened.

Fast forward to the concert. I stood next to the stage and watched nearly the whole show. At the very end, the crowd's energy was building up; it was electrifying! In the middle of it all, someone tapped me on the shoulder. As I turned around, I immediately knew what was up. A man stood behind me who was clearly under the influence of too many drugs. His hazy gaze struggled to focus. My partner grabbed the wheelchair as I bent his knees and guided him into the wheelchair to wheel him to the First Aid Room, a less stimulating environment for him to ride this wave. Every step I took was timed perfectly for an encounter I still cannot believe is real.

We were backstage at the bottom of the loading dock, when I heard the concert end, and the crowd went wild! Suddenly, Brandon Flowers ran right past me and his eyes tracked mine the entire time. At the end of every show, the band was supposed to run off stage to a getaway car. By the time the house lights came on, the band would already be on the freeway off to the next town. But Brandon stopped mid-run like he knew me. Then he turned around and bee-lined straight up to me. My eyes nearly popped out of my head as the man I just watched perform an amazing concert reached out his hand to shake mine. He reached for his pockets and said, "I wish I had something to give you." I froze, just like the man in the wheelchair that I would bring to first aid. Abruptly, Brandon blurted, "I have to go!" And just like that, he was gone.

His impression on me in that moment and through his music will forever stay with me. For his talent, my experience with Michael on that drive, and how I have used his music to heal me. He gave me enough. A year later, I would listen to his song "Life to Come" which addresses so much for me, especially all the shame and guilt I'm learning to put down.

Communication Breakdowns

In September, the Military Aircraft Air Show took place in San Diego. I had worked for the event medical company for almost a year now. This was our biggest event and my boss's first year with this contract. Over 400,000 people were expected to attend. I was so excited to be part of this. I was assigned to be a rover, which meant I would respond in a golf cart, assess the patient, and treat or bring them back to the main medical tent. It was an amazing job! I spent three days roving around, treating people, and making many fun memories.

Steve and I once again tried to break up last December for a few weeks. Then we just talked and went on dates off and on for the next few months. But at the airshow, we for sure were off. On the third day, he asked to come over. I had told him we had already done the hard work of breaking up. To see him again would be too excruciating. He said he wanted to give it a real try again. I couldn't say no. We would continue to see each other once a week for another year after this, almost always at night. He'd send me texts saying he was trying. He was trying to be in a relationship with me. He was trying to leap from boy to man and just could not. But every moment with Steve was paradise. He admitted that when he was with me, nothing else mattered, like we were on our own private island together. The problem was that when I left his sight, self-doubt crept into his thoughts like a thief in the night...

To do the air show job, I had to set up different babysitters and activities, and asked my mom to help with some odd hours that weren't covered. This was the longest I had ever been away from my children. Although I missed them, it was also the first time I could enjoy myself with little worry. The weekend flew by.

As we packed up on the very last day, as we packed up, I walked into the medical tent. A fire chief was packing up off to the side of the room. It was just us two in the tent. He asked me what my plans were after EMT. I knew most people use EMTs to start their career to go into something like firefighting or nursing. I explained that firefighting was no longer my goal and while I was very grateful to have this job, I planned to stay an EMT while my kids were in school. I didn't have a career in mind, but I'd cross that bridge when I got there.

EMTs make little money. Definitely not enough to live in San Diego. He mentioned this. So, I told him. He seemed curious. I'm a big fan of don't ask questions you don't want to know the answer to. I explained that I received social security because my kid's dad passed away, and he was in the Army. This is usually the part that makes people awkward. It's incredibly awkward for me. It is the life I was given. While I have felt a lot of guilt about this, I have also felt incredibly blessed that I do get to spend most of my time with my children.

I expected him to stutter out an apology, that he didn't know, and then to regard me with disdain like I was just another person living off the government and had no plans of making a difference in the world. Due to this insecurity, I have written off people and put my defenses up many times. I think I get that insecurity from my mom's early comments.

But what he said shocked me. He looked at me and said no one knows where we will be in a year. My wife has stage four cancer. I have kids, and we figure it out every day, day by day. He had asked about my future plans because he watched my patient care and assessments this weekend. He thought I would be a great Emergency Room nurse. It caught me off guard for sure.

I started to walk away, looked at him, and said "We may not know the future. But I do know I'll see you next year." I called my mom and told her I would be home in about 45 minutes. I just needed to drop off all the gear before heading home. She had had the kids for maybe two-three hours. She asked me if I could drop off the gear tomorrow. I asked Kacey and she said since the gear was worth thousands of dollars, she couldn't allow me to do that. I needed to drop it off tonight. I did it as quickly as I could. Kacey lived ten minutes from me, so it wasn't a huge detour. Maybe an extra thirty minutes.

Ten minutes away from home, my mom called again. I heard an "I'm hurt cry" and my mom screamed, "Come home now!" before she hung up. I was eight stoplights away and shaking with fear. When I got home, the house was silent, which was strange because ten minutes earlier, there had been distressed cries. I walked in and without a word, my mom stormed out and slammed the door. I looked around for my kids. I found them lying silently in my bed. How did they fall asleep so quickly? I thought.

I moved closer and realized they weren't asleep. They were tucked in, not moving a muscle and staring at the ceiling. Ronan's voice shook as he whispered that Grandma yelled at them not to move. That Grandma hurt Ronan. She then forced them to lay in my bed until I got home. The kids had never been that quiet in their lives. I was still confused, so I took each child aside and asked them individually. Afterward, I put both kids to bed, baffled. They said Grandma was yelling, and Ronan backed up into a wall, and Grandma grabbed him. Raela's account aligned with Ronan's, and she ran and hid under the table but saw everything.

Two days later, I still hadn't heard from my mom, so I texted her asking, "When would you like to talk about what happened with Ronan?" I didn't think my mom caused physical harm. Maybe there had been some yelling, maybe she grabbed him. But I needed to hear what she had to say. She did not respond to the text, but ten minutes later, she was at my door with David, unannounced. We all sat down, and I barely said anything before she demanded that I look at her. How dare I accuse her. When she yelled and demanded my attention, I shut down. I closed myself off like I always do because I do not engage with aggression.

Feeling uncomfortable with all the tension, my brother said, "I think we should revisit this at another time. David stepped outside, but my mom shut the door behind him. She followed me into the kitchen saying in an aggressive and forceful tone, "You really think I would hurt my grandson?" I honestly didn't think that. But I will never have a conversation that involves yelling and manipulation.

I asked her to leave. She responded, "No, we are talking about this now." I paused and took a breath to prepare my next words. I knew it would shock her enough to leave.

"Get out of my house now." It was my house. I signed the contract. I paid rent. I have every right to dictate visitors. Landlords must give 24-hour notice. She was trespassing, and she knew it. It was a power move. My entire life, my relationship with my mother was based on how much I needed her, and she used that to feel in control. I had always needed her to rescue me. Whether it be when I had Ronan, and she would watch him so I could sleep, or dropping Raela off at daycare, moving back into their house after leaving Michael, and now finally moving into this house that I lived in, but my parents property managed. But in my words, she saw that I no longer needed her in any capacity.

Our relationship of her saving me was over. And it was over in ways she could not respect. She told me I was living off the government. She no longer had to provide me with a house because I got a "handout." It was shameful to her. For the next three months, we did not speak. She did not see the kids.

Dichotomies of My Grief

It was officially one year. I sat in the rocking chair and stared out the window into the backyard. A thousand-yard stare with my headphones blaring "Fifth of May" by Zach Bryan. It was just a date. But it also signified the lineal notion that life went on. I sat there, heavy-hearted, while the children played. Every grocery order, every bedtime routine, and every alarm in the morning were reminders that life goes on. It will keep going and no one will make me better but myself. I scraped the bottom of the barrel of my emotional wellness tank many times. I suppressed feelings deep to try and convince myself I was dreaming. I tried to bathe in reality, to drown myself in it but every time I tried to feel the weight of the metaphorical water, I just floated above it. I didn't realize that it was grief. All encompassing, like I was floating and drowning simultaneously. I was so angry, shouting at a man in the sky and at Michael for abandoning us, begging for this to be made right. To be naïve again while desperate to understand everything and avoid repeating this pain for eternity.

This day marked the beginning of the timeline, where every day was the first and the last. With Michael gone, he left me everything, along with a void—a void where every cry seemed to echo endlessly, never filling the emptiness I felt. Where every cry from his babies went unheard by him. Even when he visited me in my dreams, they turned into nightmares because he was too unwell in this life to give me closure. He asked me to stand tall. To take the heat and never leave the kitchen. He stripped me of everything I was and thought I was. I lost my identity over and over again. I could not picture myself as his wife. I didn't know myself as divorced because now we would never be. And when I told people I didn't know myself as divorced they asked, "What does it matter?" It mattered because instead of a conversation, Michael made an executive decision. Whether in a diseased mental state or not. And I was once again responding, pulled by a tether to actions out of my control.

    I felt wholly valid in my sob story. And entirely wrong in it. The dichotomies of my life were carved into my skin. No one truly knew me, not even myself. The pain inside of me pulsated. It felt like an identity that others were placing on me. It was aware of every breath I took. Aware of every moment that our children experienced because of us. Guilt consumed me for bringing them into this world. For the blurred lines of Michael's love for me saturated in mental torment. For making me stand alone after my sandcastle washed away, just for me to build it again every day. Every moment. Every minute. I tried crying it all out, but it only sat in my stomach. A man was ripped from this world, and I don't know why. Anger and imbalance. Talks of gratitude that felt like I was more grateful for my life than that of another's. Weren't these evil thoughts that made me feel free? Alone I sat on every floor after my legs gave out. Again, and again.

Until one day the pain felt small enough to tuck away in my pocket. The sword I held was ready to slay anything coming my way. It was duct taped to my hand but loosened from blood, sweat, and tears that stained my denim jeans. The tornado that stood before me ceased, dropping all its contents the moment he died. There is no battle anymore. Only the one in my heart. For years, I constantly reminded myself I was not safe around him. I had to be on the defense for so long. I felt like I could only do this if he were the villain. I was afraid to feel the love I had for him lest I drop my guard and return to toxic patterns.

But when someone dies of suicide, they cannot be the villain. He was suffering; why did it have to come to this, though? Why did it come to this before everyone could believe me that he needed help? For me to understand his dragon. I fought so hard only for all the pieces to come crashing down. My mind consumed me with the lack of communication and defenses every human has. The one that is killing us all. The one my children are growing up into. We have to do better.

Psychologist, Dr. Jordan Peterson says regarding PTSD, "Nietzsche said if you look into an abyss for too long, you risk having the abyss gaze back into you. The idea is that if you look at something monstrous, you have a tendency of becoming a monster. And people are often very afraid of looking at monstrous things exactly for that reason. And then the question is, should you turn into a monster? And the answer is yes, you should. But you should do so voluntarily and not accidentally, and you should do it with good in mind. Rather than falling prey to it by possession because that's the alternative. How does it possess you? That's easy; your suffering makes you bitter. Your bitterness makes you resentful. Your resentment makes you vengeful."

I was unable to avoid looking at any of it, my depression, grief, and PTSD. While simultaneously looking at it all the time. Unwilling to acknowledge that a human did this to me, causing me to completely lose myself and all sense of security and safety. And I am also human. I have the same capabilities. Every human does. It would take me another year to unpack what it all meant and to realize how my pain had put me in fight mode—to avoid, at all costs, bringing this deep well of pain to myself or anyone else again.

The day after the one-year mark, I reflected on all the other dates. Picking out a casket from the catalog, Raela's birthday five days later, driving to Vegas, the funeral, eulogy, and then driving home to a quiet and empty house.

TAPS FAMILY CAMP

The kids and I headed to our first Military surviving families camp in Julian, California. It was a camp put on by the Tragedy Assistance Program for Survivors (TAPS). When we arrived, four people stood by the entrance to greet us. Was this for real? The badges. The goodie bags. The fundraiser blankets. *Do we belong here? Michael what have you done?* I thought. *People raised money for us to go to a camp? Because of you?* It was a slap in the face out of denial for a moment. *I don't belong here; we were getting divorced. This is not for me. It's for the children. I'm merely the chaperone.* These thoughts did their best to sooth me back out of reality.

When it was time for the first gathering, we found our seats and the program began. We broke off into groups, the kids going to their camps by age, and the parents met separately for a support group. The outside doors open, then shut. The chairs were set in a circle. As the meeting started, we were to introduce ourselves. My heart raced out of my chest even before it was my turn. I stood tall for my children.

"I was with my husband for ten years, married six. We have two children, Ronan who's six and Raela who's four. I was going through a divorce, and it was not good. I'm here for my kids but not really a spouse."

I felt the room turn, then quietly, "Yeah, me too." I looked up at the woman, Loren, who would later become a close friend. "Me too," another says. It seemed that my tragic story was actually quite familiar in this setting. I had found a room where I didn't turn heads because I was where it was normal. Thank GOD! Relief filled me, as did dismay. *How was this so common?*

As the peer support group ended, the facilitator encouraged, "While we are up here, rest. Let us entertain your kids while you rest. If they are being wild and crazy, we will tell them they are crossing a line. But allow us to do that. We want everyone to feel safe to unwind for a few days. We are in a position to help, so let us. Let your kids' freak flag fly." A phrase that I was hesitant to lean into but once I did, brought so much authenticity to my life.

Positive for Everyone

A week before Christmas, my dad implored, "Can your mom please see the kids on Christmas? Her heart is broken."

I texted my dad that they could come over but asked them to stay in the driveway, keep it to 45 minutes, and bring their dog, Miles. I figured that with these limitations and requests in place, we could have a short but peaceful encounter.

As soon as I saw them, I knew my hopes would be dashed. They came with a few presents for the kids. No dog. And walk straight into the house. I escorted them back outside to sit on the bench out there. When the kids opened their presents, they asked where Miles was. My mom responded, "Maybe when you guys come to our house, you can see the dog."

"Why haven't you come over in a long time?"

"Sometimes you have to wait to be invited, Ronan."

At first, this frustrated me. I did not want the dog used as leverage. I wanted no leverage at all in a situation where grandparents should love on their grandchildren. Then I thought about how they did need to wait to be invited. To Ronan, it meant that Ronan's mom wasn't letting Grandma come over.

When that was only part of it. I was waiting until boundaries could be discussed to allow everyone to have a peaceful time around each other.

My parents left and I was left frustrated. I would later think and discuss with my therapist more ways to better define boundaries to make the next encounter positive for everyone. The following week, my mom asked to bring the dog over and play in our backyard. I agreed. This would become a weekly event. Although it was hard for me to be around my parents without being frustrated, I could tell they were trying and that's all I could ask for. It gave me a chance to clean up Sunday afternoons before Ronan started school for the week. It was a bare minimum win-win.

Work Events of 2022/23

Throughout 2022, I was blessed to work for many concerts including Justin Bieber, Toto/Journey, opening day at Snapdragon Stadium, bull riding, Michael Bublé, The Killers, and the Lumineers. It was a year of healing, and I was grateful to be part of the team. In 2023, I got to work at a Jordan Peterson lecture, The Eagles, Muse, Blink 182, Beach Boys, Depeche Mode and many other events.

2023

Journal Entry:

He is a part of me. I don't want to say a large part. But maybe so. He's the one that for ten years, I did everything with. He's a voice in my head. He's why I formed the habits I did. He is in my children. The most fundamental part of who I am. A mother. I say that with pride. They are my world. My greatest blessing is being with them. And they are him. At first, this book was a vomit of my trauma. Then, it was a way to put it to rest. I hope my children learn about their father, but most importantly, learn about mental illness. I hope people see that I'm writing about the mask he wore. And although it is hard to remember him ever being alive, he was. The biggest gaslight of my life. Was he ever even real, or am I dreaming inside a mental institution?

IT WAS ZERO PERCENT

To say my body kept score of everything is a gross understatement. I have done everything I can to release the trapped emotions in my body. I must constantly be aware of when I tense up or forget to breathe. It had been a year and four months since Michael died. A year since I moved out of my parents' house. At this time in my life, I told everyone that there was very little I could handle when it came to aggression. I could handle an aggressive patient, but when it came to my coworkers, friends, or family, it was zero percent.

At one point, an attempt to solve a problem resulted in miscommunication between myself and another. A mild comment was made and while I might be able to handle that today, at the time, I could not. I kept my circle small along with my activities. When I explained this, the person responded "Sorry, I was stressed." I do understand why she was stressed; I just wasn't in a position to hold space for it. Within twenty minutes, my body had already taken over.

I started to lose range of motion in my shoulder. I ended up going to urgent care after a few days when I could not move it an inch. I was put on steroids for Frozen Shoulder Syndrome, which gave me such horrible nightmares I thought, "If I can imagine such evil, there must be a God." I could not sleep. Instead, I spent the night sitting on the floor in the kitchen, trembling. I wouldn't say I believed in God then, but I knew what I dreamt was demonic, and if there is evil, there must be good. There had to be a God after what I saw. That was as far as that thought went, but it changed me.

I have worked on checking in with my body and trying to control my panic attacks. What I have found most helpful with panic attacks is that I need to stop suppressing them or telling myself I am overreacting. I have to ride it out. I have to know that whatever feeling was triggering me is being brought up so I could release it. Now, I can feel when panic starts to set in. I get discouraged, shower, and try not to pass out from holding my breath. I remember to breathe and know that each negative pattern and trauma is a reminder to be mindful. When it's over, I am fine, and remind myself that I am fine. Retraining my mind to feel safe has taken a lot of time. I am not there yet, but closer every time.

Do You Believe in God?

Loren from TAPS invited me to a support group called Never Alone Widows at a church in San Clemente. I was hesitant to go to a church, a place where I felt I didn't belong. But the thought intrigued me. A place with widows sounded daunting, yet it drew me in. Before the group, the kids and I arrived early and went to the San Clemente Pier. The kids played in the sand and slowly crept their tiny toes into the waves. As I tried not to think about what I was about to walk into, I also found myself in the waves, not worried about the aftermath of this split-second decision.

Covered in the healing powers of the salty ocean, my family walked into the church. I dropped off the kids at childcare, then walked up the long, daunting stairs and into the room. Dinner was served. I grabbed a plate they so graciously provided and picked a random chair. I was around people for the first time who had the same marital status as me. They could feel the cloud of anxiety as I sat claiming my space.

"Do you believe in God?" One woman asked me. It pierced my soul. I don't belong here. It seemed to be an everlasting burn in my soul. I don't belong here.

I replied, "No, but I wish I did." *It sure would have made life easier,* I thought. I was envious that they had faith in a God to get them through their grief, but I was alone. My soul sank.

"Where are you from?"

"San Diego," I traveled so far to be in a room I didn't belong in, with people who weren't going through a divorce when their spouse died.

"Oh. So is the speaker today. He's a pastor of a church in San Diego." Interesting. And then it began.

The pastor started speaking of losing his wife to suicide. It happened three months before Michael's death.

"I've spoken to many groups of people. I've told my story many times. But this, by far, is the hardest. A room full of widows. People who understood. When I say my wife died in any other room you can feel the air sucked out. But here I am in a room where you all can say, 'Yeah, me too.'"

He talked about how he understood those in a faith crisis. It made sense, he said. He was among the broken hearts of those in the room. He spoke out loud of his nervousness, and the rawness of his words forced me to turn my head towards him and listen. I felt like a hand reached down to the center of Hell and ripped me out. I sat there, unsure what to do with the first time I felt the presence of God's love for me. It was undeniable and powerful. So powerful that I had to put the feeling away, too strong for me to acknowledge.

He finished his speech, and we started our table discussions. On the drive home, I looked at my children asleep in the rearview mirror. My world again felt upside down, or maybe, I thought, it was becoming right-side up, finally. Out of curiosity, I looked up the speaker. I started to follow his church on social media, which was, coincidentally, five minutes from my house.

AT THEIR MERCY

After three and a half months of my parents coming over once a week, one night, as I was putting the kids to bed, my dad came over unannounced. In his hand was a new rental agreement. He was raising my rent to the maximum amount the law allowed him to. I was at their mercy because I was on a month-to-month lease, and this property had been within my budget. If I refused to pay the raised rent, they could evict me. Which meant I would have to move back to Utah. My entire sense of stability and feeling like I was home disappeared. *When would they raise the rent again? When would they force me out?* I lay with Ronan and sobbed. I couldn't control myself. I looked around his room and imagined having to pack up his stability, his home. I didn't want him or me to have to start all over in a different state. I just wanted to start my life. Ronan asked why I was crying, so I told him I was in shock. I think I scared him. I texted my parents, "Do not contact me unless it is landlord related." Then I put my phone away and cried some more.

The following week was Easter. While getting ready to leave for work, I heard the doorbell ring. I figured it was the babysitter, so I answered the door. David and my mom stood there with Easter baskets for the kids. The kids ran out, grabbed all the candies, squealing, "I love you! Thank you!! Come play with us!"

In the distance, the babysitter walked up the driveway. I needed to leave for work immediately. I dragged my children inside and threw their baskets in the trash. I told them they could have some of our candies, but Grandma should have not done that.

I said, "Remember when they raised my rent? They used that money to buy this. So actually, keep it, but know it's a gift from me, not them." Maybe I should not have said that. But I did. And then I left for work. I started my drive as hot tears poured out. It was hard to breathe. I called my sister who had ironically asked me if I was open to repairing my relationship with my mom earlier that day. I told her they had come over unannounced, which made me feel like they could and would come over any time—and they did.

When I got to work, I usually managed to collect myself, but nothing I tried worked this time. I kept shaking, frustrated at myself for being unable to snap out of it. I kept telling myself, I was fine, I was safe, yet I couldn't stop shaking. My coworker approached me and told me I could sit in the back room until I could collect myself. That frustrated me more. *I am the one who is supposed to be responding to others. I can't be in the back room because of this!* But I took some deep breaths, collected myself, and enjoyed the concert. I texted David and my mom again, stating that I did not appreciate them coming over unannounced and not to contact me again unless it was landlord related. Again, we did not speak for months.

A Crushed Soul

Steve walked through the door and kissed me. We moved to the couch, where he asked about my day, and we giggled in our usual fashion. He held me close, and we were once again the only ones on the planet.

Past the four walls of the house, nothing else existed while we were together. Then, in an all too familiar tone of our fluctuating relationship, he put both of his hands over his face and cried.

After two years of trying to go "all in" with dating me and overcoming his fear of commitment, he just didn't know how to move forward because the moment he left my side, he became depressed. I was his perfect person, but he could not introduce me to his parents or friends. I became a fragmented part of his life that he entered and exited time after time. He showed up at my door, looked me in the eyes, and I'd let him in.

He felt he could be a better person out on his own, without me. Honestly, I don't know what he meant, and I don't think he did either. On my living room couch, he claimed that I was holding him back from his potential. He wanted to be someone's "number one", which was impossible since I had kids. This was the first I heard of my children being a problem for him. He wanted to go camping with just me, or maybe me and one kid, but not two. He couldn't specify which child, but when he envisioned it, there was only one child in the picture. He wanted to be spontaneous. He thought that was impossible with kids. I was utterly confused and outright enraged. Wrath filled my body, my hands balled up into fists. I stood. In my nightgown with tender sleeping children in the next room, I told him to sit down at the table. I wasn't done with him.

He shrunk into his seat. Tears welled in his eyes as my chest grew tight and I fumed over the way he treated my children so insignificantly. *When did he realize I came with children?*

"What would have happened if you got me pregnant, Steve? What would have happened then?" I questioned.

"I would have raised above and settled down," he said confidently as if to cling tightly to the dignity he told himself he had.

"Take yourself out with the trash because that is what you are. Get out. Leave!" Rage consumed every ounce of my being as he ran out and shut the door behind him. *Trash taken out,* I thought. He was trash.

I carried my sleeping children and put them in my bed. In shock, I lay awake for hours listening to their rhythmic breaths against my scattered thoughts. Anger turned to depression as I realized he would never understand the love that comes from being their parent. Beneath it all, I mourned for the fact that he used them as an excuse because there is no way that was true —and if it was, what had he been suppressing for two years to be present for me and my babies? *I did not know this man. I don't think this man knew himself.* And with that thought, I fell asleep.

The next day, he called apologizing and trying to explain himself. He held firm in his decision to end things, but changed the narrative like an improv monologue, trying to understand his own decision in real time.

He said, "We are all just wild animals living in an evolved world." That was not our previous conversation throughout the years. He flipped the script entirely. When I mentioned therapy, he yelled, "Therapy won't change the fact that you have kids, Mariah!" And that was the end. He was right. His view on that disturbed me to my core. At the beginning of our relationship, I had told him that if he ever yelled at me, there was no coming back. So he yelled. Knowing I would never contact him again after that. I sat there on the other side, stunned.

He told me he would call me later but there was only so much "feeling like sh*t he could take." He didn't call me back. There was nothing else left to say. The last thing I did was yell back "I hate you!"

My soul was broken. Depression and fury consumed me.

I felt the weight of a crushed soul. No words describe being unable to show up for your kids. A depression so deep you physically cannot move without bursting into tears. A fading friendship is nothing compared to someone actively saying, "I do not want what you have to offer," or "I would rather go my whole life not talking to you over having to figure this out or sit and have a conversation and heal myself." Instead, he chose to walk away. I didn't mean to heal himself so we could live happily ever after. I meant to heal enough to understand what scared him so much. What made our relationship "impossible?" He offered no closure. Just an eject button. All this after creating this life where he told me over and over again to rely on him and to come to him when in crisis.

Getting the carpet ripped from under me is the most accurate description I can think of. Except there was no floor beneath the carpet —just a huge hole that sent me straight to rock bottom. When I finally could shower, I lay on the bathroom floor unable to move. I remembered when I started dating Steve, I would get excited and be able to shower, able to take care of myself. It had come full circle, landing back on me to pick myself up.

As I lay wrapped in a towel on the floor, Kacy called me to drop off gear for work. I got up, dressed, and sat in her car without a word. It was one of the few moments in my life where I was brutally honest, even to myself, about my emotions. Kacy held space for it. Then, I went back into my cave and hibernated. I signed my kids up for camp because of the extreme guilt I felt that they were stuck inside and on screens because I could not move. I had no coping skills.

After I dropped the kids off at camp, I let all my pain out. At least, I attempted to. I reached out to my therapist and tried sound therapy and hypnosis. I bought crystals. I threw everything I could to pull myself out of that pit. And then on day five, I erupted. I got out of the shower and yelled at Michael. *He did this to us. He left us!* I had chosen Michael as my person for a decade. *It was supposed to be him. He didn't choose healing or rehab or amends. He died!* For a moment, I let myself blame him for everything. I sat in my disappointment that I wasn't enough for Michael to get healthy and address his PTSD.

He forced my hand to leave because he became unsafe to be around, and then he died. His children, he left them. I looked up at the sky and then down to the center of the earth, unsure where his spirit landed, and I screamed. I told him to *get us out of all this pain*, and he owed me that, I exclaimed to the Heavens or Hell. And then, standing in the middle of my room, I fell to my knees. I had nothing left in me. I was in torrential pain.

I pleaded with God to give me peace, and I would do whatever he wanted. I would go to church. I would be brave enough to walk through those doors. Just give me peace, I begged in humility and unnerving desperation.

And just like that, my pain was lifted, gone. Peace I had never experienced before filled me. I sat there and felt okay, even though it was just for a few minutes. But I felt it, and then the feeling passed. Despair consumed me again. But this time, with a deep knowledge of God, of peace. Breaking up with Steve wasn't about just losing him as a person. He was the floodgates opening to everything. He was the dam and the band aid.

I picked myself up. I walked out of my room and to my kitchen. My emotional state matched my living quarters. I pulled out a chair and stared at the dishes. I looked at the crafts everywhere. Then I thought to myself, *I feel horrible. I feel absolutely at the bottom of this hole. And yet, I do not want to live in a mess. I can still be sad and kind to myself.* I cleaned up a dish and vacuumed rugs one by one. I picked up all my broken pieces and held them in my hands. And then I cleaned. It was a slow, slow burn. I could barely see the progress in my broken heart.

However, as the days passed, I realized Steve had accepted his decision. He was okay not talking to me. That realization hurt. Rejection was deeply engraved in my heart. He chose an easier life without me than a life with me. The days he said I was his dream girl were true until they weren't. His dream girl was actually a woman with only child. She was a female mutual friend, and 50 weeks later remarked that she was so grateful they went on their first date a year prior, two weeks before he called it off with me.

Up was down, and down was up. I had to come to terms with the fact that down was down, and up was up. This was the reality of choice, for everyone. It was his choice to walk away. It was in the social contract. I felt like this was karma. I still do. When people say, "I hope you don't feel like Michael dying was your fault." The truth is, I do, and I don't. But I do know whatever pain I caused Michael; karma got me back with Steve. Please know that I have paid.

Promise To God

I had made my promise to God. I hadn't forgotten, but I was unable to decipher my next move. Growing up Mormon, going to other churches, or reading any literature not approved by the Mormon religion was deeply frowned upon and outright forbidden. Although I hadn't stepped foot in a church in over four years, it was still ingrained in me. I didn't know what being a Christian looked like. I was stepping onto the Christian's ball field with no glove. I didn't know that I didn't need one. Paralyzed by this, I did my best and made promises to myself and God. Now, I just had to figure out how to deliver. Then Ashley came over with her friend, Eunice.

My friend Ashley had shown up with divine timing many times. Michael and I had known her since 2011, when we met at a Mormon church. Eunice, who came along with her, was very vocal about being a Christian. I quickly opened up to her about my confusion. She had me pull up the church's website, register my kids for childcare, and told me everything I needed to do, including arriving 20 minutes early. She told me there would be a welcome crew and to talk to them to find out where the sermon would be. I had a rough road map and decided to go the next day.

The next day I packed my kids in the car like always. I took the wheel and wondered if Jesus would take it from me through this church. That day, I made the decision to take my children's hands and lead them into a, hopefully, hand-in-hand relationship with God. One that I was still trying to figure out myself. All I knew was I needed to hold onto my peace. Eunice texted me every step of the way. Even though I walked in alone with my children, I felt like I had support. I sat in the back pew, and astonishingly, lightning didn't strike me when I entered.

As the band played, I wept silently. I went back every week, and every week I cried. I'm not sure what was released with the music, but layers of grief melted off me.

One Sunday, the pastor spoke about his journey. It was similar to the speech I heard in San Clemente. I knew what he was going to say. But as he said it, my body crumpled, feeling the weight of his words—the ones I also experienced. As the closing song played, I ran out of church and straight to Raela. I fell on my knees in front of her, holding her and sobbing. My now friend Hannah approached me, held my hands, and prayed for me. When I could collect myself, she hugged me, and I went to get Ronan. As I pulled into my driveway and brought my children inside, I looked deeply within myself and wondered if I would ever know what it was supposed to feel like to be a widow. In that moment, I felt awfully close to that reality.

Date with Doug

After texting Doug for a few weeks as friends, he finally said it. The thing I was nervous about him saying because I didn't want to make things awkward at work. He said he liked me and wanted to take me on a date. I was also having fun talking to him, but I did not know up from down when it came to dating. I did know in my heart that I would be a good person to whoever I dated. I knew that whatever trauma I would carry over and attempt to heal would not come at the expense of the person I was with. This was my justification to date Doug.

I did not want to make things awkward, so I agreed to hang out as friends. We sat across from each other as we ate dinner. I kept reminding him we were friends, but I was oddly curious about him. I wanted to know more about him. We laughed and laughed at dinner, and when the check came, he said we still had time to see the sunset.

He drove my car, and I became the DJ. He asked me what kind of music I liked and thanks to my school bus days, there was a wide variety. I played him some favorites. We sat and watched the sunset, both proclaiming that we had had our hearts broken too many times to let that happen again. He even had a tattoo that represented that.

I told him I dug myself out of too much heartbreak and was done with that. My heart could not handle any more. It also cannot and will not handle any aggression. *I know now it will not handle excessive drinking as well.* He agreed, and we drove to a bar for his friend's birthday. The party was fun. His friends were fun. I told him this could be "not *just friends* hanging out." It could be a date if he wanted it to be. I typically never drink, but I had one with him. It felt nice. Like what normal people did.

The weeks went on, and we video called every night. We were learning everything about each other. Doug was an answer to my prayers. In more ways than one, for sure. Even as we were actively talking, I knew why he came into my life. I had hoped it was for longer than just this. But I had prayed for years to be reminded why I loved Michael. To know if I ever did. Because after everything, it was impossible to see the good. The man I married and had two kids with, I could no longer see that man. That was tragic. The grief of that was too hard to hold. So, I dissociated and survived until Doug came in.

Doug might not see the beauty in this. He might feel taken advantage of. But his playfulness, the attention he gave me, and how he made me feel special and important, transported me back to when Michael and I first started dating. When Michael thought it was cool that I was an EMT. When he was proud to show me to his family. When he answered my phone call on the first ring. When the man who got bored of everyone didn't get bored of me. Or at the very least, I could always get his attention back.

All this happened again with Doug. Doug showed me that I had fallen in love with Michael. That Michael did love me. I knew Doug loved me, too and I loved Doug right back. Not because I missed Michael, but because I saw the good. I saw the men who saw me, which makes how things ended with Doug downright tragic. Doug's pain was familiar to me, but so was his goodness. No one can take that away from us. From Michael and I. And from Doug and I.

As the weeks went by, I met Doug's children. We were fully involved and invested in each other's lives. I dove right in again. I truly meant it when I said I was up for what Doug was showing me; I allowed myself to be vulnerable, too. But there was an anger deep inside Doug that he was hiding from me. It's why he shouldn't have asked to date me. But I didn't know that yet. At the time, all of his goodness was truly genuine.

One night, he was still over after I had put the kids to bed. The sun had gone down like it naturally does every night, but the transition to night had not registered. Suddenly, my mind realized it was dark outside, and a man was in my house. Doug wasn't doing anything but standing in my kitchen, yet it flooded me with anxiety. I froze and could think of nothing but, "There's a man in my house," repeatedly until I couldn't feel my fingers or my face. I got lightheaded, and my knee buckled. I was on the floor and there was still a man in my house.

I told him the best I could that I was having a panic attack. He asked if he needed to leave because he was, after all, "the man in the house." I shook my head that it was okay to stay, and then he did something instinctual and sweet. He lay on the ground next to me while I sat, curled with my hands behind my head trying to breathe. He made himself as physically small as possible. I'm unsure if he knew what he was doing but he tried to eliminate my fear by becoming quiet, still, and small. It worked. I needed to focus on breathing. It was the first textbook panic attack that I remember getting through. Normally, I hold my breath subconsciously until I pass out. He made me feel safe and because of that, I let more of my guard down.

Doug and I attempted to work a few shifts together. I was excited because we didn't have much time together to begin with. On our first shift together, we walked into the first aid room, and he leaned in to kiss me. Before I knew what I had done, I had shoved him so hard I knocked the wind out of him. I explained to him that it was highly inappropriate. He needed to keep his hands to himself. I was not a prize. I was at work, and trying to cross that boundary is unprofessional and made me feel like a trophy. He laid off the rest of the shift.

We tried again at another event, and he was respectful but pushed to hold my hand a few times. Again, I said it may make you feel cool or look good, but it makes me sick. We were working. The answer is no. Finally, on the last shift I worked, he stopped by for about an hour. We were walking around, and he tried to kiss me again. When I told him he was no longer allowed to work with me or come to work with me, he said, "I don't care. You needed a kiss, so I gave you one." It was not worth it.

Gingerbread Houses

In December, a foundation for military families who had lost someone in service invited the kids and me to a Christmas party. I stepped out of the car and walked into the building, not knowing the divine intervention that would unfold in the next hour.

The event was on the second floor, so we took the elevator. As the elevator doors opened into the room for the event, my eyes caught someone I hadn't seen since I was a child.

"Mika?" I said, incredulously as my eyes bugged out. Mika was my childhood best friend, Emma's, father, who had been a big part of my life for four years. He looked back at me, just as surprised, and said "Mariah?" At the same time, we asked what the other was doing here. After our stunned silence, I explained, "My husband and my kid's dad died. He was in the Military."

"Oh, you should meet my wife, Susie. Her husband did as well, and I remarried her."

Internally, I froze. I already knew this. I knew Susie. I attended her husband's funeral with Emma when I was 10 years old. Nineteen years ago, I sat graveside, not knowing that I would do the same one day, except as the wife. I knew Susie because I would run up to her late husband and get his biggest hugs every time he returned from deployment and was at church. I went to Sunday school with her children. Mika brought me over to Susie, and I introduced myself. She remembered me. Her son Andy sat there with his wife and two kids. Andy remembered me, too.

"I shared a tent with your brother at a Scouts camp out."

I shot back "I'm sorry about that." We laughed.

Susie asked why I was there as well. It was a room no one wanted to be in but was grateful for its existence. I told her. She asked about my parents and my siblings. I gave her the basics. Where they lived and what they did for work. I kept it surface level. After all, she only knew me only as a 10-year-old girl running around in a dress at church, complaining about not being able to wear pants to climb trees.

She continued with the small talk, asking if my family supported me. I said I had social security and could move into my own place because of it. That's not what she meant, but it was what I was used to being asked. How am I paying my bills? Everyone wants to know. When I say this to others, they don't understand the depth of pain it brings me. But Susie did. She received the same benefits—enough to stay home and raise her children.

What most don't understand is that our spouses entered the Military and then we were handed a monetary amount that does its best to equate to their life. That's haunting. That's not Mai Tai's on a tropical island. It's an overwhelmingly disparaging feeling when your spouse's life ends, and you, as the next of kin, get funds, and live off it. They are raising their surviving children off of it and using it for babysitters so the surviving spouse can go to work. It's used for sports so a coach can teach their child to throw the ball their dad should have taught them. It's used to take them to the doctors and make decisions alone regarding the healthcare their lives provided them. These surviving spouses and children live in a shadow of grief and tragic circumstances that define them now.

She meant if my family was supporting me emotionally. I responded only with a flood of tears. After a moment, I said, "They just don't understand."

Of course, she wanted me to elaborate. I was trying to give my family an out, saying they didn't understand. That could have been enough for Susie. After all, I just started talking to her. But she continued her questions.

I told her that my mom, on multiple occasions, made comments to me, and I found myself having to recover after being around her. I found myself in a defensive position, and still, even after knowing what I was doing was right, her voice rattled in my head. When someone devalues your experience, removing their words and actions from your heart is much more complicated than actual forgiveness. It took me a long time to understand that when people say judgmental things, they are usually processing their own grief. While it's not an excuse for her actions, I think my mom was trying to process her pain and discomfort. That's how I have come to terms with it.

Shortly after Micheal died, I was in the car with my mom. I told her how hard all of this was, how I'm like the old ladies in the church's back pew, on widow's row. She scoffed and said I am not like those women. *But they are the only widows I know,* I thought, my only baseline. And yes, they were married a lot longer, didn't have a tragic almost divorce, and weren't in their 20s, but it was the only association I had with the word, that is, until now. I was put into an entire classification that I did not understand.

I asked her, "What other 29-year-old widow do you know?" It was an attempt to tell her there is no rule book. I belong here, and I belong there.

Susie understood. Suddenly, I realized I hadn't paid any attention to my children throughout our conversation. I was stuck in a vacuum and coming out of it now. I turned around and breathed a sigh of relief seeing Mika making gingerbread houses with them. He talked to and helped them for however long while I sat there and felt seen and heard for the first time in a very long time. She asked my permission to send a picture of Mika with my kids and their gingerbread houses to my parents.

Later, Susie texted me and wrote that she would like to talk to my parents about how they could support me. She was hopeful she could try to get them to understand since she had also walked this path. She asked me if there was anything I wished to tell my parents so she could pass the message along. I left it to her experience and wisdom because I didn't know how to approach them. All I knew was it felt like divine intervention for Susie and Mika to be there. On top of that, they stepped into the role to help willingly without me asking. I had to leave it in God's hands.

Susie and Mika had lunch with my parents, letting me know it went well and that it was great to catch up with them. They said my parents were open to reconciliation on my terms. I was shocked but it was, after all, divine intervention. I wrote an email to my parents to start the conversation.

The email in summary:

> There is no taking back what has been said or done. I truly do not know why things were said to me that were. I do not agree with events of the past. However, there is no way to go back and resolve it. I'm agreeing to not go over everything. If there is something that you think you need to hear an apology from me, let me know. I will

explain or apologize for whatever you need so long as they personally address something I have said or done directly to you. I will not engage in anything that was perceived or someone thinks I have done to an outside party. That party or person can ask me themselves. I welcome it.

Finally, I have always had a strained relationship with my siblings. I am not sure what cause this. I am asking that as the leaders of the family, you do your best to intervene. This could look something like coordinating one or two times a month. We all commit to getting together to share a meal possibly out at dinner or a picnic at the park. Somewhere neutral. I'm also asking that you ask my siblings to list their grievances with me and let me know what I have done to cause them to distance themselves from me.

I think some boundaries should be:

- When someone is talking about a subject that is off limits simply saying "No" means we stop all conversation and redirect.

- If a child asks a question, I will address and tell my children the truth.

My concern with bringing the kids around is that we will fall into this pattern again. I'm asking that you help develop solutions and strategies to ensure we don't put the children through this again. I'm also asking that you tell me what you need from me so that I don't potentially trigger you into saying or doing something hurtful. I understand it goes both ways. I will commit to doing my part as well once I am let known to my part.

I will meet with Mom's therapist as soon as she emails me. I had offered to meet separately with her in hopes the therapist could filter what my mom had to say as well as filter what I had to say so that we could make progress on repairing our relationship.

    My dad texted me, thanking me for the nice email and that he was sure we could find a way forward. I sunk into my bed reading that. *Was I finally home?* Peace came over me. A few other emails were exchanged, with the last one from my dad stating that he did not know anything about my perspective. He wanted to have several face-to-face conversations to iron it all out since there was a lot to discuss.

I responded in short that:

> My primary problem is that I do not feel heard when I express my concerns. I'm asking you to make the home safer and like a forever home for your daughter and grandchildren. I have a financial advisor and a budget. That is why when I look at the current situation, I see that it is not sustainable if rent continues to rise. Emotionally and financially.
>
> I appreciate that we are starting this conversation. Please understand that I love and enjoy this house, but it has never felt like home. When I sent you the other email and got your text back, I felt relieved that maybe I could actually be home.
>
> My focus is healing myself, healing my children, and creating a home of peace. We have yet to land. They feel it. I will live in this home as long as I can. I will do it in a way that protects me. I hate that I feel that I

have to defend myself from you. Put me at ease. PLEASE.

He said again that he had no idea my perspective and there was a lot to unpack. He suggested we meet again in person. My last email to him said this:

Maybe you can talk to your bishop or find a licensed professional to sit with all of us to unpack this. You said you were not aware of my perspective. That raises a lot of flags for me. I feel there is a lot more we need to discuss. I assumed a lot. I most definitely misunderstood your efforts to help me. Find an unbiased person to sit with us as we discuss because there is a lot more we need to go over.

He has yet to set up a time. Life is so short. It is so hard to put my heart in the hands of people who do not understand how quickly life goes.

On December 20th, I called Lana, a long-time friend of my mom's and a second mom to me. I owe a lot to her for my early childhood. I hear even to this day that I insisted on sleepovers at her house even at two years old. Savannah, my younger sister, and I would spend so much time there exploring Lana's backyard, making cinnamon toast, and playing with her kids and nieces and nephews. It was an endless amount of fun. Every Christmas, she would give us a bag of peanut M&M's, and we would watch Christmas movies in her recliners. I loved Mama Lana. A few years before, she had let me borrow a piano keyboard. I called her because I was ready to return it. She mentioned that she was trying to learn how to print photos, so I offered to show her how to do that on her phone.

While outside loading the piano, my mom walked by with her dog. The kids waved and said hi. She waved back and kept walking. I stood there with her friend of over 30 years and her grandkids whom she hadn't spoken to in almost a year. I thought back to Easter. She could have used this as an excuse to come over, but she didn't. She waved and kept walking. I assumed she was being respectful to me. She seemed to listen to the boundaries I requested in the email.

"Mom," I called as she walked away. My mom paused and looked back. "Do you want to come over for a bit?" I knew this would ruin any chance I would have at getting the rent to decrease. But I also hated that my children were seen as leverage. So, I took a deep breath and thought this could be divine intervention. No more leverage. The kids asked why she hadn't come over, and my mom said to ask me. Perfect. She listened. We started to walk inside, and my mom said goodbye. She wasn't pushing. "Mom, do you want to play in the backyard with the kids while I help Lana?" Silently she walked to the backyard.

After Lana left, I told the kids it was time for dinner. I offered to have my mom come in and read a book to the kids while they ate, on the condition that the kids promised to let her leave without a fit. She read the book. Divine intervention, I remind myself. Even if it wasn't, I let myself believe that it was. I had to believe that. She finished the book and left. The house was not on fire. Everything was okay.

On Christmas, she asked to bring presents to the kids. I agreed. It was the same thing; presents, outside, dinner, book, goodnight. I felt good about it. Maybe even a little hopeful about a routine. A week later, I met with my mom's therapist.

As the video call started, I tried to sum up the fracture that had occurred as quickly as possible. I explained that I had to learn to understand that my mom was not a crisis responder. I gave the example of when I had begged her to be on the next flight to come pick me up in Pennsylvania, she was not on the next flight. I didn't mean to be hurtful in any way. I knew there was no winning in the position I put my mom in. But there was a lot of learning for me.

From my childhood, and especially since I had Ronan, I had to construct a box that my mom fit in. It was the box of "friend". We went to bakeries. We went out to eat. Sometimes, we shopped. We talked about how others were doing. But we didn't talk about anything personal, and she didn't ask. It became hard to talk about it because everything seemed to be met with resistance.

Choosing to leave Michael exhausted me. I came to my parents' home for refuge, to escape and to heal. I was grateful for this, but I checked out and became numb to survive again. Healing would come, I hoped.

After I explained my side, the therapist said some interesting things. She said that when she talked to my mom, my mom disclosed, "When Mariah was younger, she was the only kid I didn't know how to comfort. Her emotions were much bigger than my other children, and I didn't know how to help her."

I was shocked to hear this. I thought about it and said, "I don't remember that. But I do know that I don't like being hugged. Maybe I pushed her away when she would try?"

Her next question took me a while to answer. I had to think about it over the next few days. She said that I had my mom in a tiny box. I added that my mom had come over to play in the backyards twice. She was shocked, as was I, that this happened. So, she inquired if I was open to expanding the box. I had never thought about it. I never imagined my mom would become open to accepting me as I was. It had taken me a lot to accept my mom as she was, albeit, in her tiny box.

I couldn't give the therapist a clear response. I said I wasn't sure I was open to that. But I disclose that if she wanted to be in my kids' life on a once-a-week or twice-a-month basis for an hour or two as a person who loves my kids, I would allow that.

Over the next six months, my mother's box grew bigger and bigger. She became a supportive person for me, and slowly, we started having more and more conversations. Ronan and Raela have grown attached to her. As their mom, that is all I desire, for people to love and invest in them. Every individual decides how deeply they do that. But it is a blessing to watch others actively want to participate in their growth and happiness. I have yet to have my conversation with my dad. The one I had requested in the emails. Dates were agreed on, but those dates came and went. I have a lot I wish to tell my dad—clarification on his end and mine. I'm not sure I will ever get a dad who understands or feels comfortable trying to understand me.

It left a hole in my heart. One that I have filled in with compassion and grace. Sealed up, even knowing closure might not come in this life. I have not received complete closure from a lot of people. There may be people out there who feel they have not received closure from me. But I do know that if I have hope that I am still worth loving., despite all the ways I have fallen or disappointed others then I need to honor the notion that so is everyone else. This doesn't excuse anyone's behavior or mine. It merely invites all to work towards an honorable life. No one is too far gone. Humility is not a hit on the ego, but the most godlike gift we can give to someone. Why wouldn't I be honored to gift that to my fellow man? It's been given to me ten-fold.

CHRISTMAS EVE

I sat there with two minutes left of therapy. Through the screen, I told my therapist, Lauren, how nice it was that Doug was on the way, and he was bringing me coffee beans. At that moment he walked in and sat down on the ground beside me. Bag of beans in hand. I waved it at the camera and Lauren smiled. It was nice. I closed the screen and hugged him. We made coffee and then went to run errands, getting last-minute Christmas presents.

I noticed Doug had been getting a little aggressive. I wasn't sure why because he had just finished a tough evaluation that he had been working on for months. When we got in the car to head home, Doug turned to the backseat and said, "Shut the fu*k up Ronan." Taken aback, I shot back, "Don't say fu*k."

Then Ronan responded, "Yeah Doug, don't say fu*k." Ronan wasn't wrong. Doug retorted, "he's seven, he needs to learn respect." All I said was, "Yeah, and you're forty-two."

Tension was high for the rest of the drive. When we got home, we unloaded the groceries and decided to go to the park. As we pulled out of the driveway, I swear I saw Steve. A truck that looked like his passed us, and I locked eyes with the man who was clearly Steve.

What was he doing? I froze. Doug asked who that was since I obviously knew him, I responded, "My ex." I didn't see how Doug could get mad at me for that. I was absolutely stunned.

We continued our trip to the park. Doug spun out of the driveway and down the hill where he bottomed out the car. Ronan yelped, "Ouch! You hurt my neck." My entire body tensed up. What was I supposed to do? I understood why Doug was thrown by the situation, but at the same time he needed to control himself.

At the park, the kids ran off and Doug sat down. I couldn't totally tell if he was mad, so I went over and sat next to him. He moved me away from him. I told him I understood why he was upset. He said he just found it weird that he was driving by. What business did he have driving by? I agreed. I told him it also upset me, but I had no answers to his questions. I had the same questions. He asked me a few times if I was still seeing him. Of course I wasn't. Doug kept pushing me away.

The following morning, Doug picked us up for church. As we sat down in the sanctuary, Doug put his arm around me. I had noticed that the first time he went to church with me he remarked that it was nice seeing me get something out of it. That progressed to him taking his hat off when he walked in and talking to me about the sermon after. I was seeing a change in him. I knew he liked church, and he said it was where he wanted to be. I believed him. I still do.

That's why it caught me off guard when, during the pastor's sermon, he checked his phone and commented about a text he got from a coworker at full volume like he expected me to join his conversation.

He moved back and forth in his chair like he couldn't sit still. While shuffling around, I asked in all seriousness, "Do you need to go walk around outside?" The truth was, I went to church before he was in the picture. I sat in the seats all by myself. It was nice to have a hand to hold, but there was no way I would have a conversation during the sermon.

He looked a little beat down but then looked forward, stopped moving, and was quiet the rest of the time. I really would not have minded if he went for a walk instead. Looking back, I wish he had listened to his body and known that he needed to do something else. In a split second, I watched him shove down whatever he was feeling and thinking to stare straight forward, almost like he was trained to do so. I went in to get the kids from childcare while Doug stayed outside. When we returned, he was on a video call with his 14-year-old daughter, Megan. He told her he would call her back once we got the kids in the car.

As he drove us through the parking lot, an elderly lady pulled her car out of her parking space in front of us. Doug had his window down and even though we weren't close to her car, he quickly pulled up alongside her and yelled, "That's what happens when you only think about yourself!" He was loud enough that those walking by stopped and looked into our car.

"Doug!" I said without thinking, "Calm down!" Seriously, what was the hurry? He called his daughter back while driving. She was on his ex-wife's phone.

"Hey baby, did you get in trouble and get your phone taken away?" She had. She had apparently asked her mom to buy her an energy drink for her friend but then drank it herself. She had also taken a permanent marker and drawn a skeleton all over her arm. Because of it, Doug hadn't been able to talk to his daughter for about a week. At first, I assumed it was because she was grounded from her phone.

The more I thought about it, though, I realized Doug always wore skeleton shirts. He had one or two Monster drinks daily, as well as multiple cups of coffee. He was profoundly influencing Megan. His daughter was acting out and imitating her dad to seem cool to him, to get his attention.

I don't think Doug would admit that out loud. I believe he would love his daughter no matter what, but when Megan gained his approval from her actions, it only incited more of that behavior. They started taking screenshots of them putting their middle fingers up, while he was driving, and they saved to his ex-wife's phone.

We got home, and Doug kept coughing. He saw Ronan's inhaler and used it. It curbed his cough while he continued talking to Megan. I was making lunch for everyone when Ronan walked in. Doug lunged at Ronan, puffing his chest like a gorilla asserting its dominance. Ronan walked right by unphased.

I told Doug it was time for him to go. Forever. I have promised my children that any anger can be resolved in a conversation. There is no room in my life for aggression. Ever. Anger, fine. It's normal to be upset, but aggression is an absolute hard stop. I have worked on myself and my relationships profusely. I have deep, meaningful friendships and family members because of this. I have done my best to clear my anxiety and PTSD from my physical reaction to aggression. I have done my best and am still working on it. But my best defense for my personal health is to have zero contact.

Doug got up and came into the kitchen saying he would leave. Then he frustratingly shook the chair in and asked to talk to me in the front yard. I grabbed some of his things and met him out front. He had asked for coconut water, so I got him one.

When I walked out and handed it to him, he spat, "I don't want that sh*t." So I threw it in the outside trash five feet away from us. Instead, I handed him his water bottle. When they say "You give people the ammunition to hurt you." Think of this: me handing

374

him the metal water bottle while he is yelled obscenities at me in the driveway. Saying Ronan is a spoiled brat. Asking me if I'm his girlfriend, or his wife, or just playing house with him. Then he yelled, "And don't get me started on Fu*k boy!" I did not know who he was talking about. I didn't have a fu*k boy. I just saw the trash being displayed on my driveway and walked inside. I was done.

As I walked away, the metal water bottle that I handed him suddenly shattered next to me. He had thrown it at my feet so forcefully it broke in two and the metal bottle clanged deafeningly against the concrete.

I turned around and said, "Do not ever contact me ever again. Do not ever show up here ever again." He picked up the evidence of the bottle and drove off with his tires screeching. I thanked God that he left and that it all was caught on the security cameras. We were done. But then he started calling me. I brought my kids inside, turned on security, and felt like a sitting duck. I was scared out of my mind. Call after all after call. Twelve calls in the first thirty minutes after he left. Two, three-minute voicemails. Then, six more phone calls.

He texted that I had his TV, and he wanted it back. With horror, I thought maybe I would just send him money for it. And then I thought I did not want his TV in my house. I dropped the kids off at a friend's house, returned home, and called 9-11. I told them about the bottle, the phone calls, and the threats. I asked them to please stay on the line with me until I had taken the TV outside. They did. I gave them my address, but I was too terrified to give them Doug's name. I put the TV on the side of the house and let Doug know it was ready to be picked up.

He texted that he had picked it up and that if I didn't answer him, he would find me. He threatened to go to my parents, my friend's house, and then call our boss. My boss. I had no control over what he did. When he said he was going to come find me, I called the police back and filled out an official report. I gave them his information. I refused when they said I had every right to a restraining order. The police officer gave me his card, wrote the incident number, and told me to contact him if I changed my mind. They said if he showed up or kept calling, to call 9-11. I agreed.

After the officers completed their report and left, I sat on the floor in Esther's house. Raela jumped on me asking when we would get to go to night church for the Christmas Eve play. They wanted to go. I didn't want to have to compromise my safety for the place I felt God's presence. I had finally found a space where I felt I could see and hear God's message at church.

I didn't know what to do. I feared Doug over trusting God. I was so upset because I worked so hard to have a peaceful life. I felt blindsided by his anger, discouraged in my judgment, and ashamed for bringing this into our lives. So, I did what I would learn to master in the coming months. I sat on the floor and closed my eyes.

I prayed to God, asking, "Is it okay to go to church?" The answer came immediately, as it still does today, and with peace in my heart. It's the answer I always go with.

A resounding yes.

I wanted to go to church, to be safe in the presence of God. So I went. I made my decision to go even as anxiety threatened to pull me down, just like Doug's threats to find me. But I knew what I had to do deep in my bones. Everything else could bog me down but I always relied back on the moment when I asked and God affirmed my decision to go to church. That is the voice I listen to.

We got a parking spot right up front. I took my children by myself hand in hand just like the first time I walked in. We sat eight rows from the front. I sat where watch the back door. I prayed to God for our peace back. I apologized for putting us in this situation. I watched my children watch the Christmas play. And then the pastor got up and gave a quick sermon about the fact that everything we do should be to benefit the next generation.

He said "As you receive the light of your candle, pass it to the person next to you as a symbol that God is making his way through our dark, broken, pain filled, confusing culture. God encourages us to let our light shine before man (Matthew 5:16). That they might see our good deeds and praise our Father in Heaven. We are called to let our light shine in our hearts, that is the posture we are supposed to have as believers to show everyone the hope that lies within us."

He continued, "Our God is familiar with pain and is near those who feel like they are far from God (Isaish 53). 'Come to me," Jesus says, 'who are weak and heavy burdened, and I will give you rest if you need rest'. The solution is not more personal indulgence, it is a personal Savior."

It is our great honor to create an environment for children to grow up strong, respectful, and having a relationship with God.

The pastor lit his candle and then went to the first row and lit their candle. The congregation started singing Silent Night. I sat and swayed with Raela in my arms. Ronan sat beside me like the big little kid he is. The kid that grew up way too fast. The kid with a mom who only has arms to hold one child at a time. The arms that were holding his 5-year-old sister. I looked up and the pastor stood before us, lighting Ronan's candle. Divinity. He lit his candle and walked away. He saw our family and noticed Ronan, the next generation. He lit his candle. In that moment, I felt God saying He sees us. That church is the place to go for peace. As the flame lit from the pastor's to Ronan's candle, a miracle grew. I denounced all patterns of craziness and hurtful, reactionary behavior that was after us in every relationship, engagement, and pursuit. Every trial I pushed through brought me to this moment where I could finally stand firm in my convictions, in my self-worth, and my love for every soul unitedly.

I spent the next few weeks terrified. I put blackout curtains on every window. I panicked deeply when a motorcycle drove by. I couldn't have my windows or doors open. I feared showing any sign that we were home. Doug had already said he would find me if he felt like it. There is so much room to say I was overreacting. But that is not the point. The point is, I knew what I could and could not handle. And I could not handle this. It is no one's right to harass me. To say they will come over uninvited. It is no one's right to throw anything at me. But I cannot stop anyone from doing anything. I do, however, have security cameras on every inch of my house. I can easily set off the alarm at a moment's notice.

I can do everything I can to keep myself safe but my plea to the world is this: if you know that you are predisposed to threaten someone, it is your responsibility to abstain from dating. Although Doug is not responsible for how I reacted, and some might say I overreacted, I came into the relationship warning him that this was a non-negotiable for me. It is an irreconcilable difference. It is a no-contact for me. I know that at the end of every day, I have to be the one who shows up for myself. I am the one who sits with myself through panic attacks and moments of deep sadness. I am the one who gets up every day, puts my jeans on, and gets things done.

The thing about boundaries is you are allowed to have them, but you have to be willing to live with the consequences. For instance, if someone has a boundary for others not to wear flip-flops anywhere around them, that is fine. That can be a boundary. However, that means that person will not have relationships with flip-flop-wearing people. They will probably not go to the beach, pool, or a surf shop. They have to recognize that their boundary will cost them.

But let me emphasize that when your boundary costs you things but saves your mental and physical life, it is worth it. Every. Time. I will not hate Doug. In fact, he was uncomfortable that I refused to hate my exes. He was uncomfortable that I would defend them even. But I wasn't defending their actions. I was refusing to say that they were terrible. I go as far as saying that I still love them. I love them because I love everyone. You cannot love one person while harboring hatred for someone else. I have compassion for my exes. I have compassion for myself. However, I will only surround myself with those willing to respect my boundaries. I vow to try my best to do the same. I will promise to apologize to others if I have hurt them, even if that wasn't my intention. Because I still hurt them. You can do your best and still hurt someone. We are human. In forgiveness, there is compassion. And above all, there is love.

Made in the USA
Middletown, DE
07 February 2025